English Masculinities 1660–1800

WOMEN AND MEN IN HISTORY

This series, published for students, scholars and interested general readers, will tackle themes in gender history from the early medieval period through to the present day. Gender issues are now an integral part of all history courses and yet many traditional texts do not reflect this change. Much exciting work is now being done to redress the gender imbalances of the past, and we hope that these books will make their own substantial contribution to that process. This is an open-ended series, which means that many new titles can be included. We hope that these will both synthesise and shape future developments in gender studies.

The General Editors of the series are *Patricia Skinner* (University of Southampton) for the medieval period; *Pamela Sharpe* (University of Bristol) for the early modern period; and *Penny Summerfield* (University of Lancaster) for the modern period. *Margaret Walsh* (University of Nottingham) was the Founding Editor of the series.

Published books:

English
Masculinities
1660–1800

Edited by
TIM HITCHCOCK and MICHÈLE COHEN

Longman
London and New York

Addison Wesley Longman Limited
Edinburgh Gate,
Harlow, Essex CM20 2JE, United Kingdom
and Associated Companies throughout the world.

Published in the United States of America by Addison Wesley Longman, New York.

© Addison Wesley Longman Limited 1999

All rights reserved; no part of this publication may be reproduced, stored in any retrieval system, or transmitted in any form or by any means, electronic, mechanical, photocopying, recording, or otherwise, without either the prior written permission of the Publishers or a licence permitting restricted copying in the United Kingdom issued by the Copyright Licensing Agency Ltd, 90 Tottenham Court Road, London W1P 9HE.

First published 1999

ISBN 0–582–31919–6 CSD
ISBN 0–582–31922–6 PPR

Visit Addison Wesley Longman on the world wide web at http://www.awl-he.com

British Library Cataloguing in Publication Data

A catalogue entry for this title is available from the British Library

Library of Congress Cataloging-in-Publication Data

English masculinities, 1660–1800 / edited by Tim Hitchcock and Michèle Cohen.
    p.   cm. — (Women and men in history)
    Includes bibliographical references (p.   ) and index.
    ISBN 0–582–31919–6 (hbk). — ISBN 0–582–31922–6 (pbk)
    1. English literature—18th century—History and criticism.
2. Masculinity in literature.   3. English literature—Early modern, 1500–1700—History and criticism.   4. Literature and society—Great Britain—History—18th century.   5. Literature and society—Great Britain—History—17th century.   6. English literature—Male authors—History and criticism.   7. Sex role in literature.   8. Men in literature.   I. Hitchcock, Tim, 1957– . II. Cohen, Michèle, 1944– . III. Series.
                  PR448.M37E54 1999
                  820.9′352041—dc21   98–51977
                                                                 CIP

Set by 35 in 10/12 pt Baskerville
Produced by Addison Wesley Longman Singapore (Pte) Ltd.
Printed in Singapore

Contents

List of Abbreviations

For brevity some frequently used journals, archives and sources have been abbreviated in the notes as follows:

BH	Frederick A. Pottle, ed., *Boswell in Holland, 1763– 1764* (1952)
BHM	*Bulletin of the History of Medicine*
BIHR	*Bulletin of the Institute of Historical Research*
BJE-CS	*British Journal for Eighteenth-Century Studies*
BL	British Library
BLJ	Frederick A. Pottle, ed., *Boswell's London Journal, 1762– 1763* (1950)
CA	*Current Anthropology*
CC	*Continuity and Change*
E-CS	*Eighteenth-Century Studies*
EHR	*English Historical Review*
G&H	*Gender & History*
GT	Frederick A. Pottle, ed., *Boswell on the Grand Tour: German and Switzerland, 1764* (1953)
HE	*History of Education*
HJ	*Historical Journal*
HRO	Hereford Record Office
HT	*History Today*
HWJ	*History Workshop Journal*
JAH	*Journal of American History*
JBS	*Journal of British Studies*
JFH	*Journal of Family History*
JH	*Journal of Homosexuality*
JHI	*Journal of the History of Ideas*
JHS	*Journal of the History of Sexuality*
JSH	*Journal of Social History*
LJ	*London Journal*
LMA	London Metropolitan Archive
LPS	*Local Population Studies*

OED   *Oxford English Dictionary*
P&P   *Past & Present*
PQ   *Philological Quarterly*
RH   *Rural History*
SH   *Social History*
TRHS   *Transactions of the Royal Historical Society*

Place of publication is London, unless otherwise stated.

Notes on Contributors

ALAN BRAY is a political activist within the gay movement and an Honorary Research Fellow of Birkbeck College, London. His *Homosexuality in Renaissance England* (1982) was a pioneering work in the study of homosexuality.

PHILIP CARTER is a Research Editor at the *New Dictionary of National Biography* and Junior Research Fellow at Wolfson College, Oxford.

MICHÈLE COHEN is Principal Lecturer in Humanities at Richmond, the American International University in London. Her recent work includes *Fashioning Masculinity: National Identity and Language in the Eighteenth Century* (1996) and '"A habit of healthy idleness": boys' underachievement in historical perspective' (forthcoming).

ELIZABETH FOYSTER is a lecturer in History at the University of Dundee. She was previously a British Academy Post-doctoral Research Fellow at Clare College, Cambridge. She has published a number of articles on marriage and the family, and her book *Manhood in Early Modern England: Honour, Sex and Marriage* will be published by Addison Wesley Longman in 1999.

JEREMY GREGORY is Principal Lecturer and head of History at the University of Northumbria at Newcastle. He was a contributor to *A History of Canterbury Cathedral* (Oxford, 1995), ed. P. Collinson *et al.*, and edited *The Speculum of Archbishop Thomas Secker* (Woodbridge, 1995) for the Church of England Record Society. He edited (with Jeremy Black) *Culture, Politics and Society in Britain, 1660–1800* (Manchester, 1991), and has written a number of articles on aspects of religion and culture in the eighteenth century. He is currently completing *Restoration, Reformation and Reform: Archbishops of Canterbury and their Diocese, 1660–1828* for the Oxford Historical Monographs series, and is writing a thematic study of religion and English society from the early sixteenth to the late nineteenth centuries.

KAREN HARVEY is a research student at Royal Holloway, University of London. She is completing her Ph.D. thesis 'Representations of bodies and sexual difference in eighteenth-century written English erotica'.

TIM HITCHCOCK is Reader in History at the University of Hertfordshire. He has published widely on the history of eighteenth-century social policy, religious millenarianism, urban history and sexuality. His most recent book was *English Sexualities, 1700–1800* (Basingstoke, 1997).

ROBERT B. SHOEMAKER is Senior Lecturer in History at the University of Sheffield. His recent works include *Gender in English Society, 1650–1850* (1998) and as editor with Mary Vincent, *Gender and History in Western Europe* (1998).

JOHN TOSH is Professor of History at the University of North London. With Michael Roper he edited *Manful Assertions: Masculinities in Britain since 1800* (1991), and his book *A Man's Place: Masculinity and the Middle-Class Home in Victorian England* will be published by Yale University Press in 1999.

DAVID TURNER is a graduate student of Brasenose College, Oxford, where he has recently completed a doctoral dissertation on representations of adultery in later seventeenth- and early eighteenth-century England. He is a former Scouloudi Research Fellow and currently holds a Past and Present Society Post-doctoral Fellowship at the Institute of Historical Research, University of London.

CHAPTER ONE

Introduction

TIM HITCHCOCK AND MICHÈLE COHEN

Woman alone seems to have 'gender' since the category itself is defined as that aspect of social relations based on difference between
sexes in which the standard has always been man.[1]

So wrote Thomas Laqueur in 1990 in his seminal work *Making Sex*.
This collection of essays, and the project of writing the history of
masculinity in general, is about de-centring and problematising this
male 'standard' and exploring the highly complex and gendered
behaviour illuminated in the process.[2]

In part, therefore, this collection represents a new direction in
historical writing. While it aims to use many of the insights gained
from the analysis of the history of traditionally excluded groups,
the history of women and of homosexual men in particular, it is
not an attempt to redraw the boundaries between exclusion and
inclusion, power and powerlessness; rather it reflects an increasing
awareness of the diversity of ways in which men constructed and
thought about themselves, and deployed those facets of self-identity
in their relations with other men and women.[3]

To have suggested that this volume attempts to do something
new is not to say that it is built from new materials. The significance

1. T. Laqueur, *Making Sex: Body and Gender from the Greeks to Freud* (Cambridge
MA, 1990), p. 22.
2. For a discussion of this problem see J. Tosh, 'What should historians do with
masculinity? Reflections on nineteenth-century Britain', *HWJ* 38 (1994), pp. 179–
202. For the most sophisticated recent analysis of Western masculinities based on a
sociological approach see R.W. Connell, *Masculinities* (Cambridge, 1995).
3. While the history of women and homosexuals is discussed in greater detail
later in this introduction, it is important to note that historical writing concerned
with other excluded groups, defined by race and class, has been equally important
in illuminating the complex relations of power and authority which characterise this
period.

1

of gender for, and its role in, male behaviour has been charted in a whole range of historical literatures.[4] However, there is currently little agreement about the nature and direction of historical change not just in gender relations as a whole but in the meanings of gender itself. Whether we look at masculinity, or indeed femininity, from the perspective of the salon or the molly house, the demographers' figures or the medical textbook, from the centre or the periphery, the elite or the plebeian, the story of eighteenth-century gender, and hence masculinities, looks different. The purpose of this volume, then, is not to subsume these different perspectives under a single over-arching analysis, a history of English masculinity, but to explore different masculinities in the various contexts in which they took shape over the course of the long eighteenth century. It has sought to bring together a range of perspectives, based on a wide variety of different sources; to juxtapose work on the gendered behaviour and culture of poor and rich men, of the articulate and inarticulate, of the metropolitan and the provincial. It has also sought to bring together work representing a diversity of methodologies, including micro-historical case studies and anecdotal and synthetic arguments. In other words, this collection is in some ways simply a mapping of the diversity of historical masculinities found in the eighteenth century. At the same time, however, that very diversity, and the debates which surround its components, suggest a broader characterisation of the field as a whole.

A brief survey of the literatures upon which most of the chapters of this book are based will highlight some of the main areas of debate and consensus. The most important and obvious of the literatures involved is women's and latterly feminist history. In one way or another, all the work included in this volume reflects and extends the concerns and agenda developed within this tradition. But the history of women does not provide the only point of departure for the history of eighteenth-century masculinity. As part of the transformation in the nature of historical writing over the past 30 years, a substantive literature on homosexuality, the family,

4. For an excellent recent survey of the history of gender in the long eighteenth century see R. Shoemaker, *Gender in English Society, 1650–1850: The Emergence of Separate Spheres?* (1998). See also R. Shoemaker and M. Vincent, *Gender and History in Western Europe: A Reader* (1998), 'Introduction'; and H. Barker and E. Chalus, *Gender in Eighteenth-Century England: Roles, Representations and Responsibilities* (1997), 'Introduction'. For surveys of the history of gender over longer time spans and broader geographical areas see A. Fletcher, *Gender, Sex and Subordination in England, 1500–1800* (New Haven CT, 1995) and O. Hufton, *The Prospect Before Her: A History of Women in Western Europe*, vol. 1 (1995).

language and manners, and sexuality and the body has appeared, and at least tangentially addressed the changing roles of masculine behaviour and identity. And while none of this historical effort has resulted in an uncontested consensus about the nature of even a small facet of eighteenth-century society, by relating each of these literatures to the material presented later in this volume, this introduction will seek to chart some of the major features which make up the geography of eighteenth-century English masculinities.

The literatures which perhaps most directly address the history of masculinity are those on homosexuality and the body. At first sight these appear to suggest that eighteenth-century masculinities were becoming more sharply defined; that the categories available to men were being gradually reduced to either a macho heterosexuality or else an effeminate homosexuality, and that these identities were being reified in relation to the body by new medical understandings of sexual difference.

Historians of European homosexuality such as Randolph Trumbach, Alan Bray and Antony Simpson have argued that prior to a transition dated roughly in the latter half of the seventeenth century, sodomy was considered a sin, but not evidence of a sexual identity. Not only could individuals participate in homosexual acts without having to reconsider their identity, but the sin was the same whether sodomy was performed with males or females.[5] In other words, before the eighteenth century, men did not define themselves in terms of their sexual behaviour, whether homosexual or heterosexual. Rather, they constructed their identity from a variety of behaviours amongst which sexual practice was only one.

5. The literature on male homosexuality in Britain in this period is extensive. See A. Bray, *Homosexuality in Renaissance England* (revised edn 1995); A. Bray, 'Homosexuality and the signs of male friendship in Elizabethan England', *HWJ* 29 (1990), pp. 1–19; A. Simpson, 'Masculinity and control: the prosecution of sex offenses in eighteenth-century London' (Ph.D. thesis, New York University, 1984); R. Trumbach, 'Sodomitical subcultures, sodomitical roles, and the gender revolution of the eighteenth century: the recent historiography', in R.P. Maccubbin, ed., *'Tis Nature's Fault: Unauthorized Sexuality during the Enlightenment* (Cambridge, 1987); R. Trumbach, 'London's sodomites: homosexual behaviour and Western culture in the eighteenth century', *JSH* XI, 1 (1977), pp. 1–33; R. Trumbach, 'Sex, gender, and sexual identity in modern culture: male sodomy and female prostitution in Enlightenment London', *JHS* II, 2 (1991), pp. 186–203; R. Trumbach, 'The birth of the queen: sodomy and the emergence of gender equality in modern culture, 1660–1750', in M. Duberman, M. Vicinus and G. Chauncy Jr, eds, *Hidden From History: Reclaiming the Gay and Lesbian Past* (1991); R. Trumbach, 'Sodomitical assaults, gender roles, and sexual development in eighteenth-century London', *JH* XVI, 1/2 (1989), pp. 407–29. For a brief survey of this field see T. Hitchcock, *English Sexualities, 1700–1800* (Basingstoke, 1997), ch. 5.

These historians have argued that in traditional European societies sodomy, while certainly a grievous sin, associated with God's
destruction of Sodom and subject to the death penalty *in extremis,* was
simply one of a range of sins into which anyone might fall – more
damning perhaps than pride or dishonesty, but not fundamentally
different from these.[6]

In extreme instances, for example fifteenth-century Florence as
described by Michael Rocke, sodomy was an aspect of power and
inter-generational relations, and was, like homosociality, one facet
of the world of young unmarried men.[7] But even in sixteenth-
and seventeenth-century Britain, pre-modern sodomy was largely
detached from the meanings we now tend to expect. It was only
with the onset of the long eighteenth century that the association
between sodomy, and exclusive homosexuality and effeminacy become commonplace. Alan Bray's chapter in this collection explores
the culture of male behaviour which preceded this transition and
which was largely swept aside by the new cultural magnetism of
heterosexuality in the eighteenth century.

In the northern European cities of Amsterdam, Paris and London, the eighteenth century witnessed the creation of what appears
to be a radically different form of homosexual identity and organisation – the molly, and the molly house.[8] For the first time, groups
of men engaged in sodomy started to present themselves in ways

6. On the relationship between sin and sodomy in the seventeenth century see
C. Herrup, 'Law and morality in seventeenth-century England', *P&P* 106 (1985),
pp. 102–23; P. Lake, 'Anti-popery: the structure of a prejudice', in R. Cust and
A. Hughes, eds, *Conflict in Early Stuart England: Studies in Religion and Politics, 1603–
1642* (1989); P. Lake, 'Deeds against nature: cheap print, Protestantism and murder
in early seventeenth-century England', in K. Sharpe and P. Lake, *Culture and Politics
in Early Stuart England* (1994). For an alternative analysis relating sodomy to honour
see C. Herrup, ' "To pluck bright honour from the pale-faced moon": gender and
honour in the Castlehaven story', *TRHS* 6th ser., VI (1996), pp. 137–60.
7. M. Rocke, *Forbidden Friendships: Homosexuality and Male Culture in Renaissance
Florence* (Oxford, 1996).
8. For literature on this transition in London see above footnote 5. For the equi-
valent transition in Amsterdam and Paris see L.J. Boon, 'Those damned sodomites:
public images of sodomy in the eighteenth-century Netherlands', *JH* XVI, 1/2 (1989),
pp. 237–48; A.H. Huussen Jr, 'Sodomy in the Dutch Republic during the eighteenth
century', in Maccubbin, ed., *'Tis Nature's Fault*; A.H. Huussen Jr, 'Prosecution of
sodomy in eighteenth-century Frisia, Netherlands', *JH* XVI, 1/2 (1989), pp. 249–62;
D.J. Noordam, 'Sodomy in the Dutch Republic, 1600–1725', *JH* XVI, 1/2 (1989),
pp. 207–28; T. van der Meer, 'The persecution of sodomites in eighteenth-century
Amsterdam: changing perceptions of sodomy', *JH* XVI, 1/2 (1989), pp. 263–307;
M. Rey, 'Police and sodomy in eighteenth-century Paris: from sin to disorder', *JH* XVI,
1/2 (1989), pp. 129–46; M. Rey, 'Parisian homosexuals create a lifestyle, 1700–1750:
the police archives', in Maccubbin, ed., *'Tis Nature's Fault.*

which set them radically apart from their contemporaries. By congregating in alehouses largely dedicated to serving a specifically 'molly' clientèle, and by adopting extreme effeminate manners, eighteenth-century mollies created a recognisable homosexual subculture. This creation was part of the changing nature of heterosexuality and, with the rise of a new homophobic discourse directed specifically at molly culture, it contributed to a dynamic of anxiety and fear within the broader culture of masculinity.

One trajectory for eighteenth-century masculinities must be seen as the development of these new extremes and roles – the effeminate molly and newly non-effeminate heterosexual. As has been forcefully argued by Antony Simpson and Randolph Trumbach, the creation of a specific ideal 'homosexual' characterised by transvestism and effeminacy provided one 'other' against which most men and women could then judge individuals now deemed to be 'heterosexual'. In this analysis sexual normality became a question of not being a 'molly'.

At the same time the significance of these developments should not be overstated. Philip Carter, for instance, has convincingly argued that the figure of the effeminate 'fop' was strongly associated with heterosexuality rather than homosexuality, with fops being ridiculed for vanity, excessive or affected refinement and, at times, failed heterosexuality.[9] In his contribution to this collection he argues, among other things, that an at least superficially foppish 'pretty man' formed one important facet of that rampantly heterosexual figure, James Boswell.

From this perspective it can also be argued that the association between homosexuality and effeminacy made by historians of homosexuality fails to address the multiplicity of ways in which 'effeminacy' was used and understood in our period. Nearly every chapter in this collection refers to effeminacy: men who fell short of the ideal of 'manly religion' (Gregory), men who, using slander, were thought to adopt a female vice (Shoemaker), men who showed an 'excessive devotion' to the ideals of politeness (Foyster), men who acted immaturely or frivolously (Carter) and men who emulated not just women but the French (Cohen) – all were labelled effeminate, though this had nothing to do with their sexual behaviour. The

9. P. Carter, 'Men about town: representations of foppery and masculinity in early eighteenth-century urban society', in Barker and Chalus, eds, *Gender in Eighteenth-Century England.* For a further discussion of this issue see L. Senelick, 'Mollies or men of mode? Sodomy and the eighteenth-century London stage', *JHS* I, 1 (1990), pp. 33–67.

concept of effeminacy highlights the crucial ways in which the 'other' to manliness in the eighteenth century was not simply the feminine, but also the effeminate. As a result, it also complicates our understanding of gender and gender boundaries in our period, and adds a new and awkward twist to the story of increasingly extreme gender identities found in the history of homosexuality.

Historians of the body and of medicine working on the understanding of sexual difference have come to a set of conclusions which is apparently consistent with the model of increasingly stark gender definitions found in the history of homosexuality. But as with the literature on molly culture, these conclusions need to be used with some caution. Following the lead of Tom Laqueur and Londa Schiebinger, a new narrative of the gendering of the body has been articulated.[10] This model posits a transition from a 'one-body' to a 'two-body' model of human anatomy and sex difference during the course of the long eighteenth century.

Essentially, this history suggests that up until approximately 1700 most Europeans thought of themselves as possessed of a single body type. Under the 'one-body' regime, the testicles and penis, and ovum and womb (or in later formulations, the vagina), were homologous, the former being driven from the body by the dry heat of the male while the latter remained inside, in the cool, wet interior of the female.[11] Thus, because one's body was plumbed in much the same way whether one was male or female, it was the experiences which the body underwent and the possession of a peculiar mix of humours which determined whether one would be male or female. As a result of this view, masculinity and femininity (both as physical and mental characteristics) were seen as part of a continuum which encompassed not only masculinity and femininity but effeminacy. While this implies that both gender and sex were unstable – maleness could degenerate into effeminacy, females could become male – it does not necessarily mean that gender

10. See, for example, C. Gallagher and T. Laqueur, eds, *The Making of the Modern Body: Sexuality and Society in the Nineteenth Century* (Berkeley, 1987); T. Laqueur, 'Bodies of the past', *BHM* 67 (1993), pp. 155–61; Laqueur, *Making Sex*; L. Schiebinger, 'Mammals, primatology and sexology', in R. Porter and M. Teich, eds, *Sexual Knowledge, Sexual Science: The History of Attitudes to Sexuality* (Cambridge, 1994); L. Schiebinger, *The Mind has no Sex? Women in the Origins of Modern Science* (Cambridge MA, 1989); L. Schiebinger, *Nature's Body: Sexual Politics and the Making of Modern Science* (1994).

11. For a concise summary of this material see R. Martensen, 'The transformation of Eve: women's bodies, medicine and culture in early modern England', in Porter and Teich, eds, *Sexual Knowledge, Sexual Science*.

boundaries were unstable as well.[12] Thus, while many eighteenth-century men were accused of being effeminate, because manliness was a virtue that could be aspired to by both sexes, women could equally be praised for their 'manly' characters.[13] In neither case was the social role of the individual fundamentally questioned.

While anatomy was not used to exclude either sex from possession of the characteristics normally associated with its opposite, 'woman' was associated with unrestrained sexuality, irrationality and openness to the influence of both the devil and God, while 'man' was seen as more rational, sexually controlled and possessed of a kind of dangerous intellectual pride which threatened his ability to experience salvation.[14] Gender, under this regime, was seen to be a predominantly cultural and political phenomenon, necessary to social order, rather than an irreducible scientific 'fact'.

Over the course of the period covered by this volume the rise of a new view of anatomy, driven by the need to redefine the 'natural' distinctions between men and women, led to the creation of a new kind of difference between the sexes. Most of the work on this material has concentrated on the history of women's bodies, but the implications of this change for the assumptions about male behaviour are equally stark. Gradually, women's generative organs came to be viewed as profoundly different from those of men. Orgasm in women ceased to be necessary in order to conceive, while the importance of sperm and semen in reproduction was valorised, in some formulations coming to take on an all-important and singular function independent of any female contribution. The older understanding of human character as being controlled by the specific humoural mix possessed by the individual was replaced by an understanding which gave central place to a more fixed anatomical difference in determining gendered behaviour. By the end of the eighteenth century, men and women were increasingly being seen as 'naturally' and predeterminedly different, and their characteristics those of 'opposite sexes'.

12. See J. Epstein and K. Straub, eds, *Body Guards: The Cultural Politics of Gender Ambiguity* (1991); in particular see the following articles in *Body Guards*, A.R. Jones, 'Fetishizing gender: constructing the hermaphrodite in Renaissance Europe'; R. Trumbach, 'London's sapphists: from three sexes to four genders in the making of modern culture'; and G. Kates, 'D'Eon returns to France: gender and power in 1777'.

13. Carolyn Williams points out that Henry Fielding's eponymous heroine, Amelia, 'is praised for her "manly resolution"'. C. Williams, *Pope, Homer and Manliness: Some Aspects of Eighteenth-Century Classical Learning* (1993), p. 9.

14. For two recent and comprehensive accounts of gender in this period see Fletcher, *Gender, Sex and Subordination* and Hufton, *The Prospect Before Her*.

The implications of this transition are usually taken to mean that 'woman' was constructed in difference from 'man', not only sexually passive but physically weaker than men and because of the presumed homology between body and mind, mentally weaker as well, culminating in the stereotype of the passive and delicate Victorian woman. However, the recent work on heterosexual effeminacy and masculinity suggests instead that the new construction of gender was deeply concerned with men. It was not just femininity that had to be clearly delineated, but masculinity. If, as increasingly appears to be the case, men possessed the more unstable and contested gender, the urge to fix the category of 'male' in the new anatomy becomes all the more significant. In other words, because the new 'two-body model' conceptualised sexual difference as mutually exclusive and 'incommensurate', man had to be constructed in difference not just from woman but from the effeminate. This new construction went a long way towards resolving the anxiety over effeminacy.[15] This transition must in part explain why the discourse of effeminacy was so much less prominent in the nineteenth century than the eighteenth. This new construction of gender entailed that, as men and women were now 'naturally' opposite sexes, men should and *would* desire women, and women alone. While sodomy had previously been seen as a part of a broader libertine sexuality, it appeared increasingly as a perversion of a new 'naturalised' heterosexuality.

This transformation has been described as a facet of the rise of a 'compulsory heterosexuality',[16] but, more than anything else, what the new understanding of the physical body did was to place a strong new pressure on men to perform sexually, and to invest their masculinity in their sexual behaviour. This is a theme explored in Karen Harvey's contribution to this volume, and suggests that men were increasingly encouraged to define themselves not just by what they did in society, but also by what they did in bed.

Of course, most of the discussion of this transition has been based on elite sources, and the products of high-professional debates. And Laqueur's model has been widely criticised as an overly schematic approach, which underplays the variety of medical

15. Michèle Cohen, *Fashioning Masculinity: National Identity and Language in the Eighteenth Century* (1996).
16. The phrase was coined by Adrienne Rich. See A. Rich, 'Compulsory heterosexuality and lesbian existence', *Signs* 5 (1980), pp. 631–60.

understandings of gender available to pre-modern Europeans.[17] There also exists a large literature on popular health texts which clearly demonstrates that the new assumptions and divisions were only very slowly adopted by the broader population. Indeed, in some ways, popular medical views seem to have remained remarkably consistent right up until the twentieth century. As a result, what one sees in the history of medicine is the creation of a new way of thinking about masculinity, but one of a variety of masculinities and one which was not universally adopted, nor even encountered by all men in the eighteenth or indeed nineteenth century.[18] Certainly, there does seem to be increasing anxiety about men's sexual performance. The pathetic figure of the male masturbator found in the increasingly hysterical anti-masturbation literature of the period is evidence enough for this phenomenon.[19] But it is important to remember that most people were blissfully ignorant of the new constructions of gender being worked out by bloody anatomists and elite physicians, and that equally powerful understandings of sexual difference remained available to individual men and women throughout our period.

What we see in the history of medicine and in relation to homosexuality are two narratives which seem to be pointing in the same direction. But in both instances we need to remember that elite medical understanding and 'molly' culture were largely metropolitan phenomena, which only slowly and occasionally impacted on the broader population.[20] We also need to be aware of the extent to which these starkly bi-polar analyses hide a range of intermediate and alternative understandings. The role of the heterosexual fop, in particular, but also the continuing existence of a popular medical world view at odds with elite medicine, add significant levels of complexity to this schema of rapidly changing definitions of gender.

17. See, for example, S. Orgel, *Impersonations: The Performance of Gender in Shakespeare's England* (Cambridge, 1996), pp. 19–26.

18. For an excellent recent synthesis of this material see R. Porter and L. Hall, *The Facts of Life: The Creation of Sexual Knowledge in Britain, 1650–1950* (Princeton NJ, 1995). For an alternative approach see M. Fissell, 'Gender and generation: representing reproduction in early modern England', *G&H* 7, 3 (Nov. 1995), pp. 433–56.

19. For a recent synthesis of this material see Hitchcock, *English Sexualities*, pp. 54–7. For an excellent collection of essays on the subject of masturbation see P. Bennett and V.A. Rosario, eds, *Solitary Pleasures: The Historical, Literary, and Artistic Discourses of Autoeroticism* (New York, 1995).

20. For eighteenth-century provincial attitudes towards sodomy see P. Morris, 'Sodomy and male honor: the case of Somerset, 1740–1850', *JH* XVI, 1/2 (1989), pp. 383–406.

While perhaps less directly concerned with masculinity, the literatures on marriage and sexuality form another important background to the chapters in this book. Essentially, there are two interrelated approaches to these issues. The first focuses on the demographic record in an attempt to specify the ages and economic conditions under which individuals married and went on to have children, while the second looks to the history of courtship and the cultural construction of marriage in order to understand the motivations and beliefs of the participants in this most common expression of gendered behaviour.

In the first of these two literatures, that on demography, a remarkable story of delayed marriage and changing patterns of courtship has been uncovered. Through the work of the Cambridge Group for the History of Population and Social Structures, it has now become clear that the first part of our period, between approximately 1650 and 1750, was dominated by a culture of sexual restraint. Men did not marry until the age of around 28, a high proportion remained single throughout their lives, and the bastardy rate was at a historically low level.[21] According to a whole raft of measures it appears that the hundred years after 1650 were characterised by a controlled sexuality in which (despite rising real wages) a significant minority of individuals chose or were obliged to remain single. In part this regime was possible because of the alternative forms of sexual behaviour available. There is a strong argument to suggest that mutual masturbation and non-penetrative forms of sex were widely practised in this period.[22] But, more than this, the demographic evidence implies a situation in which marriage (and hence heterosexual activity) was not available as a component to the construction of masculine self-identity for a significant

21. For a range of material reflecting the conclusions of the Cambridge Group see D.R. Weir, 'Rather never than late: celibacy and age at marriage in English cohort fertility, 1541–1871', *JFH* (1984), pp. 340–54; R. Schofield, 'English marriage patterns revisited', *JFH* (1985), pp. 2–20; P. Laslett, 'Introduction: comparing illegitimacy over time and between cultures', in P. Laslett, K. Oosterveen and R. Smith, eds, *Bastardy and its Comparative History* (1980); E.A. Wrigley, 'Marriage, fertility and population growth in eighteenth-century England', in R.B. Outhwaite, ed., *Marriage and Society: Studies in the Social History of Marriage* (1981), p. 156. The most substantive statement of the Group's findings is E.A. Wrigley and R.S. Schofield, *The Population History of England, 1541–1871* (1981).

22. T. Hitchcock, 'Redefining sex in eighteenth-century England', *HWJ* 41 (1996), pp. 72–90. This article expands on a suggestion made by G.R. Quaife in his *Wanton Wenches and Wayward Wives: Peasants and Illicit Sex in Early Seventeenth Century England* (Brunswick NJ, 1979) and by Henry Abelove in his 'Some speculations on the history of sexual intercourse during the long eighteenth century in England', *Genders* 6 (1989), pp. 125–30.

minority of men, or alternatively, that only a relatively small majority of men could achieve a fully formed masculine role. In either case, the existence of this pattern creates a significant challenge for our understanding of gender behaviour and more specifically masculinity. If the roles of husband, father and sexual partner were either delayed or denied, in what types of behaviour did men (and young men in particular) invest their own self-image? The specific conditions experienced by one man under this early sexual regime form the focus of Tim Hitchcock's contribution to this volume.

More than raising these questions, the demographic record also suggests a pattern of change. By the end of our period, the age at marriage for men had dropped, on average, by some four or five years, the percentage remaining unmarried had more than halved, and the bastardy rate had risen alarmingly. If the period up until the mid-eighteenth century had been characterised by sexual control and delay, the period after 1750 appears to have fostered a growing popularity for both marriage and penetrative, reproductive sex. This latter pattern can be seen to represent a newly compulsory heterosexuality, in which more men felt socially obliged and encouraged both to marry and to have penetrative sex with women outside of marriage. If we combine this observation with the rise of effeminate homosexuality and the 'naturalisation' of sexual difference described by the historians of the body, the picture which emerges is of a changing culture of masculinity in which men increasingly participated in irresponsible sexual behaviour leading to illegitimate pregnancy, as a way of demonstrating a 'normal', and increasingly problematic, masculinity.

This line of reasoning in turn reinforces a further literature on gender which suggests that the late eighteenth century saw a rising tide of misogyny, perhaps coupled with a pattern of single-sex working arrangements, leading to rising sexual violence and marital disharmony. In the work of historians such as Anna Clark, rising gender disharmony, driven by an increasingly predatory masculinity amongst plebeian men, would seem to characterise the period from mid-century. In her model, rape, violence within marriage, and the sniggering culture of the alehouse and single-sex workshop were all facets of a changing masculinity.[23]

23. A. Clark, *The Struggle for the Breeches: Gender and the Making of the British Working Class* (Berkeley CA, 1995). See also A. Clark, 'Humanity or justice? Wifebeating and the law in the eighteenth and nineteenth centuries', in C. Smart, ed., *Regulating Womanhood: Historical Writings on Marriage, Motherhood and Sexuality* (1992); A. Clark, 'The politics of seduction in English popular culture, 1748–1848', in J. Radford, ed.,

But as with the literatures on homosexuality and the body, that on demography is being vigorously contested. While few historians question the outline of demographic change described by the Cambridge Group, there is little agreement about what it means. The Cambridge Group itself sees the changes it has described as a reflection of economic change – essentially arguing that rising real wages were the prime determinant in changing patterns of behaviour, and assuming the existence of a constant and uniform underlying desire for heterosexual marriage.[24] Few historians working on the history of gender entirely accept their argument. Instead, most would argue that demography need not necessarily be seen as a good indicator of changing cultural assumptions.[25] Others have also begun to un-pick the figures upon which the aggregate picture is based. Richard Adair, for instance, has forcefully argued that the attempt to create a national picture hides a wealth of regional variations in both demographic behaviour and the culture of courtship and marriage. Similarly, urban historians have long maintained that the picture of changing marriage patterns is skewed by the overwhelmingly rural sample relied on by the Cambridge Group, and that their conclusions say little about the conditions and beliefs of the urban population.[26] As a result, the apparent confirmation of a changing pattern of masculinities which appears to be supplied by this material needs to be treated with great care. And again, as with the histories of homosexuality and the body, the straightforward story of increasingly extreme gender roles must be modified to take account of a range of exceptions and counter examples.

A further level of complexity is added by the existence of perhaps the most comprehensive, non-statistical historical treatment of the subject available. In the magisterial works of Lawrence Stone, supported by that of historians such as Randolph Trumbach, a very different story seems to emerge in which gender relations become closer and more sympathetic over the course of our period. There

---

The Progress of Romance: The Politics of Popular Fiction (1986); A. Clark, 'Whores and gossips: sexual reputation in London, 1770–1825', in A. Angerman *et al.*, eds, *Current Issues in Women's History* (1989); A. Clark, *Women's Silence, Men's Violence: Sexual Assault in England, 1770–1845* (1987).

24. The clearest statement of the Cambridge Group's view of the significance of this material is E.A. Wrigley, 'The growth of population in eighteenth-century England: a conundrum resolved', *P&P* 98 (1983), pp. 121–50.

25. For a powerful critique of the Group's conclusions from a feminist perspective see B. Hill, 'The marriage age of women and the demographers', *HWJ* 28 (1989), pp. 129–47.

26. Richard Adair, *Courtship, Illegitimacy and Marriage in Early Modern England* (Manchester, 1996).

is at the least a strong superficial contradiction between Stone's conclusions and the story which emerges from the demographic record and which is apparently supported by the history of homosexuality, the body, and in the work of Anna Clark. Stone has argued that the late seventeenth century and the eighteenth century witnessed the rise of a companionate marriage, replacing an older 'puritan' marriage style. In the process, he argues, men and women came to expect greater emotional involvement and intimacy within marriage, leading to greater reciprocity and harmony.[27] And while Stone has been widely criticised for his reliance on elite sources, his overall conclusion retains wide currency.

In part, these apparent contradictions are simply a legacy of the class and sources which the various historians involved have examined. By its nature, demographic evidence gives voice to the actions of the voiceless multitude, the poor. In a similar way, Anna Clark's work is essentially concerned with nascent working-class culture. Lawrence Stone's analysis, on the other hand, is based on the cultural productions of the middling sort and the elite. One explanation for the lack of agreement between these various studies must be that they are each talking about different groups of people, and hence reflect the diversity of experience and the variety of masculinities available to eighteenth-century men. At the same time, however, the internal contradictions apparent in the historiography reflect the gradual emergence of a more sophisticated understanding of the complexity and variety of masculinities being studied.

An alternative understanding of many of the same issues of gender identity and definition can be found in the large body of work now available on honour and reputation. This literature started off as an attempt to understand the roles of honour in high politics and elite social relations, but more recently the evidence of church court and quarter sessions material related to slander and defamation among plebeian and middling sort men and women has been mined to create a more comprehensive view of early modern social relations.

The first of these literatures, that on male honour, has charted the tensions which characterised early modern elite attitudes, suggesting that these in turn contributed to the crisis of aristocratic culture evident in the mid-seventeenth century. Drawing on ideas

27. The classic statement of Stone's views can be found in L. Stone, *The Family, Sex and Marriage in England, 1500–1800*, 1st edn (1977). See also R. Trumbach, *The Rise of the Egalitarian Family: Aristocratic Kinship and Domestic Relations in Eighteenth-Century England* (1978).

of an 'honour community' developed within anthropology, historians such as Mervyn James have described how sixteenth-century concepts of honour entailed a combination of steadfastness and aggression on the part of men, and suggested that this was largely in conflict with many of the precepts of contemporary religion. More importantly, James suggested that because religious imperatives and concepts of aristocratic honour formed two increasingly separate justifications for government and hierarchy in post-Reformation England, the growing tension between the two formed an important component in the crisis of governance associated with the English Civil War.[28] Since James published his seminal work in 1978, other historians have extended this story and given it a more markedly gendered direction. Alan Bray's contribution to this volume is a notable example of work in this field. But more than this, in work on duelling and the rise of 'civility', the history of the concept of male honour has been given an eighteenth-century epilogue which suggests the gradual decline in the emphasis on physical violence in the settling of disputes, and a rise in the ideal of 'civility', with its concomitant recourse to the law and to verbal disputation of all kinds.[29] The contributions to this volume by Robert Shoemaker and Elizabeth Foyster chart this eighteenth-century story through legal records and the contents of advice manuals and sermons respectively, while Jeremy Gregory's chapter analyses the conflict between religion and masculine identity first pointed out by Mervyn James.

In the process of delineating the transformation of sixteenth-century honour into eighteenth-century civility, a number of significant aspects of the history of gender have been highlighted. In her work on the seventeenth century, Cynthia Herrup has noted that because honour existed as a single strand within a complex elite culture, it provided a resource that helped to justify a wide range of apparently dishonourable forms of male behaviour towards women in particular. By appealing to either religion, civility or the older category of 'honour' , an excuse for most actions could be constructed.[30] There can be little doubt that these possibilities for self-justification multiplied in the eighteenth century. More than

28. M. James, 'English politics and the concept of honour, 1485–1642', first published as *P&P* , Supplement no. 3 (1978), and reprinted in his *Society, Politics and Culture in Early Modern England* (Cambridge, 1986). For a recent development of some of James's ideas see Herrup, ' "To pluck bright honour" '.

29. See, for example, D.T. Andrew, 'The code of honour and its critics: the opposition to duelling in England 1700–1850' *SH* 5 (1980), pp. 409–34.

30. Herrup, ' "To pluck bright honour" '.

this, the gradual displacement of the concept of honour by the concept of civility has been associated with the shift of elite cultural practices from 'homosociality' to 'heterosociality'. Essentially, civility required the participation of females in a way that a community of honour did not, and implied the adoption by men of what could be seen as 'female' characteristics. As a result of these caveats and observations, changing notions of honour and civility have added several layers of complexity to the story of an increasingly sharply defined set of masculine identities.

While some attempt has been made to suggest that the elite precepts associated with 'honour' had an impact further down the social scale – this is the implication of Alan Bray's argument in Chapter 4 – most work on plebeian and middling 'sort culture has concentrated instead on the idea of 'reputation'. This literature, based on the evidence created by the church courts and quarter sessions, always has been much more self-consciously gendered in its analysis than was that on honour, perhaps because it took as its starting-point the assumption of a 'double standard' in relation to sexual behaviour, or simply because women show up more frequently than men in these records.[31] The seventeenth century has been much more thoroughly investigated than the eighteenth, but what has emerged from this literature is first of all a depiction of early modern society as one in which female sexual reputation was both of supreme importance and extreme fragility.[32] By incorporating the evidence provided by charivari, broadside and chapbook literature, a popular culture has been explored in which the epithet 'whore' was the almost universal insult directed against women. Less susceptible to sexual insult, men were generally attacked through the reputations of their wives: being accused of having been cuckolded, or else, in a more generic manner, of allowing their wives to 'wear the breeches' and exercise authority in the household.

At the same time, and while acknowledging this disparity in the construction of sexual reputation, it appears that similar character traits were valued in men and women. Honesty, financial probity, religious seriousness, domestic calm and good order were looked

31. The classic statement of the role of the 'double standard' in seventeenth-century England is K. Thomas, 'The double-standard', *JHI* 20 (1959), pp. 195–216.

32. Some of the best of this literature includes Martin Ingram, *Church Courts, Sex and Marriage in England, 1570–1640* (Cambridge, 1987); L. Gowing, 'Gender and language of insult in early modern London', *HWJ* 35 (1993), pp. 1–21; L. Gowing, *Domestic Dangers: Women, Words and Sex in Early Modern London* (Oxford, 1996); and J.A. Sharpe, *Defamation and Sexual Slander in Early Modern England: The Church Courts at York*, Borthwick Papers 58 (York, 1980).

for in the lives of men and women alike in this period.[33] And while there was certainly a double standard whereby a degree of sexual laxity was condoned in men but not in women, and a strong sense in which reputation played significantly different roles in the lives of men and women, this was by no means the end of the story. Several historians, most notably Polly Morris, have suggested that as the eighteenth century progressed, the disparity between the types of reputation expected between men and women grew stronger. In an important study of male reputation in Somerset, Morris found that men's sexual activities were increasingly tolerated, as long as they eschewed the pitfalls of bestiality and sodomy, while the reputations of women became if anything more fragile and more directly concerned with sexual probity.[34] Apparently associated with this shift, popular rituals such as ridings and charivari which used to shame cuckolds and husband-beaters in the seventeenth century came to be more frequently directed at wife-beaters towards the later part of the eighteenth century. Morris has related this change in the construction of sexual reputation to both the rise of an effeminate homosexual sub-culture and its associated stereotype, the molly, and the redefinition of female anatomy. Other writers have associated it with the rise of a more fully articulated culture of libertinism after the Restoration.[35] But, however this change is explained, this literature argues that during the long eighteenth century, assumptions about gender which underpinned reputations in English society became polarised. Men's reputations became if anything less connected to their sexual behaviour, while those of women became more fully dependent on just that aspect of their lives.

But again, we have to be careful about how we understand these developments. In the case of elite male honour, Cynthia Herrup's comments on the multiple uses of honour suggest just how transient a phenomenon this could be, making it difficult to trace its meaning for a single generation, much less over 300 years. And in the case of defamation and slander, the conclusions arrived at are based on the products of a set of courts whose function changed dramatically over the course of our period. It is as yet unclear that the evidence of these courts can be used to chart change over

---

33. See, for instance, Ingram, *Church Courts*, p. 303.
34. See Morris, 'Sodomy and male honor'; these ideas have been enlarged upon by F. Diabhoiwala, 'The construction of honour, reputation and status in late seventeenth- and early eighteenth-century England', *TRHS* 6th ser., VI (1996), pp. 201–14.
35. Diabhoiwala, 'The construction of honour', pp. 205–7.

time.[36] More than this, recent work on the seventeenth century has begun to complicate our understanding of the functioning of reputation in early modern society by pointing out the variety of roles defamation played in the lives of individuals depending on their age, gender or economic position.[37] The work of David Turner and Robert Shoemaker in this volume suggests that any attempt to draw hard and fast rules about how reputation and honour fitted into a specific gender regime is difficult to substantiate. Likewise, the limitation of this analysis to material arising from verbal defamation circumscribes its usefulness. Written and literary libel were also important components in eighteenth-century culture. This is suggested by Wendy Frith's argument that a 'discourse of vilification' was available to eighteenth-century literate elite culture, so that Pope and Walpole, for example, could use extraordinarily vindictive and degrading language in poems and letters to 'castigate and contain' a transgressive woman, Lady Mary Wortley Montagu.[38] A complete picture of the role and meaning of reputation in this period would have to analyse the whole range of material from elite literary sources to that produced by church court cases brought by plebeians.

As we have seen, there currently exists a series of contradictory story lines within the history of eighteenth-century gender. According to a wide range of historical literatures it appears that masculinity in our period became more sharply defined as the long eighteenth century progressed. At the same time, it is clear that a range of caveats and exceptions have problematised this narrative, and that other literatures, such as those on the companionate marriage, honour, reputation and civility, suggest the growth of a heterosocial world in which men and women increasingly shared emotions, values and experiences.

The nature of the contradictions within and between these literatures is perhaps most clearly reflected in the current state of the most substantial literature on gender identity in this period. Under

36. For a discussion of the changing nature of church courts in our period see T. Meldrum, 'A woman's court in London: defamation at the Bishop of London's consistory court, 1700–1745', *LJ* XIX, 1 (1994), pp. 1–20.

37. Gowing, *Domestic Dangers*.

38. W. Frith, 'Sex, smallpox and seraglios: a monument to Lady Mary Wortley Montague', in G. Perry and M. Rossington, eds, *Femininity and Masculinity in Eighteenth-Century Art and Culture* (Manchester, 1994), pp. 115–18. As Frith's aim is to discuss how Lady Mary was perceived to transgress the 'feminine', she does not analyse the letters and poems directed against her in terms of their 'insulting' nature, nor does she mention Montagu's reactions.

the rubric of the 'rise of separate spheres' , the hardening of gender boundaries during the late eighteenth century has become an
orthodoxy within women's and feminist history which is supported
by a wealth of collateral historical analysis. The current state of this
literature and the debates that surround it are discussed at length
in John Tosh's concluding chapter in this volume, but here we need
to address directly the implications for the earlier development of
eighteenth-century masculinity.

Underpinning much early women's history, and achieving its most
sustained and powerfully stated expression in Davidoff and Hall's
*Family Fortunes: Men and Women of the English Middle Class, 1780–
1850* (1987), is the idea that from the middle of the eighteenth
century, women were increasingly restricted to a domestic and
'private' sphere of the home while men monopolised the 'public'
spheres of business and politics. This has both become a historical
commonplace, and has been under sustained attack for a number
of years.[39]

Within women's history and the history of gender this question-
ing of separate spheres orthodoxy has been based on new archival
work and a new understanding of the actual behaviour of elite
women. It suggests that whatever the content of conduct manuals
and sermons, late eighteenth- and early nineteenth-century women
pursued much more active and public lives than can be subsumed
under the rubric of the 'domestic'.[40] Similarly, the concomitant
conclusion that men increasingly invested their self-identity in
their public performance of a masculine role tied to a strong and
authoritarian position within the family, has been problematised by
historians such as John Tosh. His analysis of the internal dynamics
of nineteenth-century middle-class families suggests that men's roles,
both public and private, were far less clearly defined than the ideology of 'separate spheres' might suggest.[41]

Within the history of gender the older model of gradually
hardening gender boundaries is currently being reassessed, with
many historians (including John Tosh, in this volume) choosing
to emphasise the continuity of gender relations which underlay the

39. L. Davidoff and C. Hall, *Family Fortunes: Men and Women of the English Middle
Class, 1780–1850* (1987).
40. For the fullest development of this alternative view see Shoemaker, *Gender
in English Society*. See also A. Vickery, 'Golden age to separate spheres? A review
of the categories and chronology of English women's history', *HJ* 36, 2 (1993),
pp. 383–414.
41. J. Tosh, *A Man's Place: Masculinity and the Middle-Class Home in Victorian England* (London and New Haven, forthcoming 1999).

undoubted changes in public rhetoric upon which much earlier analyses had been based.[42]

Proponents as well as detractors of the idea of 'separate spheres' in women's history have been largely concerned with the period between 1780 and 1840, and as a result have concentrated their efforts on the origins of an essentially nineteenth-century, or Victorian stereotype of gender identities. But a more fundamental reassessment of the nature of social divisions has been taking place, concerned primarily with the preceding 120 years. The rapidly expanding literature on the eighteenth-century 'public sphere' has forced historians to modify significantly many of the assumptions which underpinned earlier analyses. In particular, the growing literature concerned with the 'public sphere' and the sociability and politeness practised in that space, has led to a series of conclusions which makes a model of separate and sharply delineated gender practices difficult to maintain.

Though the concepts of public and private have long been thought to be gendered, it was the consideration of gender in the eighteenth century which highlighted the limitations of a simple sexualisation of space into male and female spheres. An important impetus to the rethinking of the notion of gendered separate spheres and of the meanings of public and private in the eighteenth century has been the work of Jürgen Habermas on the formation of what he termed the 'authentic public sphere', a space for rational, critical debate, whose institutions were the salons, coffee houses and taverns so emblematic of our period. In contrast to the court, which Habermas locates in the sphere of public authority, the authentic public sphere was constituted by private people in essentially private spaces.[43]

One important consequence of the ideas developed by Habermas and taken up by a growing number of writers has been the realisation that women were central to the sociability and conversation constituting the main practices of this 'public' sphere. The more the public roles of women have been recognised, the less possible it has been to map gender onto conventional notions of public and private. It is not that historians working on the public sphere have

---

42. See in particular Shoemaker, *Gender in English Society.*
43. J. Habermas, *Struckturwandel der Offentlichkeit* (1962). English translation, *The Structural Transformation of the Public Sphere: An Inquiry into a Category of Bourgeois Society* (Cambridge MA, 1989). For two excellent assessments of the impact of these ideas on British scholarship see J. Brewer, 'This, that and the other: public, social and private in the seventeenth and eighteenth centuries' and J. Barry, 'A historical postscript', both in D. Castiglione and L. Sharpe, eds, *Shifting the Boundaries: Transformation of the Languages of Public and Private in the Eighteenth Century* (Exeter, 1995).

abandoned gender as a significant marker, but that they have had to consider that boundaries were more ambiguous and shifting than a simple and static demarcation between public (male) and private (female) spaces would allow. However, because mixed conversation as the ideal social arrangement was predicated on the pivotal role of women in this 'public' sphere, it is the 'publicity' of women that has been celebrated and been the main focus of interest to historians.[44] And because the 'public' is a space men normally inhabit, their presence in that space has been taken for granted and the dangers which mixed conversation, with its refining and civilising functions and its female company, held for eighteenth century masculinity have generally been overlooked.

The tensions between the 'polite' and the 'manly' have been most clearly analysed by Michèle Cohen in relation to the role of conversation in the fashioning of the gentleman. Politeness, a dominant ideal of behaviour for both sexes and the main technique of male self-fashioning in the eighteenth century, was best expressed in conversation.[45] However, to achieve politeness, English gentlemen had to look to women and to the French. Not only was women's conversation, 'naturally' delicate and elegant, considered essential to refine men's, but the best models of conversation were the French. Given the powerfully ambivalent role France played in British culture in this period, and the ambiguous gender of both politeness and the spaces in which it was deployed, the anxieties for men – anxieties embodied, for instance, in the Frenchified and effeminate fop – can be readily imagined.[46]

Modern feminist linguistics provides a further insight into these same issues. If, as linguists such as Deborah Cameron argue, men and women are who they are because (among other things) of the way they talk, the question arises of how eighteenth-century men used linguistic resources to produce gender differentiation?[47] One

44. See L.E. Klein, 'Gender, conversation and the public sphere', in J. Stills and M. Worton, eds, *Textuality and Sexuality: Reading Theories and Practices* (Manchester, 1992) and 'Gender and the public/private distinction in the eighteenth century: some questions about evidence and analytical procedure', *E-CS* 29, 1 (1995), pp. 97–109.

45. For sources on this topic see Cohen, *Fashioning Masculinity*; see also L.E. Klein, *Shaftesbury and the Culture of Politeness: Moral Discourse and Cultural Politics in Early Eighteenth-Century England* (Cambridge, 1994) and P. Langford, *A Polite and Commercial People: England 1727–1783* (Oxford, 1989).

46. Cohen, *Fashioning Masculinity*; P. Carter, 'An "effeminate" or "efficient" nation? Masculinity and eighteenth-century social documentary', *Textual Practice* 11, 3 (1997), pp. 429–43.

47. D. Cameron, 'Performing gender identity: young men's talk and the construction of heterosexual masculinity', in S. Johnson and U.H. Meinhof, eds, *Language and Masculinity* (Oxford, 1987). Cameron is referring to Judith Butler's notion of

solution was that apparently increasingly practised in the nineteenth century. They simply shut up.

In the light of work on language, of Habermas's 'authentic public sphere', and the critique of the rise of separate spheres, the straightforward model of increasingly dichotomous gender roles whose boundaries were hardening and becoming more exclusive over the course of the long eighteenth century looks increasingly threadbare. But, having provided an effective critique of a 'separate spheres' model, historians have been less eager to present a clear vision of what should replace this older orthodoxy.

In conclusion, we are left in a fundamental conundrum. On the one hand there is substantial evidence that people (both men and women) thought about their own genders and sexes in more extreme ways over the course of the 140 years covered by this volume. The emergence of a specific homosexual identity, the evidence of the history of medicine and of demography all suggest this, as does some of the work on reputation. At the same time the overarching model of separate spheres, which seemed at one time to provide a powerful analytical framework for these literatures, is losing its explanatory force and looking increasingly unsatisfactory. The observation that women were not just increasing the variety and number of their public activities but that they were central to cultural production, and that the mutuality of the companionate marriage required the active engagement of men at the heart of the domestic sphere, combined with the contradictions for male identity and behaviour in the practice of civility and politeness, makes any simple linear model of the historical development of masculinity difficult to sustain. The model of a straightforward transition from a single early modern masculinity based on social reputation to a modern version in which men defined themselves through sexual behaviour (both heterosexual and homosexual) and through their control of women (newly confined to the domestic sphere) can now be seen to be inadequate. Such a model assumes that the main problems masculinity engages with are sexual and patriarchal in nature and that there exists a single unified masculinity available for historical analysis. The articles collected here show that once masculinity is problematised, anxieties and unresolvable contradictions emerge from the very heart of the identities examined.

---

gender as 'performative' – 'if gender attributes are not expressive but performative, then these attributes effectively constitute the identity they are said to express or reveal'. J. Butler, *Gender Trouble: Feminism and the Subversion of Identity* (1990), pp. 141 ff.

But then, why should the historical development of masculinity be any less complex than that which has already been mapped for femininity?

The sheer variety of masculinities described in this volume, and indeed practised by a single individual in the case of James Boswell, suggests that a single story line is almost certainly going to be insufficient. Essentially, what emerges from this volume is the gradual breakdown of older forms of gender identity and behaviour. Alan Bray's contribution suggests convincingly that the latter part of the seventeenth century witnessed the loss of a consistent set of signs and assumptions about masculine behaviour. And while it is certain that this older model was as riven by regional and class variation as was any later gender formulation, its unravelling set the stage for a long period of contest and anxiety centred on masculine identity. Indeed, the intense concern about 'manliness' conveyed by the many conduct and advice manuals published at the time, as well as in the individual experiences of men like James Boswell, suggests that the masculinities of the eighteenth century were a varied and continually contested set of roles and categories, while the attitudes towards the male body explored by Karen Harvey suggest a similar conclusion. The heterosexual fop, the libertine, the homosexual; the pretty man and blackguard; the man of religion and polite gentleman; the reader of erotica and the violent aggressor, all were possible male identities. The contributions in this volume suggest that each was brought into existence or modified over the course of our period, and that each was in some ways in conflict with the others. More importantly, perhaps, they suggest that the contradictions between them are not and were not resolvable.

It is in the unresolvable nature of this burgeoning variety of masculinities that the force for change must be located. Because these roles and categories were uncertain and open to debate, they inevitably became more fully defined and rigorously policed over time. As a result, what we see in the various literatures which describe the development of more sharply defined forms of masculine behaviour is not the story of a unified male culture, but a growing variety of acceptable and unacceptable forms of male behaviour. The undoubted rise of an ideology of separate spheres at the beginning of the nineteenth century, while obscuring a varied reality, was perhaps, like the new 'naturally' sexed body, an attempt to provide more clearly defined boundaries than were provided by the diverse and often contradictory expectations about male behaviour which characterised the eighteenth century.

PART ONE

Sociability

CHAPTER TWO

Sociability and Misogyny in the Life of John Cannon, 1684–1743[1]

TIM HITCHCOCK

> One evening I went to see my femall schollar, being somewhat in-
> toxicated in liquor. After some love toyes & amourous expressions
> dropt between us, I must confess I attempted a great piece of inde-
> cency. Being smitten deeply with love (or other lust) I put my hand
> under her coats to her knees. But she resisted & pray'd me not to be
> guilty of such folly & the more she resisted the more I was fired.
> Then we kissed & using some alluring words I told her if I offered or
> did her any injury I would repare it with sufficient satisfaction, and
> withal attempted a second time . . .[2]

This apparently unsolicited sexual assault on a young female student was committed by John Cannon in 1709 and was reasonably
typical of his behaviour as an excise officer in Reading, Watlington
and Wycombe between 1707 and 1721. During this fourteen-year
period Cannon was living at inns and lodging houses, and socialising almost exclusively with his fellow, male, excise officers. His sexual
behaviour was marked by a high level of aggression, occasional
violence and an assumption that women were sexually available. He
had not, however, always behaved in this manner. Prior to his entry
into the excise service and his socialisation by this all-male community, while a youthful farm servant in West Somerset, his sexual
conduct was marked by calm and negotiated gender relations in
which women seem to have exercised a relatively high degree of

1. I would like to thank Penelope Corfield, Robert Shoemaker, John Broad and
Michèle Cohen for commenting on this piece and saving me from many egregious
errors. I would also like to thank Tim Wales and Mary Fissell for independently
suggesting that Cannon's memoir might interest me. They were right.
2. John Cannon, 'Memoirs of the Birth, Education Life and Death of: Mr. John
Cannon. Sometime Officer of the Excise & Writing Master at Mere Glastenbury &
West Lydford in the County of Somerset', 1684–1742. Somerset Record Office, MS.
DD/SAS C/1193/4, p. 87.

authority, frequently instigating the process of courtship. This chapter will examine John Cannon's behaviour during these two very different periods of his life, and in the process assess the forces contributing both to his more negotiated relationships and to his later sexual aggression.[3]

John Cannon was born in 1684 to a family of butchers and smallholders in Somerset. A precocious, if intemperate, student, Cannon gained an excellent grasp of accounts and English literature and a smattering of Latin before being removed from school at the age of thirteen to be put to farm service, first with his own father, and then with an uncle living nearby.[4]

In his early twenties Cannon fell out with the uncle, and in the process lost a number of small legacies he felt were his due. At the age of 23 he gained a commission in the excise, and for the next fourteen years served as an excise officer in Reading, Watlington and Wycombe, small market towns 30 to 40 miles west of London, before losing his commission and becoming master to the charity school at Mere near Glastonbury, and occasional surveyor and accountant. He was almost continually broke throughout his life, never had any substantial success in any business, and finally died in 1743 at the age of 59, leaving behind him a wife, several children, and a 700-page manuscript. The fact that he wrote an autobiography or memoir is the only noteworthy aspect of his otherwise apparently provincial and pedestrian life. Having said this, however, the memoir is of supreme historical importance. As a document it is on a par

3. Cannon's disparate behaviour fits well within two very different historiographical traditions in relation to gender in the early eighteenth century. In the works of historians such as Susan Amussen, Margaret Spufford and perhaps most fundamentally Alice Clark, this period has been depicted as one characterised by relatively equitable and calm gender relations based on a household economy. At the same time the work of historians such as Felicity Nussbaum and Phyllis Mack suggest the period should be seen as one dominated by a brutal misogyny. Cannon's behaviour and experience supports both these perspectives. See Susan Amussen, *An Ordered Society: Gender and Class in Early Modern England* (Oxford, 1988); Margaret Spufford, *Small Books and Pleasant Histories: Popular Fiction and its Readership in Seventeenth-Century England* (Cambridge, 1981); Alice Clark, *The Working Life of Women in the Seventeenth Century* (1992 edn); F.A. Nussbaum, *The Brink of All We Hate: English Satires on Women, 1660–1750* (Lexington KT, 1984); P. Mack, *Visionary Women: Ecstatic Prophecy in Seventeenth-Century England* (Berkeley CA, 1992).

4. The two most comprehensive published accounts of Cannon's life can be found in John Money, 'Teaching in the market-place, or "Caesar adsum jam forte: Pompey aderat": the retailing of knowledge in provincial England during the eighteenth century', in John Brewer and Roy Porter, eds, *Consumption and the World of Goods* (1993), pp. 335–77 and Tim Hitchcock, *English Sexualities, 1700–1800* (Basingstoke, 1997), pp. 28–38.

with the diaries of Pepys and Boswell as a source for social historians – having the added advantage that its originator was of a
markedly lower social standing than either of these two more famous
diarists.[5] Tentatively it is possible to conclude that the memoir was
created from a set of diaries or day books, and that the judgements
recorded in it represent a mixture of Cannon's views at the time
the events took place with a gloss added several decades later.[6] Because the volume itself was put together at the end of Cannon's life,
it is difficult to distinguish between the views of the elderly school
master and those of the young farm servant and excise officer. But
overall, the depth of detail contained in the memoir suggests the
dominance of the 'diary' over an older man's memory in the construction of the memoir. And while we must be cautious in how
we use this source, there is no reason to suggest that the details
it records are wildly inaccurate.

The two periods on which this chapter will concentrate are,
first, John Cannon's life in farm service at West Lydford, and second,
his experience and behaviour as an unmarried excise officer at
Watlington and Wycombe. In the first instance, Cannon's attitudes
and behaviour while living in a generally heterosocial household
economy will be examined, while in the second, we will see how he
responds to the homosocial world of the inn, alehouse and excise.[7]

Cannon's description of his early life at West Lydford details
a wealth of information about his relationships with friends and
relatives, both men and women, and provides both an insight into
Cannon's own attitudes and an important point of comparison with
scholarship on the nature of early modern gender relations. In
the early sections of the memoir he is assiduous in recording his
opinion of individuals and passing judgement on their behaviour,
spreading both his praise and opprobrium evenly between men
and women.

In relation to adult men, he is particularly concerned with their
financial honesty, social ability and charity, and criticises them most

5. Surprisingly few historians have made use of Cannon's memoirs, and while
John Money is reportedly in the process of editing the volume for publication, it is
as yet unclear when this edition will appear.

6. Cannon regularly puts the specific date of the events he describes in the
margins of the memoir, suggesting that he was working from a pre-existing diary.
He also frequently mixes contradictory views on specific subjects. His actual descriptions of his masturbatory habits, for instance, are relatively value free, but are almost
always followed by a separate condemnation of its ill-effects. See Cannon, 'Memoir',
p. 29.

7. For a discussion of the meaning of homosociability for seventeenth-century
men see Alan Bray's chapter in this volume.

severely for having cheated him out of his due, either in gambling, or, in connection with his own relatives, in regard to legacies and bequests. A typical example of the traits he valued in men can be found in those he ascribes to his grandfather: 'a sincere friend and good benefactor and upright, honest dealer and a liberal advocate for the poor, being merry, facetious and pleasant in his deportment, whose jests and sayings [have been] . . . rendered proverbial in these parts'. By contrast his greatest censure was reserved for people like William Berryman, a local journeyman. Cannon describes Berryman as 'a great reprobate [who] would not only cheat us all but curse swear, bully & lye'. It gradually emerges that Cannon had been cheated at cards by Berryman, and that Berryman had further borrowed some money which he then refused to repay.[8]

During this early period in his life, Cannon was also scathing about some, but not all, forms of male sexual incontinence. His description of two boys he supervised on his uncle's farm gives a sense of the sorts of things for which he had a particular dislike:

> I had under me two very bad loose and debauched boys, one of which was James Billing. He was loose and profligate and a profane swearer and vainboaster, and full of shameless actions to our maid . . . , oftentimes showing her his privities. And with his hand holding it up to her would brag what he could or would do if she would consent, for which base actions I often beat him . . .[9]

Of course, one has to be careful in assessing what this disapprobation actually means. In some ways, it seems more directed at Billing's very public behaviour in approaching the maid so directly and aggressively than with Billing's suggestion that these two unmarried servants should have a sexual relationship. Indeed, Cannon's own contemporaneous behaviour towards maidservants reinforces this conclusion. Cannon spent many hours masturbating while staring through a hole he had carved in the back of the privy for the purpose of observing the genitals of a particular maidservant.[10] The

8. Ibid., pp. 12, 43.
9. Ibid., p. 55. Exposing one's genitals as part of a rough sexual invitation seems to have been a traditional form of behaviour in Somerset. G.R. Quaife devotes three pages to a recitation of numerous examples of similar behaviour in the same county during the first half of the seventeenth century; *Wanton Wenches and Wayward Wives: Peasant and Illicit Sex in Early Seventeenth Century England* (New Brunswick NJ, 1979), pp. 165–7.
10. Ibid., p. 41. Cannon's masturbatory habits are recorded in detail and form a significant counterpoint to the growing literature on the rising anxiety about masturbation in the early eighteenth century. See, for example, P. Bennett and V.A. Rosario, eds, *Solitary Pleasures: The Historical, Literary, and Artistic Discourses of*

fact that he was not caught in this practice seems to have excused him, in his own mind at least. Similarly, Cannon is full of praise for the good sense, honesty and erudition of a local man, John Read, despite Read's being rumoured to have sodomised a mare and his confirmed, although unobserved, habit of sexually abusing a local, mentally retarded girl.[11] To the extent that Cannon could essentially excuse the sexual misbehaviour of individual men, his attitudes conform to those described in the secondary literature on gender and reputation in this period, which suggests that sexual reputation was of little importance to men. His attitude towards women seems to fit less neatly.[12]

Cannon's views on women are strong and clearly expressed. Among the positive attributes he noted in his female contemporaries were sobriety, piety, charity and intelligence. A second cousin was 'very charitable to all people, pious to God & sober in all . . . dealings & conversation'; while another cousin was 'sober, vertuous & pious'. His greatest praise was reserved for Mary Rose, a covenant servant employed by his uncle, whom Cannon courted for

---

Autoeroticism (New York, 1995); T. Engelhardt, 'The disease of masturbation: values and concepts of disease', *BHM* 48 (1974), pp. 234–48; Thomas Laqueur, 'The social evil, the solitary vice and pouring tea', in M. Feher, ed., *Fragments for a History of the Human Body*, Part Three (New York, 1989), pp. 334–43; R.P. Neuman, 'Masturbation, madness, and the modern concepts of childhood and adolescence', *JSH* VIII (1975), pp. 1–27; Peter Wagner, 'The veil of medicine and mortality: some pornographic aspects of the *Onania*', *BJE-CS* VI (1983), pp. 179–84.

11. Cannon, 'Memoir', pp. 47–8. Bestiality in this period has been little studied, but the Somerset variety has been analysed in P. Morris, 'Sodomy and male honor: the case of Somerset, 1740–1850', *JH* XVI, 1/2 (1989), pp. 383–406, and Quaife, *Wanton Wives*, pp. 176–7.

12. There is a wide and impressive literature on early modern reputation and gender, based on the evidence of defamation cases brought before the consistory courts. This literature suggests that female sexual reputation was of overwhelming concern to early modern litigants, and that they were far less worried about the sexual reputation and behaviour of men. Essentially, scholars working in this area have argued that the nature of reputation was highly gendered, and starkly divided between a view of women in which sexual continence was central to the individuals' ability to maintain personal authority in their community; and a view of men according to which honesty, financial probity and the ability to govern a patriarchal household formed the locus of a man's social standing. See, for example, Laura Gowing, *Domestic Dangers: Women, Words and Sex in Early Modern London* (Oxford, 1996); Martin Ingram, *Church Courts, Sex and Marriage in England, 1570–1640* (Cambridge, 1987); T. Meldrum, 'A woman's court in London: defamation at the Bishop of London's Consistory Court, 1700–1745', *LJ* XIX, 1 (1994), pp. 1–20. See also the chapters by David Turner and Robert Shoemaker in this volume. Two excellent studies of reputation and sexual behaviour in Somerset, based on court records, have been published. Unfortunately, they deal with the periods on either side of Cannon's life span, and do not use the 'Memoir' as a source. See Morris, 'Sodomy and male honor', and Quaife, *Wanton Wenches*.

many years. She was 'sharp, keen & a compleat country girl, of a
true natural wit & quick genius, hansome in feature, of a ruddy
complexion, but low in her stature'. Cannon describes at considerable length and with great enthusiasm Mary's able management of
his uncle's business affairs, and suggests that her success was largely
a result of her own ingenuity. At the same time he is markedly
critical of many women. He disliked and resented his mother, whom
he blamed both for not allowing him to continue his education
and for favouring his younger brother and sister over himself.
Likewise, he reproached his younger sister for wasting money on
flowers and plants for an ornamental garden, money which he felt
could have been more usefully spent providing him with further
educational opportunities.[13] Cannon is particularly critical of women
for lack of generosity, pride and a sharp tongue (characteristics
he frequently found mixed together in the same individual). A
cousin, Margaret, he finds 'naturally covetous', a second cousin is
'of haught, proud and a great dissembler and a great talkative', and
he describes an aunt as 'a haughty clamorous woman and withal
very expensive and selfish in her apparel when she attended the
markets, which pride of hers occasioned a great decay in their
circumstances'.[14] At the same time, however, he does not criticise
either men or women for sexual incontinence alone, although he
does record a number of occasions on which various individuals
apparently left themselves open to such criticism. His own father,
for instance, had an adulterous affair with a maidservant named
Margaret White resulting in the birth of a bastard child. Besides
passing over the actual sexual behaviour without a word of criticism,
Cannon describes the issue, a girl called Edith, with great affection,
and avers that 'She ever very much affected our author & his children and both acknowledged each other as brother and sister,
their children respectively calling, uncle & aunt'.[15]

Nor does Cannon's apparent lack of concern over sexual impropriety stop at the bounds of his extended family. Throughout his
time in service he is part of a group of friends who spend their free
time bell-ringing. With three friends Cannon travelled about the
neighbourhood, ringing bells and visiting fairs, and pursuing what
opportunities he could for experimenting with courting.

One instance that seems reasonably typical of the circumstances
Cannon and his colleagues found themselves in and the attitudes

---

13. Cannon, 'Memoir', pp. 12, 16, 55, 34, 40.
14. Ibid., pp. 40, 13, 16, 15.   15. Ibid., pp. 21–2.

they expressed is provided by his description of a meeting that took place in 1704, when Cannon was 20 years old. Having spent a long Sunday ringing at the church at Balston, Cannon and two companions, by prior arrangement, went on to the house of Mary Withers, 'a clean tite girl & had some share of beauty & handling her tongue'.

> So coming to the door she gave us invitation to enter, which we made no scruple as being our intent. Her father as it happened was not at home, but Mary (for so was her name) made us wonderful welcome, & although Sunday we were merry & free, she being sole commander of the house (her mother being dead) . . . & there was then in the house a buxom jolly widow named Hester . . . & another young woman with her . . . with whom we pass'd away the evening till near midnight in eating & drinking & pretended courtship . . . but in this I had no great inclination to any love or binding affection . . . Our present diversion was no more than innocent & harmless . . .

Cannon goes on to describe a long night spent in the company of these three women, and a subsequent visit to the Widow Hester, during which she upbraids him either to seriously consider marriage, or else to leave her alone. He chooses the latter option, but remains remarkably positive about both Widow Hester and his own experience.[16]

Perhaps more telling than the actual circumstances, is Cannon's account of the fate of one of the principal actors. He records that Mary Withers, whose house formed the stage for these actions,

> sometime after was deluded by one Thomas Hayme, who got her with child & pretended marriage, but never effected it, notwithstanding vows & promises, but maintained the child. It was [also] reported that Ambrose fframpton [one of Cannon's bell-ringing companions] had carnal knowledge of her at the same time. She was married afterwards to one Wadman, a tailor, by whom she had many children and was living at Castle Cary in 1740.[17]

---

16. Ibid., p. 53. For scholarly treatment of the nature of courtship at this period see I.K. Ben-Amos, *Adolescence and Youth in Early Modern England* (New Haven CT, 1994), ch. 8; J. Gillis, *For Better, For Worse: British Marriages 1600 to the Present* (Oxford, 1985); J. Gillis, 'Married but not churched: plebeian sexual relations and marital nonconformity in eighteenth-century Britain', in R.P. Maccubbin, ed., '*Tis Nature's Fault: Unauthorized Sexuality During the Enlightenment* (Cambridge, 1987); B. Hill, *Women, Work and Sexual Politics in Eighteenth-Century England* (London, 1989), ch. 10; D. Levine, '"For their own reasons": individual marriage decisions and family life', *JFH* (1982), pp. 255–64; G. Parfitt and R. Houlbrooke, eds, *The Courtship Narrative of Leonard Wheatcroft* (Reading, 1986).

17. Cannon, 'Memoir' p. 53.

When combined with the lifelong, close relationship Cannon maintained with his half sister Edith, the bastard daughter of his father
and a maidservant, this suggests that Cannon and his contemporaries in rural Somerset had a relatively relaxed attitude towards illegitimacy, and were willing to tolerate a degree of sexual incontinence
in both men and women. Indeed, on balance Cannon's disapproval
seems more fully directed at Thomas Hayme than Mary Withers,
despite his belief in her promiscuity, and the fact Cannon believed
that Hayme was being misled about the certainty of his own patern-
ity of the bastard child. This at least suggests that at this point in his
life Cannon saw male sexual incontinence as a serious problem,
and that the sexual behaviour and reputation of women was of less
concern than other forms of evidence might lead us to expect.
Indeed, while there does seem to have been a 'double standard' in
Cannon's opinion of his male and female contemporaries, it cannot be characterised as a simple dichotomy whereby men's reputation rested on their financial probity and sociability while that
of women rested exclusively on their sexual continence. Instead,
Cannon's assessment of the reputation of both men and women
seems to have been based on a mixture of their financial honesty,
social probity, charity, intelligence and sexual behaviour.[18] And while
he does seem to make a distinction between men and women,
criticising the former for failures of financial honesty and the latter
in relation to talkativeness and pride, there also appears to have
been a high degree of overlap in the characteristics he looked for
in each.

More than this, the interchange quoted above, in combination
with Cannon's attitudes towards women in general, begins to suggest some of the patterns which characterise the gender relations
Cannon participated in at this time. Certainly, it appears to have
been Mary Withers who largely organised and controlled the events
of the evening rendez-vous described above. And while Cannon's
animus towards a number of his own female relatives can be viewed
as an expression of an incipient misogyny, it must likewise reflect
the real authority and power exercised by the women involved.

Indeed, the clearest fracture lines between approval and disapproval in the earlier sections of Cannon's memoir centre not on
sexual behaviour or even around gender so much as on the specific
variety of relationship Cannon had with the individual involved.

---

18. The classic statement of the early modern 'double standard' is Keith Thomas,
'The double standard', *JHI* XX (1959), pp. 195–216.

The women of whom he disapproves are those who have some sort of power over his own life, while those on essentially equal footing, who dealt with him in a manner he perceived to be 'honest', whether male or female, were treated with much less vitriol, and even a degree of indulgence.

The relationship between authority and contempt in Cannon's account extends beyond the immediate family. One instance that exposes the tensions between Cannon and those with whom he had an unequal relationship arises from a confrontation between himself and a covenant maidservant of his father's:

> it was my fortune one morning to assist in milking the cows, and our maid living so long in the service was impertinent & took upon her to command others at her will. She this morning peremptorily commanded me to fletch into the backside the cows then in a close not far off. [I] deny'd to do it by her order, upon which she complain'd to my father & aggraved my refusal to a high pitch, so that my father gave me a blow or two for disoblieging his servant . . . but it grated me much to be beaten for the maids complaint, [and] therefore meditating revenge I found a favourable opportunity for my design, for one of the cows being near a pool in the yard, & she sitting on a stool milking her, I came unawares behind her & wilfully jostled the stool from under her, giving her a slight push in to the water, but sav'd the milk . . . This was nuts to me to see her sprawl and sqwal in the water.[19]

What irked Cannon in this instance was receiving orders not from a woman, but from a subordinate. And indeed, his position in relation to the servant was ambiguous. On the one hand he was the son of the household, and yet, on the other, his role was that of a younger fellow servant.

Similarly, one of the few women who is not associated with his family's household but whom Cannon actively dislikes and disparages is Mary Brown, a woman Cannon's parents encourage him to court, and of whom Cannon can say little more than that she was 'very pale of complexion, of a peevish temper and naturally covetous, which qualifications was very disagreeable to me'. What Cannon appears to have disliked most in Mary Brown was the authority his

---

19. Cannon, 'Memoir', p. 52. Service in husbandry has received a deal of scholarly attention. See in particular A. Kussmaul, *Servants in Husbandry in Early Modern England* (Cambridge, 1981) and Hill, *Women, Work and Sexual Politics* ch. 5; K.D.M. Snell, *Annals of the Labouring Poor: Social Change and Agrarian England, 1660–1900* (Cambridge, 1985).

parents had vested in her in their attempt to find him a suitable match.[20]

At the same time, Cannon was still happy to approve of a large number of people. Farm labourers, the women he met at fairs and entertainments, most of his fellow servants and relatives met with Cannon's measured approval. Indeed, in the case of men there had to be some peculiarity, as in Berryman's cheating at cards, or James Billing's sexual displays, for Cannon to express real disapproval. In relation to women, he seems most concerned about individuals who affected his life in a negative way, who wielded some power over him, and in the process frustrated his own ambitions and expectations.

The reflection of these aspects of Cannon's attitudes in his sexual behaviour towards women can be seen most clearly in his account of his first serious courtship, with Mary Rose. Against the advice and will of his family, Cannon pursued a relationship with Mary Rose for some ten years. In the end, after his move to the excise, he treated her rather badly, courting three other women simultaneously and marrying someone else; but during the first part of their relationship, he presents himself and their exchanges as a model of restrained and reasonable courtship, conforming in almost all regards to the pattern of rural courtship outlined in the works of historians such as John Gillis.[21]

Cannon and Mary had an active sexual life composed of long sessions of mutual masturbation. They exchanged the halves of a broken shilling and promises of marriage, and, in the end, were deemed in the neighbourhood to be fully married, but for the final capstone of a ceremony. But what is important here is that this relationship was carried out while the two principals were essentially fellow servants, and that what Cannon depicts is a loving relationship which builds up over several months. In Cannon's own words, 'our jesting compliments began to burn up to a fervent ardour & earnest . . . [which] brought on by degrees a more close familiarity, even to a plain discovery of such matters & concerns which modesty teaches me to omit'. The point being that this

20. Cannon, 'Memoir', p. 54. While Cannon does not seem to have criticised male authority figures with the same vitriol as their female counterparts, he did have real problems getting along with men in authority over him. His entry into the excise was precipitated when he allowed himself to strike his uncle and putative patron with a 'paddle' during a dispute about the best way to plough a field. Ibid., p. 57.

21. Gillis, *For Better, For Worse*. For a detailed treatment of Cannon's courting practice see Hitchcock, *English Sexualities*, ch. 3.

relationship grew gradually and that Mary had an active role in its initiation. It was not, as his later encounters would prove to be, the result of some drunken assault on his partner's chastity, but rather a natural outgrowth of the intimacy forced upon them in their roles as servants. Cannon was able to maintain his good opinion of Mary Rose for many years, and seems to have preserved an affection for her to the end of his life.[22]

Throughout his period of farm service, Cannon seems able to behave towards both his male and female contemporaries with a degree of easy sociability. His relationship with his three male bell-ringing companions, with the women he engages in mock-courtship at fairs and in more intimate surroundings, and finally his more serious courtship of Mary Rose, seem devoid of much of the aggression and sheer peevishness which were to characterise the next stage in Cannon's life. And while his obvious dislike and resentment of many of his female relatives and co-workers suggests an underlying problem with authority and perhaps with women in particular, there is little actual violence towards women. During his ten years of farm service, up until the age of 23, he is certainly critical of both men and women – finding fault with the former in relation to their honesty, civility and temper, and with the latter in relation to their covetousness, pride and talkativeness. At the same time, however, there is little evidence that he subscribed to the contemporary view that women were sexually voracious, or that they were intellectually inferior to men.[23] Women seem to have been able to exercise a degree of control over the pace and outcome of courtship during this period, and Cannon seems to get on with them reasonably well, developing a form of heterosociability which allowed him to work and play with his female contemporaries and to maintain a good opinion of them during the course of their relationships.

What is evident is the extent to which all of Cannon's relationships, and the attitudes expressed about them, were embedded in, and the result of, a complex network of authority and power in which Cannon himself was relatively powerless. In part, this reflects his youth – the behaviour described thus far was characteristic of the period up until he reached the age of 23.[24] But more than this,

---

22. Cannon, 'Memoir', pp. 55, 57, 64.

23. See, for instance, P.M. Spack, ' "Ev'ry Woman is at Heart a Rake" ', *E-CS* VIII, 1 (1974), pp. 27–46.

24. See Ben-Amos, *Adolescence and Youth*, and Keith Thomas, 'Age and authority in early modern England', *Proceedings of the British Academy*, LXII (1976) pp. 205–48.

it reflects the type of household and community in which he was living. In a mixed arable and dairying community on the boundary between what historians of the seventeenth century have described as the chalk and the cheese of the English countryside, Cannon was surrounded by men and women labouring together in a complex, heterosocial working environment noted for its low bastardy rate.[25] A brief description of the beginning of Cannon's working day gives a flavour of the culture of gender relations he experienced:

> A custom there was . . . to get up before day light to bake, and it was often my fortune to arise & heat the oven, whilst the women did prepare the batch, & they would make bread cakes which were soon got ready for breakfast which we eat with butter or sopp'd in beer, ale or cyder before our other employment . . . As soon as this regale was ended then to help the maids at milking, afterward into the barn, or to the herd as the season was. And sometimes to faggot making, digging [the] garden, or ditch, or dressing lands, or otherwise as we had orders or was directed by our father or sometimes rather as our mother would have us to do.[26]

While this description reflects a highly gendered division of labour, the ascription of authority and power to individuals within this system was complex. Cannon's attitudes and behaviour towards women and sexuality reflect this complexity.

Cannon's life as a farm servant came to an end in 1707, when, after a dispute with his uncle left him effectively disinherited, he gained a commission in the excise, moving to Reading, then Watlington and finally Wycombe.[27] This was Cannon's first experience of living

25. On the role and authority of women in dairying and its changing character over the course of the eighteenth century see Deborah Valenze, 'The art of women and the business of men: women's work and the dairy industry *c.*1740–1840', *P&P* 130 (1991), pp. 142–69. For a recent survey of English agriculture in this period see Mark Overton, *Agricultural Revolution in England: The Transformation of the Agrarian Economy 1500–1850* (Cambridge, 1996). For a study of the social and political implications of different types of agriculture see David Underdown, *Revel, Riot and Rebellion: Popular Politics and Culture in England, 1603–1660* (Oxford, 1985), and for a regional analysis of bastardy rates which maps this aspect of sexual behaviour onto agricultural regions see Richard Adair, *Courtship, Illegitimacy and Marriage in Early Modern England* (Manchester, 1996). West Lydford is in the middle of the 'Waterlands' of Somerset, an area in which G.R. Quaife found a remarkably controlled sexual regime characterised by an extremely low bastardy rate, falling to an all-time low towards the end of the seventeenth century, *Wanton Wenches*, pp. 56–7.

26. Cannon, 'Memoir', p. 41.

27. For an excellent account of the workings of the eighteenth-century excise see John Brewer, *Sinews of Power: War, Money and the English State, 1688–1783* (1989), pp. 101–14.

outside of a farming household and his first taste of relative financial independence. Living either at inns or else in rented lodgings, Cannon spent long periods socialising with his male workmates, while the few women with whom he came in contact were restricted either to the one or two private students to whom he taught reading and writing, or else the servants of the establishments in which he was now a paying and powerful resident.

Cannon himself was very conscious of this transformation in his fortunes, and struggled to fit into his new surroundings, and while no stranger to predominantly male company and strong drink, he worked hard to develop the new skills required. Indeed, one of the remarkable aspects of this period of Cannon's life is his self-conscious pursuit of a new form of sociability. At one stroke his love of bell-ringing disappeared, as did his frequent jaunts to fairs in search of courting opportunities. In their place, he spent long evenings in pubs and alehouses in search of good, by which he meant male, company.[28] This transformation was not simply of Cannon's own desire, it was expected of him as an important part of his job. A flavour of the pressures which were brought to bear, and Cannon's response to them, can be gleaned from his description of learning to smoke. Soon after arriving at Watlington, his supervisor, a Mr Godfry, took him aside and 'importuned me to learn to smoak tobacco, saying that it would be more agreeable to him if I would learn to smoak, not failing to set forth that noble qualification in & towards company keeping'. Cannon dutifully set about learning the art.

> I gott me an ounce of the best tobacco, a penny worth of tavern pipes, and two or three quarts of beer & ordered the maid to carry these materialls into my room & make a fire there ... And late at night I came home, all being silent & in bed, [and] I entered my room & fastened my door & sat me down, drinks & fills a pipe, then smoakt, then drank, & then take another pipe, fills it, lights & smoaks, then drank. & so alternatively fills, smoaks & drinks till all my tobacco was wasted & burnt, my pipes, some foul, some broken, my liquor drunk or spilt about the room, & my self very much intoxicated & my head whirling about like a windmill or like a weather cock in April. Then re[t]ching, then spewing and sick, that my room resembled a jakes or a boghouse more than a lodging room.[29]

---

28. Even though this period witnessed the growing respectability of inns and alehouses, women remained a small minority among the clientèle. Peter Clark, *The English Alehouse: A Social History, 1200–1830* (1983), p. 225.

29. Cannon, 'Memoir', p. 89.

Cannon attempted to keep his naiveté a secret from the household in which he was living by pretending to have had a group of male friends over, and in the process exposed some of his most deeply felt anxieties about how he should fit in and be regarded in his new position.

But smoking for the sake of sociability was not the only lesson Cannon learned. More important in this context is a new and highly critical view of women, and in particular their sexual behaviour. The content of these new attitudes comes through clearly in Cannon's account of incidents he and his contemporaries in the excise found particularly funny. At one point, Cannon relates how, towards the end of his service in the excise, he was inspecting a brew house with two companions:

> Suddenly a board broke over our heads & down came a young woman between the joysts . . . The place being so narrow . . . it carried up all her cloths, leaving her naked up to her very navel or breasts, & hanging by her arms kicking & screaming, & could no ways relieve herself. On which we all set about to extricate her from her captivity. With the landlord taking her by one leg & I by the other. But Cottell would need be more efficacious, laid his hands on her secrets which she being sensible of began to curse, & swearing in a hard manner, & at last she let fly a full shower, and also her paten . . . like a devil about Cottell's ears . . . . We made the more laugh to get her at liberty, . . . which at length was brought about. But for all that our kind service, she abused us grosly.[30]

The basis for the humour of the situation is difficult to unpick, but what is most striking is that Cannon stood back and allowed what amounted to a sexual assault on someone in difficult physical circumstances. For Cannon, at this stage in his life, it was acceptable that a man's first response to finding a woman trapped over his head was to touch her genitals, and think this was a great joke.

The extent to which these attitudes could then lead to the preconditions for sexual aggression and possible violence are well illustrated in a further episode. Having spent a long evening drinking with two companions at the Antelope Inn at Watlington, the three men

> went to our chamber, being guided by the wench. & stripping our selves went all into one bed. & being frolicksom, pull'd the wench into bed to us, also tumbling her about & putting up her cloths . . . Neither of us did anything else with her, tho she fain would have had to do with us. . . . Next morning, ashamed of our folly we parted & each went our ways.'

30. Ibid., p. 145.

In this instance sexual assault is depicted as an amusing part of being 'frolicksom', while the woman herself is described as essentially 'asking for it'.[31]

It is not difficult to see some of the origins of this humour and mode of behaviour. Whereas, during his period in farm service, Cannon was surrounded by women possessed of equal or greater authority and power, which naturally forced him to treat his female contemporaries with greater circumspection, his life in Watlington and Wycombe was devoid of such figures. He lived continually in either an inn or rented lodging. The women he met on a day-to-day basis were almost exclusively servants employed to look after him and his wants, and his daily companions were for the most part made up of young, unmarried male excise officers, who were themselves similarly waited on by women of a social status inferior to their own.[32] As an excise officer who was frequently transferred in order to avoid fraud, Cannon would have had few links to the broader community, and hence few opportunities to participate in heterosocial gatherings with women of a similar social standing.[33] In this context, it is little wonder that Cannon's relatively easy sociability should be transformed into something rather different.

Gradually, over the course of his fourteen years service in the excise, Cannon developed what can only be described as a disparaging and insinuating humour and a pattern of behaviour characterised by aggression and drunken assaults on women.

During his time in the excise he embarks on at least three new sexual relationships, at least two of which contain an element of coercion and contempt. The first of these is described in the quotation which began this chapter, and was clearly the result of a combination of drink and an assumption that Joanna, a seventeen-year-old student to whom Cannon taught reading and writing, was playing a sexual game when initially resisting his drunken assault.

Cannon's next sexual farrago is similarly drunken and violent, but in this next instance leads to pregnancy and disgrace for the woman involved. Coming home late one night to the inn at which he lodged, Cannon found a young servant waiting up.

31. Ibid., p. 109. See also Spack, '"Ev'ry Woman is at Heart a Rake"'.

32. Cannon described a typical evening in 1713 as consisting of a game of cards, well oiled by drink, in the front room of the Catherine Wheel Inn where Cannon was lodging. His companions included his four fellow, unmarried excise officers, and any other unattached young men they could find. Cannon, 'Memoir', pp. 109–10.

33. Brewer, *Sinews*, pp. 101–2.

I drew a chair & sat down by her. & ungartering my stocking, talk[ed]
to her merrily and waggish, being . . . in liqueur, suddenly slipt my
hand under her coats to her knee which she not resisted, I boldly
ventured higher, she suffring it patiently, laying aside modesty &
shame, consented to whatsoever I did, which at that time was by no
more than by feeling . . . [But the following] Sunday . . . the wench
was above in my chamber making the bed & being fired with lust I
goes up stairs into my chamber to her & without real opposition lays
her on the bed & had carnal knowledge of her, which I believe no
man before ever had . . . we had more of the same sport frequently,
that at last she was grown so impudent as to get out of her own bed
& in the dead of the night & come to mine, & if she found me asleep
she would deal with me till she was satisfied, & often times she would
say she would use all ways & meanes with me till she was with child in
hopes to force me to marry her . . .[34]

'Lais', a classical reference essentially meaning whore, is the only
name Cannon gives his correspondent. Eventually she becomes pregnant, and after an attempt to procure an abortifacient, swears the
child on Cannon. He denies fatherhood, but eventually posts an
anonymous bond for the upkeep of the child, who dies in infancy.[35]

All the calm humour and negotiation which had seemed to
characterise Cannon's relationship with women while a farm servant were replaced in the homosocial world of the excise with the
assumption that women were likely to respond positively to his
unsolicited sexual assaults, but that they were culpable if they did
have sex with him. Underpinning this behaviour was an attitude
towards women which seems significantly misogynist. In the instances
already cited and in several other encounters, it is largely the women
themselves who are blamed for the outcome. 'Lais' is roundly condemned as an opportunist and a whore, while even Joanna (his first
sexual partner while in the excise) is blamed for having misman-
aged Cannon's sexual desire in such a way as to naturally lead to
his fornication with Lais.[36] In general, while at Watlington and
Wycombe, Cannon's willingness to condemn men for sexual licen-
tiousness is replaced by an overwhelming tendency to blame women.
It is at this point in his life that he depicts women as sexually
voracious, deceitful and exploitative, interested only in trying to
entrap him into marriage or fornication.

Eventually Cannon married, was booted out of the excise, and
went home to the rural communities of mid-Somerset. In the process he returned to a more heterosocial world characterised by

34. Cannon, 'Memoir', p. 89.   35. Ibid., pp. 102–3.   36. Ibid., p. 103.

more tolerant attitudes. But there can be little doubt that during his fourteen-year stint in the excise he developed a significantly different attitude to women and a markedly aggressive approach to sexual encounters.

In part, the transformation Cannon seems to have undergone during his twenties and early thirties can be seen as a reflection of his stage in a relatively common life-cycle. The majority of eighteenth-century plebeian and middling sort men would have found themselves most free of the bounds of the power relations of a patriarchal household at precisely this point during their lives.[37] To the extent that his lifestyle mirrored that of his friends who remained behind in West Lydford, Cannon's growing sexual aggression reflected his independence from constraint rather than an entirely different culture of gender relations. As such, it was part and parcel of eighteenth-century patriarchy. But, whereas Cannon's contemporaries in West Lydford would have only gradually assumed a more powerful position within a heterosocial household, Cannon was rather abruptly faced with almost complete freedom from these constraints. So, whereas his friends would certainly have slowly gained greater authority, they would never have been completely free from the complex power relations created by the demands of mixed agriculture. Women's roles in dairying and cheesemaking and running a productive household would have ensured that, whatever their beliefs about women, Cannon's contemporaries would have necessarily dealt with these women as individuals possessed of significant authority.[38] It was, in other words, Cannon's almost complete isolation and autonomy within the excise, his removal from the economics of household production which most fundamentally impacted on his attitude towards women, and set those attitudes apart from those he acted out both before and after this period of his life.

In part, therefore, what we see in Cannon's experience is precisely the division between heterosocial work patterns and negotiated gender relations on the one hand, and homosocial employments with their associated misogyny on the other, described by historians such as Anna Clark for early nineteenth-century Britain and Merry Wiesner for sixteenth-century Germany. Anna Clark's characterisation of British working-class culture as comprising two types of communities, one dominated by household production, shared labour between men and women, and a relatively tolerant

37. Ben-Amos, *Adolescence and Youth*; Kussmaul, *Servants in Husbandry*; Amussen, *An Ordered Society*.
38. Valenze, 'The art of women'.

and negotiated gender regime, and the other dominated by artisanal work patterns in single-sex workshops and extreme misogyny, could be applied to the two communities with which Cannon was involved. In a similar way, Merry Wiesner's suggestion that the single-sex housing and working arrangements experienced by sixteenth-century German journeymen encouraged the adoption of a markedly antagonistic attitude towards women and the patriarchal household, exacerbating differences between men and women and between employees and employers, could likewise be taken as a model of the forces at work helping transform Cannon's attitudes and behaviour. As with the men described in the work of both Clark and Wiesner, Cannon's sexual aggression and incipient misogyny were embedded in a specific set of economic and power relations, and flourished in a context where men and women were positioned in substantially unequal places in the social and economic hierarchy.[39]

At the same time, we need to be careful in how we treat this evidence and these comparisons. Cannon's experience was not only unique, it was also unusual. The excise service Cannon joined in 1707 was an organisation of the future, and has been cited by historians such as John Brewer as a significant staging post in the process of creating the modern state.[40] More than almost any other job could have done, the excise placed Cannon in a modern bureaucracy with its generally homosocial culture. In some ways his move from West Lydford to Watlington was a move from the seventeenth to the nineteenth century. As a result, it is difficult to generalise about the relationship between early eighteenth-century male culture and Cannon's changing attitudes towards women. In part, the excise, with the freedom from constraint it allowed and the alehouse culture it encouraged, simply gave voice to attitudes and beliefs which Cannon already possessed. But at the same time, the very radical social departure the move represented for someone from Cannon's background must have helped to create the beliefs about and contempt for women evident in Cannon's actions.

Cannon possessed strong views about the roles and natures of men and women throughout his life, aspects of which were probably

---

39. See Anna Clark, *The Struggle for the Breeches: Gender and the Making of the British Working Class* (Berkeley CA, 1995); Merry E. Wiesner, '*Wandervogels* and women: journeymen's concepts of masculinity in early modern Germany', *JSH* 24 (1991), pp. 767–82; Merry E. Wiesner, 'Guilds, male bonding and women's work in early modern Germany', *G&H* 1, 2 (1989), pp. 125–137.

40. Brewer, *Sinews*.

misogynist in character, but the significant thing here is that these beliefs were turned into *actions* primarily through the encouragement and reinforcement provided by the specific circumstances of life in an all-male service. In other words, while, as literary historians such as Felicity Nussbaum have suggested, there was an underlying misogyny inherent in the system of patriarchy which characterised the late seventeenth and early eighteenth centuries, the evidence of Cannon's memoir suggests that this was most readily translated into sexual aggression and contempt in circumstances in which women had significantly less authority than men, and in which men looked exclusively to their own fellows for social validation.[41] As a corollary to this, we can conclude that early eighteenth-century male culture contained the extremes of both misogyny and relatively positive attitudes towards women at one and the same time. The expression of the various points on the continuum between these disparate poles was shaped by the specific circumstances in which individual men acted and was not the predetermined outcome of a unified masculinity.

41. Nussbaum, *Brink of All We Hate.*

CHAPTER THREE

Manliness, Effeminacy and the French: Gender and the Construction of National Character in Eighteenth-Century England[1]

MICHÈLE COHEN

'If there were no other Use in the Conversation of Ladies', declared Jonathan Swift, 'it is sufficient that it would lay a Restraint upon those odious Topicks of Immodesty and Indecencies, into which the Rudeness of our Northern Genius, is so apt to fall.'[2] Thus, the present 'Degeneracy of Conversation', which he attributed to the custom of excluding women from the society of men, would be remedied. Swift was not alone in suggesting this role for women's conversation. From the beginning of the century to its close, the most diverse voices – moralists and essayists, educationalists and clergymen, earls and philosophers – were unanimous that 'one of the best Methods' for making men polite was the conversation of women.[3] It appears, then, that in eighteenth-century England, as in France since the seventeenth century, conversing with women was believed to enable men to acquire and develop the appropriate conduct of body and tongue, the politeness which fashioned them as gentlemen or *honnêtes hommes*. Thus a space was opened for women's voice, a space that represents a shift in respect

1. I would like to thank Phil Bevis, Tim Hitchcock and John Tosh for their comments on earlier versions of this chapter, and Anne Goldgar for her encouragement and support.
2. 'Hints Toward an Essay on Conversation', in *The Works of Jonathan Swift*, ed. Thomas Roscoe, 2 vols (1880), II, p. 294.
3. Bishop Berkeley (1724), cited in David H. Solkin, *Painting For Money: The Visual Arts and the Public Sphere in Eighteenth-Century England* (New Haven and London, 1993), p. 71.

of the traditional discourse on women's talk which urges them only to be silent.[4]

This may be one reason why it is the 'publicity' of women, their centrality to the discursive practices of sociability in England and France, that has led historians to reassess women's role in the formation of Habermas's 'ideal speech community', the 'public sphere' – a sphere located in the *private* realm, made up of *private* people coming together to form a public through sociable discussion and rational-critical debate. In the wake of Habermas's work, important questions have been raised about his conceptualisation of a public/private dichotomy, and the lack of attention he paid to gendered aspects of the public sphere.[5] This criticism has been highly productive, and has led not just to re-considerations of the complex relations between public and private in the eighteenth century, but to complicating these categories in relation to women. John Brewer's 'unpackaging' of the meanings of public and private in the eighteenth century, for example, reveals not just their interpenetration but the unstable, shifting boundary between them, 'as if public and private are shifting territories on a map'; and women have been rescued from being positioned in private spaces synonymous only with domesticity.[6]

Scholars rethinking the eighteenth-century public sphere in terms of gender have not, however, raised questions about its relation to men, and masculinity. This is not just because, as we argue in the introduction to this book, gender has for a long time signified 'women', nor because of assumptions about the way gender differences are mapped onto public and private spaces,[7] but because the

4. See, for example, Lisa Jardine, *Still Harping on Daughters: Women and Drama in the Age of Shakespeare* (Hassocks, 1983), especially ch. 4.

5. Jurgen Habermas, *Structural Transformation of the Public Sphere* (Oxford, 1989); Keith Michael Baker, 'Defining the public sphere in eighteenth-century France: variations on a theme by Habermas', and Seyla Benhabib, 'Models of public space: Hannah Arendt, the liberal tradition, and Jurgen Habermas', both in Craig Colhoun, ed., *Habermas and the Public Sphere* (Cambridge MA and London, 1992).

6. John Brewer 'This that and the other: public, social and private in the seventeenth and eighteenth centuries', in D. Castiglione and L. Sharpe, eds, *Shifting the Boundaries: Transformation of the Languages of Public and Private in the Eighteenth Century* (Exeter, 1995), pp. 8–9; L.E. Klein, 'Gender and the public/private distinction in the eighteenth century: some questions about evidence and analytic procedure', *E-CS* 29, 1 (1995), pp. 97–109.

7. See Robert B. Shoemaker, *Gender in English Society 1650–1850: The Emergence of Separate Spheres?* (1998), and Amanda Vickery, *The Gentleman's Daughter: Women's Lives in Georgian England* (New Haven and London, 1998) for the most recent contributions to this debate.

conceptualisation of the public sphere as *public* has, itself, contributed to producing *women*'s publicity as the object of inquiry.
For even as women's publicity is acknowledged and celebrated, it
requires explanation. Thus, when Dena Goodman, for example,
argued that the nature of the Habermasian public sphere makes it
possible to explain the 'public' position of women in French salon
culture, she explained that it was because 'this public sphere was
within the private realm' that 'a "public" role for women was legitim-
ated'.[8] On the other hand, because the 'public' is conceived as a
sphere that men occupy 'naturally', as it were, *their* presence in that
sphere has been taken for granted and assumed to require no
accounting.

Politeness, a 'complete system of manners and conduct based
on the arts of conversation', was at the heart of the sociability
that developed in the social and cultural spaces of the new urban
culture of early eighteenth-century England.[9] The practice of the
polite arts was central to men's self-fashioning as gentlemen, but,
as this chapter will argue, participating in the 'associative public
sphere'[10] elicited a number of tensions for *men*, tensions expressed
in particular as anxieties about effeminacy. In other words, my
claim is that the conceptualisation of the public sphere as 'public'
has contributed to eliding problematisations around masculinity by
producing *women*'s publicity as the sole object of concern. The aim
of this chapter is to describe these problematisations and to make
suggestions as to how they were resolved.

My starting-point is to propose that we imagine the spaces for
eighteenth-century sociability not as public but as *social* spaces. This
would avoid the term 'public' and its problematic connotations[11]
and enable us to rethink the historically specific social, cultural and
discursive relations deployed in those spaces. The defining feature
of eighteenth-century social spaces is that they were spaces for the
mixed company of the sexes, since their conversation was one of
the conditions for the refinement and self-improvement at the heart

8. Dena Goodman, 'Public sphere and private life: toward a synthesis of current
historiographical approaches to the old regime', *History and Theory* 31, 1 (1992), p. 18.
9. John Brewer, *The Pleasures of the Imagination: English Culture in the Eighteenth
Century* (1997), p. 111.
10. Klein, 'Gender and the public/private distinction', p. 104.
11. Joan Landes, for example, traces the etymology of the term public to '*publicus,*
"under the influence of *pubes,* in the sense of "adult men", "male population"' and
goes on to argue that 'A public action is then one authored from or authorized by
the masculine position'. Joan B. Landes, *Women and the Public Sphere in the Age of the
French Revolution* (Ithaca and London, 1988), p. 3.

of politeness. Social spaces were neither fully public nor private but rather a space-between, created in part by the nature of the activities that took place there,[12] and comprising all the spaces for 'society' both inside or outside the home: coffee houses as well as tea tables,[13] state rooms in great houses as well as the 'pump rooms, assembly rooms, theatres, walks, gardens, squares' which, Borsay argues, were built to 'enable company to congregate simultaneously'.[14] Social spaces accommodated both women's publicity and men's self-fashioning, since the presence of women was pivotal for men to achieve politeness. But it was in those spaces, too, that masculinity could be compromised.

Explorations of gender in terms of the public sphere have yielded a variety of perspectives pertaining mostly to women and their relations to publicity, privacy and an ideology of domesticity; explorations of the public sphere as a discursive arena have been concerned in the main with the development of a print culture and the printed word. If we look at gender from the perspective of masculinity and conversation in social spaces, a different pattern can be seen to emerge. This chapter addresses the tensions of politeness and conversation for the eighteenth-century gentleman. Referring to conduct and educational literature, and moral and periodical essays, it argues that politeness and conversation, though necessary to the fashioning of the gentleman, were thought to be effeminating not just because they could be achieved only in the company of women, but because they were modelled on the French. The question is, could men be at once polite and manly?

> It is to the Fair Sex we owe the most shining qualities of which our's is master . . . Men of True Taste feel a natural complaisance for women when they converse with them, and fall, without knowing it, upon every art of pleasing . . . An intimate acquaintance with the other Sex, fixes this complaisance into a Habit, and that Habit is the very Essence of Politeness.[15]

12. I am here adapting a remark of John Brewer's about Habermas's public sphere – that it is the nature of the activities in specific spaces that creates the public sphere. 'This, that, and the other', p. 5.

13. See, for example, Solkin's discussion of Van Aken's painting 'English Family at Tea', in *Painting For Money*, p. 73.

14. Steven Pincus has recently challenged the view that coffee houses were spaces for men only, ' "Coffee politicians does create": coffeehouses and Restoration political culture', *Journal of Modern History* 67 (1995), pp. 807–34; Peter Borsay, *The English Urban Renaissance: Culture and Society in the Provincial Towns 1660–1770* (Oxford, 1989), p. 273.

15. James Forrester, 'The Polite Philosopher' [1734] Part I in *A Present for a Son* (1775), pp. 67–8.

For James Forrester, it was the very mechanism of politeness that explained why the company of women was necessary to its attainment. Conversation with ladies as 'the Shorter, Pleasanter and more Effectual method of arriving at the summit of genteel behaviour' was the advice a father might give his son, as did Forrester in *Present for a Son*.[16] It was also the counsel that spiritual fathers might bestow on their daughters: in his widely read *Sermons to Young Women* (1770), the Presbyterian divine James Fordyce declared that 'nothing' formed the manners of men so much as 'the turn of the women with whom they converse . . . Such society, beyond anything else, rubs off the corners that give many of our sex an ungracious roughness.'[17] Mixed conversation was a 'Golden State'[18] of social relations, and the free intercourse between the sexes that it epitomised was so central to eighteenth-century society that it came to be held as *the* index of a nation's refinement.[19]

A gentleman, declared the *Tatler* in 1709, is 'a man of conversation'.[20] But how could this gentlemanliness be achieved, when, as Addison remarked, 'the *English* delight in silence more than any *European* Nation'. Though Addison, who devoted the whole of *Spectator* No. 135 to language, was prepared to be indulgent towards English taciturnity, he conceded that it adversely affected conversation: 'Our Discourse is not kept up in Conversation but falls into more Pauses and Intervals than in our Neighbouring Countries'.[21] Despite Addison's gently ironic tone, English taciturnity was not a *valued* trait in the first part of the century, and many of his contemporaries were more caustic about it. Taciturnity was the antithesis of politeness and sociability; it was the effect 'not of Wisdom, but of a morose and suspicious Humour' which made the gentleman 'unworthy of the Name on this very Account'.[22] It was the result of 'a clog upon the tongue', a national 'Laziness'. 'Silence and difficulty of speaking and fewness of words, are a kind of National Character', argued Thomas Wilson in 1730. This was a problem

16. Ibid., p. 62. See also Stanhope, Philip Dormer, Earl of Chesterfield, *Letters to his Son 1737–1768* (1774).

17. James Fordyce, *Sermons to Young Women*, 2 vols (1st edn 1766, 1770), I, p. 17.

18. *An Examen of Mr Sheridan's plan for the Improvement of Education in this Country* (1784), p. 40.

19. See David Hume, 'Of national characters', in *The Philosophical Works*, ed. T.H. Green and T.H. Grose, Reprint of the new edition London 1882, 4 vols (Aalen, 1964), III; William Alexander, *The History of Women from the Earliest Antiquity to the Present Time*, 2 vols (1779); John Millar, *The Origin of the Distinction of Ranks* (1779); Hannah More, *Essays on Various Subjects* (1785).

20. *Tatler* No. 21 (26–28 May 1709).   21. *Spectator* No. 135 (4 August 1711).

22. [John Constable], *The Conversation of Gentlemen* (1738), pp. 90, 190.

because, he explained, conversation, though enjoyed, is 'less pleasant to us; and in solitude, silence and spleen gain ground'.[23]

Despite the importance of conversation to the fashioning of the
gentleman, and the many virtues that were supposed to accrue for
men who achieved the fluency of tongue required by politeness,
the English saw themselves as a nation with 'a sullen and uncom-
municative disposition'. Englishmen's reputation for taciturnity had
even crossed the Channel and was the subject of satire in a number
of French plays. In Boissy's *Le François à Londres* (1727), a French
marquis, discussing the conversation of the English, comments

> leur conversation? ils n'en ont point du tout. Ils sont une heure sans
> parler, et n'ont autre chose à vous dire que *how do you*... cela fait un
> entretien bien amusant.'[24]
>
> (Their conversation? they haven't any. They spend an hour without
> talking and then the only thing they say is 'How do you'... This
> makes for a very entertaining encounter.)

Englishmen's reluctance to partake in 'conversations of mere amuse-
ment'[25] is the chief trait of a character in *L'Anglois à Bordeaux* (1763):
Mylord, who does not speak much, is seeking lodgings where he
might 'vivre seul dans l'ombre et le silence' (live alone in darkness
and silence).[26]

However, what struck visitors from the Continent was not just
Englishmen's silence but their 'disagreeable bluntness'.[27] 'The desire
of pleasing is here seldom found among the great', remarked Abbé
Leblanc. He attributed this bluntness to Englishmen's scorn for
those 'polite and insinuating manners which conciliate us to the
good will of others', and to their failure to converse with women.
'The English, unless in love, fear the company of women, as much
as the French delight in it.'[28]

23. Thomas Wilson, *The Many Advantages of a Good Language to Any Nation, with an
examination of the present state of our own* (1729), pp. 30, 36.
24. Louis de Boissy, 'Le François à Londres', in *Théâtre des auteurs du second ordre:
comédies en prose*, 40 vols (Paris, 1810), IX, first produced in Paris in 1727. The play
was reviewed as *The Frenchman in London* in the *Monthly Review* 12 (Jan–June 1755),
p. 384, and in the *Connoisseur* IV (16 September 1756), p. 252.
25. Nicolas Charles Joseph, Abbé Trublet, *Essays Upon Several Subjects of Literature
and Morality* (1744), p. 23.
26. Charles Simon Favart, *L'Anglois à Bordeaux* (Paris, 1763), Sc. VI, p. 23.
27. Trublet, *Essays*, p. 23.
28. Jean Bernard, Abbé Le Blanc, *Letters on the English and the French Nations*, 2 vols
(Dublin, 1747), I, p. 24, II, p. 237. Eliza Haywood claims that, by contrast with the
French, in England 'Ladies, even of the first Quality are treated with very great
Indifference', *Female Spectator*, 4 vols (1744–45), I, p. 281. See M. Cohen 'The Grand
Tour: constructing the English gentleman in eighteenth-century France', *History of
Education* 21, 3 (1992), pp. 241–57.

Religious and secular advice literature, essays and conduct books all recommended the mixed conversation of the sexes as the ideal social arrangement, because, as Addison had already made clear earlier in the century, 'Man would not only be an unhappy, but a rude unfinished Creature, were he conversant with none but those of his own Make'.[29] Yet, there seems to have been considerable resistance, on the part of elite men, to the 'hegemonic character ideal' of the polite gentleman.[30] The question is why.

The concern that, away from women's company, men would display not just 'roughness of behaviour'[31] but 'indelicate language of everykind'[32] was matched by another, equally or perhaps more compelling: the anxiety over effeminacy. The essence of politeness was 'pleasing'. Indeed, it was in their 'Endeavours to please the opposite Sex' that men were refined and polished 'out of those Manners most natural to them'.[33] But here is the nub of the problem. If 'natural' manliness was, as many repeatedly noted, rough and brutal, ungracious, rugged, then in fashioning themselves as polite, men became 'other' – softer and more refined, but not necessarily more manly. What is more, because of what Chesterfield called the 'inevitable contagion of company',[34] the anxiety was that in desiring to please women, men might become *like* them. A remark of Joseph Spence encapsulates the tenor of the concern: while 'some conversation with the ladies is necessary to smooth and sweeten the temper as well as the manners of men . . . too much of it is apt to effeminate or debilitate both'.[35]

The tensions generated by the requirements of politeness did not arise from the necessity of women's company alone. For the gentleman to fashion himself as a 'man of conversation', he also had to imitate the best models of polite conversation – the French. 'It will be hard', John Constable claimed in 1738, 'to find any

29. *Spectator* No. 433 (17 July 1712). See also M. Cohen, *Fashioning Masculinity: National Identity and Language in the Eighteenth Century* (1996).

30. The phrase 'hegemonic character ideal' referring to the gentleman comes from Raphael Samuel, 'The figures of national myth', 'Introduction' to vol. 3, *National Fictions*, in Raphael Samuel, ed., *Patriotism: The Making and Unmaking of British National Identity*, 3 vols (1989), p. xxxii.

31. Alexander, *History of Women*, I, p. 314.   32. Fordyce *Sermons*, p. 18.

33. *Spectator* No. 433 (17 July 1712).

34. Chesterfield, *Letters to his Son* (1890), Letter CCXIV (18 January 1750). All further references to Chesterfield are from this edition.

35. Joseph Spence, *Letters from the Grand Tour 1730–1741*, ed. S. Klima (1975), pp. 9–10. Spence was Professor of Poetry at Oxford and went to France and Italy as tutor or 'bear leader' to young aristocrats in the 1730s and 1740s.

where more agreeable Conversation than among the *French.*' It was they who had best developed the 'art of pleasing' at the heart of politeness.[36]

It is not surprising, then, that the fop should have been such a ubiquitous figure in the eighteenth-century imaginary. The fop is a parody of the man who has, precisely, followed the prescriptions for achieving politeness: he seeks the company of ladies, whom he resembles, and he is Frenchified. He is also the quintessential inhabitant of social spaces, where he is a favourite of the Ladies whom he seeks to charm with his 'Pretences to Wit and Judgement'[37] and his mastery of the 'insinuating arts';[38] and his conversation is not just peppered with French smatterings but, like the French, he is voluble and talks too much. Fops' 'rattling Volubility of ... tongue',[39] 'empty prattle'[40] and 'fast running tongue'[41] distance them from the sober gravity of 'Men of Sense'.[42] The fop embodies both the dilemma and the danger of politeness: in becoming polite, one risked forfeiting one's identity as *English* and as a *man* and becoming 'all outside, no inside'.[43]

Thus, though it had been suggested, early in the century, that men ought to imitate women's conversation, with its 'readiness of Fancy ... Vivacity of Imagination ... Acuteness of wit', and that they need not 'scorn nor blush' to imitate it,[44] there must have been those who, like Shaftesbury, felt that men's

> language and style, as well as our voice and person, should have something of that male-feature and natural roughness by which our sex is distinguished. And whatever politeness we may pretend to, 'tis more a disfigurement than any real refinement of discourse to render it thus delicate.[45]

The polite ease of the French and their mastery of the arts of conversation were admired, but not without reservations. In David

---

36. Constable, *Conversation*, p. 89. See also John Andrews, *A Comparative View of the French and English Nations* (1785).
37. *Spectator* No. 92 (15 June 1711).
38. *Town and Country Magazine* (August 1771), p. 413.
39. Constable, *Conversation* p. 139.
40. James Fordyce, *Addresses to Young Men* (1777), p. 186.
41. James Moore Smythe, *Rival Modes* (1727), Act IV, p. 34.
42. *Spectator* No. 128 (27 July 1711).
43. N. Holland, cited in S. Staves, 'A few kind words for the fop', *Studies in English Literature* 22, 3 (1982), p. 413.
44. Samuel Parker, *Sylva, Letters Upon Occasional Subjects* (1701), p. 77.
45. Anthony Ashley Cooper, third Earl of Shaftesbury, *Characteristics*, 2 vols (Indiana, 1964), II, Treatise V: 'The moralists, a philosophical rhapsody', p. 6.

Fordyce's *Dialogues upon Education*[46] two characters, Simplicius and
Cleora, are discussing the differences between polite conversation
and the 'Plainness and Bluntness' of native English intercourse.
Cleora claims that many of the polite forms of conversation are
just 'a more specious kind of Lies' and, more importantly, that
these forms of conversation are alien to the British character. Is
there a way, she asks, of being polite and agreeable 'without polish-
ing ourselves out of our old British Plainness and Sincerity'?[47]
What was at issue was not politeness as such, but the pivotal role of
women's conversation, and the relation of politeness to the French.
If Addison and Steele's project of promoting a 'well mannered
masculinity'[48] was to be realised, what was required was the creation
of a *British* politeness. For David Fordyce, in the 1740s, like for Lord
Chesterfield in the same period (though for different reasons),
gentlemanliness was inconceivable without politeness, and each
parodies the consequences of its lack. Fordyce's reclusive scholar
transgresses the most elementary rules of polite sociability: he knows
nothing about the modern world, wears singular clothes, and when
he appears in polite company he not only looks like 'the inhabitant
of another world', but his conversation is about such recondite
subjects that no one can converse with him. Chesterfield's 'awkward
fellow' stumbles over his own sword, does not know what to do
with his hands or where to put them, and is 'frightened out of
his wits when people of fashion speak to him; and when he is to
answer them, blushes, stammers, and can hardly get out what he
would say'.[49]

Politeness on the French model could not be achieved without
'pleasing' and the conversation of women. But gallantry and what
Cleora contemptuously called its 'Flowers of Speech'[50] eroticised
verbal commerce. Conversation, Cleora argues, should subdue men's
passions rather than exacerbate them. To remove desire and danger, conversation must be unsexed either by erasing or silencing
women's sexuality (as was Cleora's) or by dispensing with women
altogether. As long as politeness was located in social spaces – i.e.
where women were – it would endanger manliness. The French
were the model and the warning. To ensure that English politeness

46. David Fordyce, *Dialogues Concerning Education*, 2 vols (1748). David Fordyce
was Professor of Moral Philosophy at Aberdeen, and James Fordyce's older brother.
47. Fordyce, *Dialogues*, I, p. 45.   48. Solkin, *Painting for Money*, p. 60.
49. Fordyce, *Dialogues*, I, pp. 97–8. Chesterfield, *Letters*, Letters XLIV, 29 October
1739, LXIX, n.d., and LXXIV, 25 July 1741.
50. Fordyce, *Dialogues*, I, p. 43.

would be free of the effeminacy of French politeness, it was necessary to find sites other than social spaces for its production. Fordyce's
solution was to recommend that young men should converse not
with women but with a variety of men, and

> frequent Coffee houses, and all Places of public Resort, where Men
> are to be seen and practiced, go to the shops of Mechanics as well as
> the Clubs of the Learned, Courts of Justice and particularly the Houses
> of Parliament, in order to learn something of the Laws and Interests
> of [their] Country, and to inspire [them] with that Freedom, Intrep-
> idity and public Spirit which does, or should, animate the Members
> of that August Body.[51]

Such conversations, Fordyce insisted, would provide the necessary
polish and produce men of civic virtue, free men, not fops.[52]

By the 1760s, however, the necessity of politeness had begun to
be questioned. Richard Hurd, Lord Bishop of Worcester's *Dialogues
on the Uses of Foreign Travel*, an imaginary conversation between
John Locke and Lord Shaftesbury,[53] is ostensibly one of many books
published at the time about travel to the Continent as a 'finish' to
the education of young men of rank. In fact, in the voice of the
character Locke, Hurd challenges the whole edifice upon which
politeness is constructed and rewrites the definition of the gentleman. He begins by demoting politeness from its central position in
the fashioning of the ideal gentleman:

> No very great man was ever what the world calls, perfectly polite.
> Men of that stamp cannot afford such attention to little things, as is
> necessary to form and complete that character. And even to men
> of common make, that excessive sedulity about Grace and Manner,
> which constitutes the essence of good breeding would be injurious;
> and it tends to cramp their faculties, effeminate the temper, and break
> that force and vigour of mind which is requisite in a man of business
> for the discharge of his duty, in this free country. So that . . . this
> exquisite ease of good breeding should be left to the ambition of still
> inferior spirits, of such indeed as are conscious to themselves of an
> incapacity for any other.[54]

Whereas David Fordyce's educational project still aimed to shape a
polite and 'compleat' gentleman, Hurd's critique reveals a major

---

51. Ibid., II, pp. 304–5.   52. Ibid., pp. 305–9.
53. Richard Hurd, *Dialogues on the Uses of Foreign Travel Considered as a Part of an
English Gentleman's Education: Between Lord Shaftesbury and Mr Locke* (1764).
54. Ibid., pp. 114–15. A similar argument was suggested by Vicesimus Knox, in his
essay 'Men of genius do not always excel in conversation', *Essays Moral and Literary*,
2 vols (1779), I, XXIV.

shift: he sets up a distinction between 'men' and 'fine gentlemen', and what his character Locke, as an educator, is seeking is 'the proper method of building up *men* . . . [not] fine Gentlemen'.[55] Hurd opposes politeness for the usual reasons – its connection with women and the French. The 'mighty value, that is set upon manners, comes from . . . the Ladies' who 'may perhaps have advanced the credit of it something higher, than such an accomplishment deserves', and the refinements of good breeding 'have had their birth from correspondent policies. . . . In the more absolute monarchies of *Europe*, all are courtiers. In our freer monarchy all should be citizens.'[56] Politeness suits the French because in their political system 'insinuation, not merit, brings favour or distinction'. But it is his conclusion that is different. More appropriate to the English character is the 'plainness, nay the roughness' of their manners. Knowing that he is courting contention, Hurd declares that this 'defect' is amply compensated by his countrymen's 'useful sense, their superior knowledge, their public spirit, and, above all, . . . their unpolished integrity'.[57]

There had always been an uneasy relation between politeness and sincerity. As John Constable reflected,

> It were to be wished that, not only Humanity, but also true Christian Sentiments always animated mutual Civilities. Then they would not be only sincere, but also Acts of true Virtue. However, taking the matter, as it is in the common Course of the World, Civilities are very fitting in themselves, and necessary to agreeable Conversation . . . without a due regard to such Rules, as are commonly established among polite Persons, the World would soon become Savage . . . Excess of ceremony is troublesome; but Rudeness is offensive, and brutish. Polite behaviour is not only a sign of good Nature, but also calls for, and naturally gains a Return.[58]

These sentiments were echoed by the French Abbé Trublet, whose apology for politeness was that without politeness, there was no society. 'Sincerity', he argued, 'is a natural, universal disposition of mankind.' Man 'loves to speak what he thinks, and to give vent to his own sentiments'. The difficult achievement is to be polite and hold back what might offend. It is this that demands self-control. Indeed, 'constant dissimulation is a violent state'.[59] This is probably why Gerald Newman, in his analysis of sincerity and 'English

55. Ibid., p. 71.   56. Ibid., pp. 117, 159.   57. Ibid., p. 160.
58. *Conversation*, pp. 190–1.   59. Trublet, *Essays*, pp. 291–2.

National Identity', assigns the status of 'cultural turning point' to the following incident: in a letter written in 1751, the poet William Shenstone tells of being in an embarrassing social situation when, having to choose between 'offending either against the *Rules* of Politeness or . . . the *Laws* of Sincerity', he opts, against convention, for sincerity.[60] My point, however, is that what is radical about Hurd is not his association of Englishness with sincerity, but his exaltation of rough manners and lack of polish as integral to English manliness.

The shift signalled by Hurd's attitude to politeness was soon reflected in attitudes to language. This is not accidental since it was thought, on both sides of the Channel, that language and national character were interrelated.[61] The 1780s saw what seems to be a complete reversal of the *values* that had, since the early century, been associated negatively with the English language and character, and positively with the French. In the first part of the century, Englishmen's taciturnity had been considered problematic for the practice of social conversation. For Addison, English taciturnity and the 'Genius' of the English language were inextricably interwoven. 'To Favour our Natural Taciturnity, when we are obliged to utter our thoughts, we do it in the shortest way we are able.' It was English 'Aversion to Loquacity' which had generated the contractions which have 'much disfigured the Tongue, and turned a tenth part of our smoothest Words into so many Clusters of Consonants'. These changes which have 'added to the *hissing* in our Language' noted by foreigners 'humour[s] our Taciturnity, and ease[s] us of many superfluous Syllables'.[62] At the time Addison was writing, not only were the French the best models of conversation, but the French language itself was held to be the language of politeness *par excellence*. Refined and polished by the Académie Française, it was considered a musical, graceful tongue with a 'melting tone', airy and soft.[63] But even then, English admiration of the French tongue (like that of French mastery of the polite arts) was not without reservation; French was also considered to have been *so* refined and

---

60. Cited in Gerald Newman, *The Rise of English Nationalism: A Cultural History 1740–1830* (1987), p. 132.

61. 'The language of a people is a sort of mirror that shews them', Abbé Leblanc, *Letters*, I, p. 65.

62. *Spectator* No. 135 (4 August 1711).

63. Henry Felton, *A Dissertation on Reading the Classics and Forming a Just Style* (1723), pp. 87, 89; Thomas Stackhouse, *Reflections on the Nature and Property of Languages in General and on the Advantages and Defects and Manner of Improving the English Tongue* (1731), p. 181.

polished that it had lost its strength and 'sinews'.[64] Monosyllabic
English might be unrefined and 'full of harsh sounds',[65] but it was
'strong', 'substantial' and 'manly'.[66] The point is, in the early part
of the century, manliness alone was not sufficient. Languages, like
men, needed to be polished. By the 1780s, priorities had been significantly altered. It was not so much that English and French were
now seen in a new light. Indeed, the language used to describe
English echoed Addison's words, half a century earlier. The crucial
change was a polarisation of attitudes relying, as Joan Scott would
put it, on gendered coding to establish its meaning.[67]

    The particular affinity between French and politeness which,
early in the century, had served to deplore English monosyllabic
harshness and taciturnity, now served as a foil to celebrate these
very same traits. While French was a 'language naturally made for
graceful trifling', wrote Captain Alexander Jardine in 1788, English
was a 'plain rational and monosyllabic tongue', suited to its 'manly
and laconic speakers'.[68] For John Andrews, who compared both
languages in some detail, French 'like a person of an artful, insinuating address, deals much in hints and circumlocutions', whereas
English, 'like a plain, blunt man, avoids prolixity, and comes to the
point at once'.[69] Even the 'attention to the nicety of diction' necessary for speaking French (which so many young men on their Grand
Tour had spent months trying to attain in damp Blois) was now
said to destroy 'manliness of thinking'.[70] French *esprit* and social
brilliance, essential in France to the 'male intellectual persona'[71]
and conversation, were now derogated as 'incogitative loquacity'[72]

64. Felton, *Dissertation*, p. 89; Stackhouse, *Reflections*, p. 181. See also G.S. Rousseau,
'Towards a semiotic of the nerve', in P. Burke and R. Porter, eds, *Language, Self and
Society: A Social History of Language* (Oxford, 1991), for a discussion of the gender of
nerves and sinews in the eighteenth century.

65. *Tatler* No. 230 (26–28 September 1710). It was also said that a monosyllabic
tongue was one that was not yet polished.

66. Stackhouse, *Reflections* p. 181; Felton, *Dissertation* p. 89.

67. Joan W. Scott, 'Gender: a useful category for historical analysis', *American
Historical Review* 91 (1986), pp. 1053–75.

68. Captain Alexander Jardine, *Letters from Barbary, France, Portugal, etc.*, 2 vols
(1788), I, pp. 268, 360.

69. John Andrews, *A Comparative View of the French and English Nations* (1785),
p. 319.

70. Ibid., p. 318. It was in Blois that the French accent was thought to be most
pure. See Cohen, 'Grand Tour'.

71. Linda Walsh, '"Arms to be kissed a thousand times": reservations about lust in
Diderot's art criticism', in Gill Perry and Michael Rossington, eds, *Femininity and
Masculinity in Eighteenth-Century Art and Culture* (Manchester, 1994), p. 164.

72. *The Art of Speaking and Holding One's Tongue* (1761), p. 4.

and mere flexibility of the tongue, traits associated with fops and women.[73] Taciturnity, the 'clog upon the tongue' of Englishmen, was now evidence of the strength of mind and manly restraint which the French so conspicuously lacked. At the beginning of the century, men had been invited to imitate women's language; at its close, it was women who were summoned to employ 'the simple and masculine language of truth' instead of the 'jargon of affected softness, in which smooth and pliant manners are substituted for intrinsic worth'.[74]

'Sincerity' had long been the excuse given for Englishmen's bluntness. As Vicesimus Knox put it, 'bluntness is said to be one of the characteristics of the English, and is allowed to be a natural consequence of their sincerity'.[75] What was different now was the positive, almost necessary connection between bluntness and manliness, a manliness that affirmed English identity as incommensurably different from the French, whose willingness to 'substitute politeness in the place of truth' confirmed *their* national lack of manly integrity.[76] What can account for such a dramatic shift?

This chapter has attempted to show that looking at practices of sociability from the perspective of masculinity throws a different light on eighteenth-century 'publicity'. In particular, it has argued that as politeness, conversation and the social spaces in which they were deployed came to be construed as French and effeminating, resistance to these practices was developed. The concluding section of the chapter will suggest that these tensions were resolved by recasting a feminised politeness in a domestic space that was free of social spaces' French corruption, and by celebrating sincerity, especially blunt sincerity, as a defining characteristic of English manliness.

Social spaces, produced by and framing a historically specific sociability, required, at least in theory, the mixed company of the sexes. As Addison had envisioned it, mixed company was mutually

---

73. Rousseau coined the phrase women's 'flexible tongue', see J.J. Rousseau, 'Emile', in *Oeuvres Complètes*, 4 vols (Paris, 1969), IV, Livre 5, p. 718. It was taken up in England, for example, by Henry Home, *Loose Hints upon Education* (Edinburgh, 1781), p. 135.

74. See Samuel Parker, quoted above; Hannah More, *Strictures on The Modern System of Female Education*, 2 vols (1st edn 1799, 1811), II, p. 99.

75. Knox, *Essays*, I, VII 'on conciseness of style', p. 49. Constable, *Conversation*; Fordyce, *Dialogues*; Hurd, *Dialogues*. See also Frank Felsenstein, ed., introduction to Tobias Smollett, *Travels through France and Italy* (Oxford, 1981).

76. Andrews, *Comparative View*, p. 145.

regulatory and improving – in the presence of men, women's femininity was enhanced, and in the presence of women, men would
become refined. Though Addison's idealisation would produce a
well-mannered manliness, politeness, like all the practices which
could secure men's status as gentlemen, simultaneously threatened
to compromise their masculinity. The Grand Tour was caught in
the same paradox: indispensable as a means of 'completing' young
men's education, it could also make them effeminate.[77] Nevertheless, well into the second part of the century, the importance of
refining and civilising men's rude nature and language prevailed
over potential threats to their masculinity, and men were continually enjoined to seek the refining company of women. 'Commerce
[with the ladies] . . . is the best nursery of those qualities which
constitute a man of the world.'[78] By the 1780s, however, John
Andrews reflected that though Englishmen 'might gain in delicacy
and refinement' if they spent as much time in the company of
women as the French did, they 'might lose in manliness of behaviour and liberty of discourse, the two pillars on which the edifice
of our national character is principally supported'.[79] This is why the
moment when it became possible to consider that politeness, not
just 'French politeness', was incompatible with manliness and
national character indicates a profound cultural shift. It is not
just that English bluntness, recast as a 'forcible and manly' way of
speaking, was now valued over the French's 'many pretty ways of
insinuating what they mean[t]'.[80] 'Manly frankness of speech' is at
odds not only with the language of politeness and its 'unmeaning
terms', but with all the 'ceremonies' of social spaces.[81]

But while politeness could be rejected for men, this was more
difficult to do in the case of women, especially as the main characteristics of politeness – the desire to please, softness, and 'the graces'
– were precisely those that delineated and enhanced the feminine
ideal. 'Gentleness of manners', John Burton advised, 'is perfectly
consonant to the delicacy of [the female] form.'[82] Could politeness
be preserved for women, and if so, how? By constructing a 'true'

77. See Cohen, 'Grand Tour' and *Fashioning Masculinity*; see also Marcia Pointon's
discussion of what she calls the 'dilemma of masculinity' in 'The case of the dirty
beau', in K. Adler and M. Pointon, eds, *The Body Imaged: The Human Form of Visual
Culture Since the Renaissance* (Cambridge, 1993), pp. 175–89.
78. *Monthly Review* 8 (Jan–June 1753), p. 257.
79. Andrews, *Comparative View*, p. 72.   80. Jardine, *Letters*, I, p. 268.
81. Andrews, *Comparative View*, pp. 145, 159; see also John Burton, *Lectures on
Female Education and Manners*, 2 vols (1793).
82. Ibid., II, p. 83.

and a 'false' politeness.[83] False politeness consisted of 'unmeaning ceremonies', 'affectation', 'dissimulation', 'ostentation', and was the politeness displayed in social spaces.[84] True politeness, what 'gives lustre to all qualities',[85] was to be found within: 'Your behaviour at home, when withdrawn as it were, from the public eye ... will be the real criterion of courtesy'.[86] Thus, when Sir John Fielding declared that 'the utmost of a woman's character is contained in domestic life', this 'domestic' space was set in contrast to 'society', where girls become 'intoxicated' and women think only of 'how to appear ... with the greatest advantage'.[87]

Social spaces were increasingly associated with danger both to men's masculinity and to women's virtue. What the 'domestic' sphere that emerges at this time represents is not a 'private sphere' where women would become isolated, but an idealised space for the production of a virtuous and moral nation. If, as we argue in the introduction, the new construction of gender in the late eighteenth century entailed that 'men should and *would* desire women', it was in this 'domestic' sphere that this heterosexual desire was to be nourished and fulfilled. This is why 'domesticity' could be and was extolled for men as well as women.[88] Though domestic spaces, like social spaces, were shared by men and women, there was a crucial difference: social spaces were spaces where women reigned, but domesticity implied a reordering of gender relations epitomised by the gender hierarchy of men's 'mastery in the home'.[89]

At the same time, as John Tosh argues, 'the relationship between domesticity and masculinity' is ambiguous.[90] Even if men ruled the household, domesticity alone could not eliminate the anxieties about effeminacy that attended their being where women

83. Ibid. See also Rev. John Bennett, *Letters to a Young Lady*, 2 vols (Dublin, 1789).

84. Burton, *Lectures*, II, p. 91; Bennett, *Letters*, p. 121. As Brewer argues, politeness 'thrived on being watched and seen', *Pleasures of the Imagination*, p. 102.

85. Bennett, *Letters*, II, p. 121.   86. Burton, *Lectures*, II, p. 92.

87. Sir John Fielding, *The Universal Mentor* (1763), p. 250; James Fordyce, *Sermons*, I, p. 20. See Cohen, *Fashioning Masculinity*, ch. 5, on which this discussion of social spaces and domesticity is based.

88. At the same time as John Bennett rhapsodises about the 'domestic' woman, he complains about how 'undomesticated' many young men are. *Letters*, II, pp. 96, 98, 124–5. See also Knox, *Essays*, II, VI 'On the happiness of domestic life'. The use of the term 'domestic' here does not necessarily entail acceptance of the analytical model of separate spheres. It would be valuable to explore further the meanings of 'domestic' and 'domesticity' for the late eighteenth century and disrupt some assumptions, as John Tosh has begun to do in his contribution to this volume, 'The old Adam and the new man: emerging themes in the history of English masculinities, 1750–1850'.

89. Ibid., p. 223.   90. Ibid., p. 228; Knox, 'On the happiness of domestic life'.

were. As William Alexander observed, though the society of women is one of the most powerful influences on men's conduct and manners, if men are 'perpetually confined to [women's] company, they infallibly stamp upon us the effeminacy, and some other of the signatures of their nature'. It is Alexander's solution to this problem that is significant. Men must spend some time with women (if only to ensure they will not 'contract a roughness of behaviour, and slovenliness of person'), but, to 'retain the firmness and constancy of the male', they must also spend time 'in the company of our own sex'. Homosociality alone could secure manliness. The question is how this balance was to be achieved.[91]

While politeness could be redeemed for femininity by shifting the site of its production from the social to the domestic, sincerity, the opposite of politeness, became a defining feature of English manliness. Though sincerity has a long history,[92] it was in mid-eighteenth century that it was constructed as the obverse of politeness, defined in opposition to it to represent a 'distinctively English possession, worn as the badge of a superior culture.'[93] Both politeness and sincerity were expressive systems, but whereas the language of politeness consisted of 'refined phrases' and 'fulsome compliments',[94] sincerity was the plain language of truth. The true English*man* was characterised not just by sincerity but by *blunt* sincerity and a 'courageous forthrightness of address'.[95] If, as I have argued above, the association of politeness with France had been an abiding problem for the English, sincerity, especially unpolished, resonated with echoes of a proud national ancestry, the ancient Briton.[96] Masculinity was re-defined in terms of a patriotic lineage, the 'manly . . . ancient nobility and gentry . . . rough, bold, and handy to pursue the sports in the field, or wield the spear and battle ax against the enemies of their country', unlike the present

91. Alexander, *History of Women*, I, p. 314. See also Tosh's discussion of this issue on pp. 228–30. I have argued that this is one factor in the expansion of public school education in the late eighteenth century. Cohen, *Fashioning Masculinity*, ch. 7.

92. See Leon Guilhamet, *The Sincere Ideal: Studies on Sincerity in Eighteenth-Century English Literature* (Montréal and London, 1974).

93. Newman, *Rise of English Nationalism*, p. 128; see his analysis of sincerity, pp. 127–39.

94. [Rev. John Harris], *An Essay on Politeness* (1775), p. 18; Bennett, *Letters*, p. 121. Politeness could even be a 'cloak for insincerity', Burton, *Lectures*, II, p. 96.

95. Newman, *Rise of English Nationalism*, p. 131.

96. For similar views on this topic, see Newman, *Rise of English Nationalism*; Samuel, 'Figures of national myth'.

weak, sickly . . . puny successors, who know no toils but those of the
toilet . . . a motley kind of beings who having caught the contagion
of every vice and folly on the continent . . . import them on their
return to contaminate the principles and customs of their native
country.[97]

Rejecting the 'false' politeness of social spaces made it possible,
once and for all, to shake off the cultural hegemony of the French
and the effeminating effects of their social practices. Regenerated
in a domestic space emblematic of national virtue, 'true' politeness
could become women's province, and conversation, the prerogat-
ive of the frivolous, the feminine and the effeminate: women and
the French.

97. *Town and Country Magazine* (March 1771), p. 134.

PART TWO

Virtue and Friendship

CHAPTER FOUR

The Body of the Friend: Continuity and Change in Masculine Friendship in the Seventeenth Century

ALAN BRAY AND MICHEL REY

In 1987 I heard Michel Rey, a student of J.-L. Flandrin in the University of Paris, give a lecture entitled 'The Body of My Friend'. The lecture was only an outline, and his early death left his doctoral thesis uncompleted and his loss keenly felt by many. But in the years that followed that lecture Michel and I often discussed the history of friendship, and I have sought in this paper to complete that paper as he might have done had he lived, as a tribute to his memory. It is a paper about the body of the friend at the onset of the modern world and its loss.

In seventeenth-century England friendship was dangerous. That is the principal difference between the friendship of the modern world and the friendship I shall describe in this paper, and it was so because friendship was then a public relationship not the private and comforting relation the word is apt to suggest today. To the inhabitants of seventeenth-century England the 'friend' was readily a patron (or a client), a landlord, or creditor or debtor, someone who could use influence on your behalf, obtain a payment, or settle a dispute; and that evocative collective term 'our friends' (or its counterpart 'friendless') represented your hold on a potentially hostile world.[1]

It is easy to consign a past instrumental friendship of this kind to history as a 'feudal' relic, a stepping stone on the way to modernity, but this is not how I shall approach it. Rather the argument of this paper is that in the year 1660, the year with which this collection of

---

1. On the dangerous nature of friendship in seventeenth-century England, see David Wootton, 'Francis Bacon: your flexible friend', in J.H. Elliott and Laurence Brockliss, eds, *The World of the Favourite* (New Haven, forthcoming).

papers opens, the public signs by which friendship between men was created and recognised had a history that visibly stretched back into medieval England. Within only a single generation these signs had gone. This paper is an account of that change and of the echo from it that is still with us.

The embrace

The symbolic world that at this point was poised on the edge of change is caught in the gesture described below. Its setting is the hunting lodge that James I maintained at Royston among the woods and fields of Hertfordshire; but the account, published 35 years after the event, assumes that the gesture will be readily intelligible to its readers. It also proves to have a ready meaning far beyond the conventions of the court. The description appears in the memoirs of Sir Anthony Weldon, who at the time of the incident recounted was an office-holder in James I's court. The Earl referred to is Robert Carr, James's friend and now the Earl of Somerset, who is saying his farewells to James before returning to London and to the commission of enquiry that was to lead to his ruin. The date is the autumn of 1615.

> The Earl of Somerset never parted from him with more seeming affection than at this time, when he knew Somerset should never see him more; and had you seen that seeming affection (as the author himself did) you would rather have believed he was in his rising than setting. The Earl when he kissed his hand, the King hung about his neck slabbering his cheeks, saying 'For God's sake when shall I see thee again? On my soul, I shall neither eat nor sleep until you come again'. The Earl told him on Monday (this being on the Friday) 'For God's sake let me'. Said the King 'Shall I? Shall I?', then lolled about his neck, then 'For God's sake give thy Lady this kiss for me' in the same manner at the stair's head, at the middle of the stairs, and at the stair's foot. The Earl was not in his coach when the King used these very words (in the hearing of 4 servants, of whom one was Somerset's great creature and of the bedchamber, who reported it instantly to the author of this history) 'I shall never see his face more'.

Anthony Weldon's charge is that these gestures were a formality and a sham, that James had no intention of fulfilling what they indicated. For the social historian that is curiously helpful, for it detaches the gestures being described from what we might or might not make of James's relationship with Robert Carr and leaves them floating free as public signs with an understood meaning. What then was that meaning?

In one respect at least the picture Anthony Weldon gives needs a hefty discount, for this is the account of a man with a grudge. By the time Anthony Weldon came to prepare the manuscript from which this account was probably drawn by its editor he was no longer the courtier we see here. He had lost his post and was a bitter man. We therefore need to make some allowance for his malice. To slabber Robert Carr's cheeks was certainly to kiss him and to hang about his neck was to embrace him, but the colourful language in which these are described is Anthony Weldon's own.

The clue several centuries later on as to how to read this gesture lies in that reference to the staircase at Royston, where James chose to embrace Robert Carr. This was no casual choice. It was there, at the midpoint of the stairs, that James chose in 1623 to welcome back his son Charles and the Duke of Buckingham (who was to be the successor to Carr in the King's favour) from the Spanish journey, unseduced by Popery or Spanish princesses and when the church bells rang for them across the length of a mightily relieved Protestant England. On that occasion James had descended the stairs to their midpoint to meet them, a piece of carefully symbolic domestic geography. In Weldon's description James has not only accompanied Carr to that point but has done so all the way to the foot of the stairs and at each point – at the head of the stairs, at the midpoint, and at their foot – he had embraced Carr before the eyes of all the court.

The embrace he gave Robert Carr was a gesture not only expected of a King or of King James. Indeed it was so readily intelligible a gesture precisely because it was so familiar. When James had sought to reconcile Robert Carr to the rising George Villiers (the Duke of Buckingham to be) by encouraging Carr to take Villiers as his client, it was this gesture he asked Carr to give Villiers, as Anthony Weldon recounts it in the memoirs from which the above extract is drawn. The speaker is the King's servant Sir Humphrey May:

> 'My Lord, Sir George Villiers will come to you to offer his service and desire to be your creature; and therefore refuse him not, embrace him, and your Lordship shall still stand a great man, though not the sole favourite'. My Lord seemed averse. Sir Humphrey then told him in plain terms that he was sent by the King to advise it, and that Villiers would come to him to cast himself into his protection, to take his rise under the shadow of his wings. Sir Humphrey May was not parted from my Lord half an hour, but in comes Sir George

Villiers and used these very words 'My Lord, I desire to be your
servant and your creature and shall desire to take my Court preferment under your favour and your Lordship, and your Lordship shall
find me as faithful a servant unto you as ever did serve you'.

The displaced Robert Carr, however, did not embrace George Villiers
but rather offered to break his neck (a reply, Anthony Weldon
added, that savoured more of spirit than wisdom). Had the gesture
been given as James had asked, it would have been the public sign
of a patron and client: a man under Carr's protection, his faithful
servant and friend, his creature as George Villiers put it. For Anthony
Weldon, the cynical nature of James's hypocrisy was that James had
given Robert Carr this gesture before the eyes of all the court on
the very eve of Carr's fall. As Anthony Weldon put it, one would
have rather thought that he was in his rising than in his setting.[2]

This publicly displayed intimacy is what Francis Bacon, writing at
the time in his essay *Of followers and friends*, called 'countenance',
the appearance of a patron's evident favour; and the influence it
advertised was a gift that could readily be turned to advantage.[3]
The material gifts that turned the wheels of seventeenth-century
society are still readily apparent, the gift of offices especially and
the flow of fees and sweeteners they could bring. Less apparent are
the symbolic gifts that could be as readily exploited. Arguably the
most eloquent of these was the physical intimacy we see here, from
which a wider intimacy could be read: the gift of the body.

Both Robert Carr and James potentially benefited through a
gesture like this. Carr benefited from being powerfully reinforced
as James's friend and James as his good lord. James benefited
through the tacit obligation it placed Robert Carr under. But while
the benefit for Carr was immediate in the 'countenance' it gave
him, for James the benefit was deferred to when he might call on it.

---

2. Sir A[nthony] W[eldon], *The Court and Character of King James* (1650), pp. 102–
3 and 97–8. Three editions of Anthony Weldon's book were published in 1650 and
a fourth was published in 1651. I have quoted from the edition of 1650 catalogued
in the British Library as 610. a. 32. All four editions differ in spelling and punctuation, and the 1651 edition contains some alterations and additional material not
contained in the earlier editions; these appear to be of an editorial nature. If Anthony
Wood is correct, all four editions were published after Anthony Weldon's death:
Anthony A. Wood, *Athenae Oxonienses*, ed. Philip Bliss, 4 vols (1813–20), II, p. 868.
'Naturally': I have emended the apparent misprint 'naturall' (in line with other
editions). Page 103 of Weldon is misprinted as '130'. 'Slabbering' (spelt 'slabboring'
in Weldon): to wet. 'Let': to allow to go. 'Villiers': I have used the more familiar form
than the 'Villers' used in the text. I have used 'Humphrey' rather than 'Humfrey',
which is the spelling in the text.

3. Francis Bacon, 'Of followers and friends' in *Essayes* (1597) p. B4ᵛ.

The gesture he had given Carr was for James a form of symbolic capital – part of what contemporaries characterised as 'honour' – and it was the deferral of its return that created a continuing relationship between them. This gift – in this case false coin according to Anthony Weldon – was what James gave Carr that day.[4]

The table

The public embrace was though only one of the bodily signs of friendship. Another was eating together; and this was the point of James's claim that he would not eat without the departing Carr. It was the table that most of all transformed the stranger into the friend.

The common table was part of the symbolic geography of all the great houses of seventeenth-century England, centres of influence far beyond their roles as homes for the English aristocracy; and James's lodge at Royston shared in this symbolism. The buildings themselves were often constructions of the sixteenth century or later, but well into the seventeenth century their domestic symbolism was still visibly of a kind with the great houses of the medieval aristocracy; and in the courtesy books of the Middle Ages the 'service' of a lord was firstly service at the table, in cutting the food, filling the cup and so on. These were tasks that were carried out for a lord by his gentry supporters acting as his personal servants, and they conferred the same 'countenance' as the public embrace of the kind we see here. But they did so because the wider role of the great house required it to contain different levels of society as part of one household, whether or not always physically present, and the symbolism of the body and the bodily functions such as the common table readily represented its nature.

By the seventeenth century one can see this visual symbolism most clearly in the colleges of the universities. The fellows and fellow commoners (the more wealthy students) would eat at the high table in the great hall. The scholars would sit apart in the great hall, and the numerous poorer students (often working their way as servants in the colleges) would sit further apart or be waiting on

4. The classic anthropological account of gift-giving is Marcel Mauss *The Gift*, trans. Ian Cunnison (1954). This has been utilised in understanding sixteenth-century friendship: by Natalie Zemon Davis, 'Beyond the market: books as gifts in sixteenth-century France', *TRHS* 33 (1983), pp. 69–88; by Felicity Heal, *Hospitality in Early Modern England* (Oxford, 1990); and by Lorna Hutson, *The Usurer's Daughter: Male Friendship and Fictions of Women in Sixteenth-Century England* (1994).

the tables. The visible effect would not have been greatly different from that produced by the crowds of tenants and visitors eating or drinking in the hall of a great house. The great halls in the seventeenth-century universities reflected an older architectural pattern that had largely been abandoned in the great houses by the later fourteenth century, but the move of the high table that had taken place then in the great houses from the dais in the great hall to the great chamber above only further emphasised the procession of the dishes first to the high table and then back down for what was left to be eaten by those further down the social scale.

The eating and drinking in the great hall illustrates a part of the workings of seventeenth-century friendship that is not apparent when a gesture such as the friend's embrace is seen in isolation. The formal nature of such friendship was not a mutuality of interest but a mutuality of obligation. The obligation to reciprocate that the gift of the embrace tacitly imposed on the recipient was not necessarily an obligation to the giver. It could be met, or rather passed on, to a third party and by doing so reaffirm the solidarity of a group. The progress and return of the food in the great hall reflected an obligation of that kind, identifying those taking part as common insiders at precisely the points where the symbolic system emphasised social divisions. Those at the high table ate first and so on down the social chain; but the dish was the same, and your restraint was the gift that passed on.

Gestures of this kind did more than indicate bonds of friendship, as a signpost might indicate a town: they created them. This perhaps most of all now requires an act of imagination on our parts, as it is a way of thinking that is now largely alien to us, in which representation is constitutive and not merely mimetic. There is a curiously similar survival of this way of thinking in the Catholic doctrine of the Mass. When in Catholic theology the bread is taken, blessed, and broken, it is *changed* into the body of Christ. It was through a mechanism of that kind that the table changed the stranger into the friend.

The bed

What then of that other claim that James made, that he would not sleep until Robert Carr returned? If eating and drinking created friendship, so too did sleeping together. The inhabitants of seventeenth-century England slept in beds or pallets set up at night, and (as one can see from their size) such make-shift beds were usually shared, and the epithet 'bedfellow' readily suggested the intimacy of a friend. This is the significance of the comment in Anthony Weldon's account that Robert Carr's 'great creature' was 'of the bedchamber', and the symbolism it drew on was as old as that of the common table. This is John Paston writing home hopefully to his mother in 1479: 'I think that Sir George Brown, Sir James Radcliffe, and other of mine acquaintance which wait most upon the King and lie nightly in his chamber will put to their good wills'.[5] The implication is the same as in this gratified note from early in the seventeenth century: 'His Majesty understanding of our coming presently sent for us into his bed-chamber and did use us very graciously'.[6] That gesture was still fully alive in 1678 when John Evelyn proudly recorded in his diary: 'I had a private audience of his Majesty in his bed-chamber'.[7]

The intelligibility of the gesture was not restricted to the royal bedchamber. John Chamberlain glossed the epithet 'bedfellow' as indicating who was 'the chief man' about William Cecil, Lord Roos;[8] and the glamour it could exercise is played out to comic effect in George Chapman's play *The Gentleman Usher*, when the gullible gentleman usher is seduced into acting as pander by the embrace and shared bed of a young nobleman, who then broaches the delicate subject in the intimacy of their lying together.[9] As the audience would have been well aware, it was not only a woman's seduction that could be discussed in the intimacy of a shared bed. When William Laud dreamt of the great Duke of Buckingham sharing his bed, a dream he noted in his diary, it was that intimacy that he was dreaming of.[10]

In the universities the sleeping arrangements were as carefully orchestrated as the eating and drinking in the great hall. It was common for a tutor to share his room with a student who acted as his personal servant. Where the student might act as the tutor's patron the dependence was reversed, so much so that a tutor in

5. Norman Davis, ed., *Paston Letters and Papers of the Fifteenth Century* (Oxford, 1971), p. 617. 'Radcliffe': Radclyff'.

6. Sidney Sussex College, Cambridge, Ward papers/ 'Some passages of the synod of Dort'.

7. E.S. de Beer, ed., *The Diary of John Evelyn* (1959), p. 647.

8. Norman E. McClure, ed., *The Letters of John Chamberlain*, 2 vols (Philadelphia, 1939), II, p. 80.

9. Allan Holaday, ed., *The Plays of George Chapman: The Comedies* (Urbana IL, 1970), pp. 161–7 and 213.

10. James Bliss, ed., *The Works of . . . William Laud*, 7 vols (Oxford, 1847–60), III, p. 170.

sixteenth-century Oxford discovered that he was in danger of having surrendered his rights over a valuable young man by allowing him to share the cubicle of another tutor.[11]

Historians of the royal court have persuasively demonstrated how the gentlemen of the royal bedchamber were deliberately employed as a tool of government, but what was being employed in this was not the sacred nature of monarchy. The stratagem it employed was so effective because it was so common and readily intelligible.[12]

The chamber pot

Perhaps the most striking illustration to us now of bodily symbolism of this kind is that which arose out of the emptying of the chamber pot, a ubiquitous fact in pre-modern housing of all kinds. For someone to dispose of someone else's bodily wastes could carry the same indication of intimacy as sleeping or eating together, to which it was of course an adjunct. The Groom of the Stool at James's court at Royston was Sir Thomas Erskine and he was able to write with some pride on the precise details of the state of the King's stool. His pride was not misplaced for his role fixed his position by the King. He was also entitled to sleep on a pallet at the foot of the King's bed and to be alone with the King in the coach.[13] His role though was in its effect the same one that Lady Anne Bacon had complained of Antonio Pérez occupying in the household of Francis Bacon 'as a coach-companion and bed-companion',[14] and was but the same role writ large of a poor student in a Cambridge college in emptying his tutor's chamber pot.

Gender and society

It is not greatly difficult to reconstruct this symbolic system from the pieces one sees. They cohere too easily. But identifying the

11. Rosemary O'Day, 'Room at the top: Oxford and Cambridge in the Tudor and Stuart age', *HT* 34 (February 1984), p. 34.

12. David Starkey *et al.*, *The English Court: From the Wars of the Roses to the Civil War* (1987).

13. Neil Cuddy, 'The revival of the entourage: the bedchamber of James I, 1603–1625', in Starkey *et al.*, *The English Court*, pp. 185–6. Also David Starkey, 'Representation through intimacy: a study in the symbolism of monarchy and court office in early-modern England', in Ioan Lewis, ed., *Symbols and Sentiments* (1977), pp. 187–224.

14. Lambeth Palace Library 653/318. In Gustav Ungerer, *A Spaniard in Elizabethan England: The Correspondence of Antonio Pérez's Exile*, 2 vols (1974), I, p. 219.

place this symbolism occupied within seventeenth-century society more widely is a great deal more precarious. In the evidence I have used, this symbolic system appears as part of the life of the great houses of seventeenth-century England. But is it simply that the light is strongest here?

The evidence available to any historian of pre-modern England is overwhelmingly that left by the elite. That is true even of evidence in administrative records that appear to provide accurate information about ordinary people, such as court records. The information recorded (and the information excluded) was at the choice of those who controlled those records, and it is the outline of their concerns that we see in the evidence remaining. No sources automatically relieve the historian from the extremely difficult decision of how to generalise from the evidence that remains. It is that question I propose now to turn to in the context of this symbolic system.

One reason for being open to the possibility that this symbolism was not uniquely a function of the great houses is that the great houses were far from being populated only by the gentry. I have already mentioned the tenants and visitors that would have been part of the crowd in the hall. Nor was the way of life in the great house altogether different from that of the farmer living and eating in the same house with the farm's labourers. Similarly the colleges, whose halls replicated those of the medieval great houses, were by no means wholly places of education for the wealthy. They contained also others studying alongside them, who might be maintained there by a bishop or a local corporation. More likely though such students would be maintaining themselves by working as servants to the colleges or to the wealthier students. Would the signs I have described not then potentially be intelligible to them in other contexts also?

Arguably the most abrupt difference between the great houses and society more widely is the point I have so far avoided: that the great houses were overwhelmingly a world of men. At first sight, this fact more than any other seems to make it impossible to generalise from them to society at large. It is, I would suggest, the guide we are looking for, or rather it leads us to it if we follow its trail.

James's lodge at Royston was almost entirely composed of men, members of the Court and servants alike. The point was true of all the great houses of the time. The names of the members of the household of the Earl of Derby in 1587 for example contain only two female servants in comparison to the overwhelming roll call of male names – the Johns and Henrys and Edwards and Richards and so on, in the hall, the chamber, the kitchens, the offices, the stable, the pantry, and the cellar.[15] The Northumberland household earlier in the century[16] and the Warwick household a century before that[17] show a similar overwhelming majority of men. The same was true of the colleges at the universities, which admitted only male students and employed only male servants, insofar as the work was not carried out by the poorer students themselves.[18] It is difficult to imagine a wider view of this gift of the body that I have described that did not take account of the apparent fact – in this evidence at least – that the body being given was male.

The explanation is not that the great houses and the colleges were masculine enclaves cut off from contact with women. They had extensive links with the many women who were traders supplying its needs, or who were its tenants, or worked on the land or with the animals belonging to the house. The point is rather that these women did not live and work within it. When a great house needed work that women normally did – work such as washing clothes or looking after cattle – this work was carried out by women outside the house whenever it could be, by the river or a well or in the fields. In this respect the women associated with the great house were in a position not fundamentally different from that of the women who supplied the house's needs as traders rather than servants. They ate, they drank, and they slept outside the great house. When they were unmarried (as many would have been given the stage of life service represented) they would have lived together with other single women in a tenement or in a group of cottages. Such groups of women are a visible feature of sixteenth- and seventeenth-century England and were often organised around the fact of shared work.[19]

15. *Remains Historical & Literary Connected with the Palatine Counties of Lancaster and Chester*, Chetham Society (1853), pp. 23–7.

16. *The Regulations and Establishment of the Household of Henry Algernon Percy* (London, 1827).

17. C.D. Ross, 'Household accounts of Elizabeth Berkeley, Countess of Warwick', *Transactions of the Bristol and Gloucestershire Archaeological Society* 70 (1951), pp. 91–2.

18. John M. Fletcher and Christopher A. Upton, '"Monastic enclave" or "open society"? A consideration of the role of women in the life of an Oxford college community in the early Tudor period', *HE* 16 1, (1987), pp. 1–9.

19. P.J.P. Goldberg, *Women, Work, and Life Cycle in a Medieval Economy* (Oxford, 1992), pp. 313 and 317–18. Peter and Jennifer Clark, 'The social economy of the Canterbury suburbs: the evidence of the census of 1563', in Alec Detsicas and Nigel Yates, eds, *Studies in Modern Kentish History* (Maidstone, 1983), pp. 79–80. Derek Keene, *Survey of Medieval Winchester*, 2 vols (Oxford, 1985), I, p. 388. Charles Pythian-Adams, *Desolation of a City* (Cambridge, 1979), p. 203. In France such groups of women continued into the eighteenth century. Olwen Hufton, 'Women without men: widows and spinsters in Britain and France in the eighteenth century', *JFH* 9 (1984), pp. 361–2.

The maleness of the great house is the corresponding phenomenon to these groups of women living and working together but in
a male context; and one can see the same phenomenon also with
unmarried itinerant male journeymen living with other men working in the same trade in the town.[20] Nor was it only with unmarried
men and women that work in large measure determined where the
inhabitants of seventeenth-century England ate, drank and slept.
This was true for most people, as little domestic housing of the
time allowed for food to be cooked safely or for washing, either
the body or clothes. Hence the ubiquitous bakers and laundresses
of this society and the stalls and street vendors where cooked food
could be bought. When survival was as pressed as it was for most of
the inhabitants of this society, then eating, drinking and sleeping
tended to be carried out as close as possible to where someone
worked, whether or not they had a marital home. Sundays and
holidays apart, it was the place of work that often then determined
where these needed to be carried out; and these pressures would
have applied to a married servant as much as to an unmarried one.
It was in this way that the constraints of work shaped the greater
extent to which in this society, in comparison to our own, the daily
cycle of working, eating and drinking, the bodily functions and
sleeping was carried on outside the marital home.

Service in the great houses was men's work, and that fact in large
measure determined for its inhabitants where this daily cycle was
carried out. But service in the great house was characterised alike
in this way when the service was carried out by gentlemen as well as
by menial servants, as such work was not labour alone. When social
life was shaped as widely by work as this, 'work' was not only an
economic activity. It was also a means by which social relationships
could be established and given meaning. The symbolism of the
body of the friend was such an instrument.

From this vantage point, the symbolic gift of the friend's body
does not appear as necessarily a gift between men, nor was it only a
gift that carried a meaning in the context of a great house. The
guide to its place in seventeenth-century society is the nature of the
sign itself rather than the immediate context in which we now see
it several centuries on. It is no accident that the meaning of this
symbolic system is now clearest to us in such a context of power and
place. The gift of the body was a sign of power and security in the
friend, and wherever power was diffused – into whatever levels

20. E.J. Hobsbawm, 'The tramping artisan', in *Labouring Men* (1968), pp. 34–63.
R.A. Leeson, *Travelling Brothers* (1979).

it seeped – so too was potentially diffused the gift of the friend's body.

In seventeenth-century England the word 'love' could comprehend as easily the relationship between a generous lord and a dutiful servant as the more private meaning we give the word today, but wherever on that wide spectrum the gift of a friend's body might lie it gestured towards a place of comforting safety in an insecure world.

Bodily humour

This is a conclusion that puts in focus the bodily humour in this society that does not fit at all easily with our own anxious assumptions about homosexuality. It is a humour that could be rough and cruel, as in the message James I included for Henry Howard in a letter to James's secretary Robert Cecil. The letter is heavily laden with earthy humour, and in James's rough way it was intended to be affectionate. This was despite the reminder to Howard of his father's execution by Henry VIII. James's message for Howard was a response to his jocular annoyance at seeing James's sons prospering so well. James's reply was his intention of producing more such sons to annoy Howard: 'but be he sure I will immediately upon my return have his head for this labour and in as great haste as King Henry my noble predecessor got his father's, who could not go *ad centrum terre* without it, but in one point I am greedier than he was, for whereas the head alone served him, I will have body and all together'.[21]

It could be teasing, as in the prospect John Stubbe offered his college friend Michael Hickes concerning a certain John Drury, of whose friendship Michael Hickes had been jealous (Which of us both, he had written, do you love best?). 'This term', Stubbe cheerfully volunteered, 'he is like enough to be your bedfellow.'[22] Or it could be charmingly salacious, as in the affectionate wish James Thickness included in a letter to John Evelyn, who was in Rome and had written to his friend about the things he had seen: 'The scholar's wife wished herself a book: and I a statue, to be the object of that fair mind, those dear eyes, those curious hands, which enliven antiquity as well in a friend as in a ruin'.[23]

21. Hatfield House, Cecil Papers, 134/71.
22. BL, Lansdowne Manuscripts, 21/26 and 12/217.
23. BL, Evelyn Correspondence, 11/1229. The words 'to be' have been deleted before 'a statue', and I have omitted the character before 'friend'. My thanks to Douglas Chambers for this reference.

James Thickness's letter, for all its insouciance, was a formal ('familiar') letter of friendship. When he wrote his letter to John Evelyn they were still young men with hopes of preferment, practising between themselves the eloquent gestures they hoped preferment would bring them; and one can trace in its good-humoured homoeroticism, as much as in that of King James, the social cohesion that could be signified by the symbolic gift of the friend's body. Humour like this is a long way from the imprecations against the abhorred but exotic figure of the 'sodomite' that one sees in seventeenth-century England. The image of the sodomite we see there, who was variously assumed to be an atheist or a papist (and as likely as not an agent of the King of Spain and a companion of witches and werewolves), was held at a distance for much of the time from the label one might attach to one's neighbour or oneself. Such a response must have been especially easy in a reassuring context like this, for what after all was being given here but the body of the friend? [24]

Desire

A desire for such a gift does not correspond easily to anything in our culture several centuries on, but one can recapture the magnetism it could then exert through one of the stories in William Painter's *The Palace of Pleasure*. For the modern reader this needs some teasing out, as the immense popularity of this collection of stories lay in the purchase they exercised on the fantasies of their sixteenth-century readership.

The story opens with a symbolism that may by now be familiar.

> Besides the country of Perche, there were two gentlemen, which from the time of their youth lived in such great and perfect amity, as there was between them but one heart, one bed, one house, one table, and one purse.

The one bed, one house, and one table is something we have already met, as the physical intimacy that was the friend's gift. The story's first readers would also have been alert to that final addition, the one purse, to which the narrator returns.

---

24. I have discussed the extent to which this was the case in seventeenth-century England in my *Homosexuality in Renaissance England* (London, 1982 and New York, 1995), especially pp. 67–80.

Long time continued this perfect friendship: between whom there was but one will and one word, no difference in either of them. Insomuch as they not only seemed to be two brethren, but also they appeared in all semblances to be but one man. One of them chanced to marry. Notwithstanding they gave not over their friendship, but persevered in their usual amity as they were wont to do. And when they happened to be strained to straight lodging, the married gentleman would not stick to suffer his friend to lie with him and his wife. But yet you ought for friendship sake to consider that the married man lay in the mids. Their goods were common between them, and the marriage did yield no cause to hinder their assured amity.

In time that amity was poisoned, by the married friend conceiving a suspicion of his wife's fidelity with his friend. The curious twist to the modern reader is that the story does not present the problem as one of jealousy or sexual desire but in the *secrecy* that led the one friend to keep his suspicions from the other.

I know well enough that jealousy is a passion so intolerable as love itself. And when you shall conceive that opinion of jealousy, yea and it were of myself, I should do you no wrong, for yourself were not able to keep it. But of one thing which is in your power, I have good matter whereof to complain, and that is because you will conceal from me, your malady, sith there was no passion or opinion which you conceived, that before this time you kept secret from me. Likewise for my own part if I were amorous of your wife, you ought not to impute it as a fault unto me, because it is a fire which I bear not in my hands, to use at my pleasure. But if I kept it to myself from you, and endeavour to make your wife know it by demonstration of my love, I might then be accounted that untrustiest friend that ever lived.[25]

The moral of the tale, as Painter goes on to recount it, is that what destroys their friendship is not jealousy over a woman but secrecy between friends.

Within the setting of the story is the Elizabethan 'secretary', a role which has since changed both in status and usually in gender also. The 'secretaries' of Elizabethan noblemen were those highly educated and able men who were part of their households and acted as their go-betweens with the world: the coveted route to advancement for the army of poor but able graduates that the

25. William Painter, *The Palace of Pleasure* (1575), pp. 256ʳ–8. 'Accounted': spelt 'accompted'; see Oxford English Dictionary (Oxford, 1980) 'Account . . . *v*.'. 'Mids': now obsolete in English, meaning 'the middle'. 'Sith': in the now archaic sense of 'seeing that'. The 1566 edition (folios 336ʳ–338ᵛ) differs in some textual respects. It is Lorna Hutson who has taught us how to read William Painter, in *The Usurer's Daughter*.

sixteenth-century universities produced in such numbers. The origin of their title was that they could keep a 'secret'.[26] It is that role that is being decked out here in the trappings of this fable about secrecy and that animated the story for its sixteenth-century readership.

The setting of the story as that of two intimate friends unveiled rather than concealed its placing in sixteenth-century society for its original readers, for the one heart the two friends shared is that stance of a disinterested affection one sees in the formal ('familiar') sixteenth-century letter of friendship that was the textual counterpart to the gift of the friend's body.[27] It was often passionately expressed in ways reminiscent of James's protestations to Robert Carr. The story's open secret is that of a sixteenth-century secretaryship, and from this setting comes the symbolism of the body of the friend with which the story opens and the intimacy on which it then turns. The one house and the one table are the coveted position in the household of a patron, the one bed is the intimacy they gave access to, and the one purse is the reward these could bring. The readers of William Painter's book were most unlikely though to have had such a coveted post; they were rather the kind of men that dreamed of having one, and that dream was the fantasy this story played on: its moral was that they should be trusted and its fantasy was that one day they might be. This was all the more so because the author tantalisingly presents himself in the 'familiar' letter to the Earl of Warwick that opens the volume as in actuality himself possessing just such a relationship. The excitement the story was designed to arouse – almost pornographic in its virtual setting – is directed then not towards the body of the friend's wife, the tale of adultery that we might now be inclined to see as the narrative structure, but towards the body of the male friend himself.

Change

Why did the symbolic system I have described, a system of such apparent enduring strength, so abruptly fall away, as it appears to

26. The role is explored in Richard Rambuss, *Spenser's Secret Career* (Cambridge, 1993).

27. They were designed to be copied, preserved and circulated and by this means advertise the same 'countenance' as the bodily gestures I have described here but in an enduring and circulating form. Their role as concrete and visible tokens of friendship is the explanation for their preservation and their subsequent survival in such numbers. It is arguably their survival that now tells us most about the role they played.

have done?[28] The conclusion to this paper will consist of some suggestions as to the possible reasons for that change, but to do this I will need to move away from the close detail of seventeenth-century culture that I have been following so far, to the changes taking place within English society in the closing decades of the seventeenth century.

One of these changes was a radically different attitude to homosexuality, which might appear to be a determining element in this broader transformation. It is towards the end of the seventeenth century in England that the image of the sodomite lost the alien associations that had kept it at such a distance from an image that one might normally apply to oneself, to one's neighbour or one's friend. The change gave the 'sodomite' a new actuality and was quickly evident in violent action directed against homosexuality on a scale without precedent in English history. It also provided a radically new meaning to the desire for the body of the friend; and when in 1749 an Englishman described the practice of two men kissing each other as a foreign and sodomitical practice, he seems to have been unaware that it had ever been thought otherwise. Was it in this change that the symbolic gift of the friend's body was lost?[29]

One might be uneasy about so neat an explanation, as this symbolic system not only became unacceptable, it also became unintelligible. Most visibly, it is at this point that the great houses of the English countryside cease to be able to provide the stage for the

28. The continuity in the symbolic system described in this paper is illustrated by the joint tombs of Sir William Neville and Sir John Clanvowe from the end of the fourteenth century and that of Sir John Finch and Sir Thomas Baines from the end of the seventeenth century (Siegrid Düll, Anthony Luttrell and Maurice Keen, 'Faithful unto death: the tomb slab of Sir William Neville and Sir John Clanvowe, Constantinople 1391', *Antiquaries Journal* 71 (1991), pp. 174–90, and Jean Wilson, '"Two names of friendship, but one Starre": memorials to single-sex couples in the early modern period', *Church Monuments* 10 (1995), pp. 71–9. The embrace depicted in the first is the embrace that would have been the public sign of their sworn brotherhood many years before. In the second monument the final union of the two friends' bodies, represented by the common funerary urn depicted on their memorial, repeats the embraces of the two men that the monument also reverently records. In each monument the representation is that of the two friends lying together in their final bed and in their final embrace.

29. I described this change in *Homosexuality in Renaissance England*, particularly in ch.4: 'Molly'. My book was concerned with male homosexuality, but in a seminal paper Valerie Traub has argued for a comparable development at the same point for female homosexuality: 'The perversion of "lesbian" desire', *HWJ* 41 (1996), pp. 19–49. The thesis outlined in these paragraphs on the creation of the 'perversions' and their wider significance is set out by Valerie Traub in this paper.

[Anon] *Satan's Harvest Home* (1749), p. 51.

expansive gestures I have described. In part this was due to physical changes in the layout of such houses. The introduction of back stairs and of servants' dormitories located in basements removed the servants of the late seventeenth-century great house from view (and with the backstairs the removal of the chamber pot finally ceased to be a public sight). The open 'prospect' of the eighteenth-century country house was an illusion produced by this seventeenth-century removal of servants from sight; and with these changes the crowds of male servants sleeping close at hand or by a door, once so ubiquitous, disappeared from view.

The companions to these physical changes were corresponding changes in the way of life being carried on in the great houses and by those affected by them. These similarly imply that bodily intimacy of the kind I have described was no longer an intelligible sign. At the same point as the lower servants disappeared from sight and from looking on, one ceases also to see the crowds of tenants and visitors drinking in the great hall; and it is significantly also at this point that gentlemen cease to serve at the table, the bed, or the stool and such service begins to be regarded as menial or degrading.[30]

Changes of the same kind are also apparent in the universities at this point, which had long reflected the symbolic geography of the great houses. It was during the course of the eighteenth century that the practice fell away of the poorer students waiting on the table or acting as personal servants, changes which reflected the same change in attitude apparent in the disappearance of the gentlemen servants in the great house. Students could still be required to share rooms and beds when there was overcrowding, but as one can see from their letters home this was now thought to be onerous and inconvenient. There is no sign in these complaints of the meanings that had once been attached to such intimacy.[31]

It seems from the comments of visitors that England was diverging in this from a way of life that still continued across the Channel. The separation of servants that was the norm by this point was noted as surprising both by the German visitor Johann Wilhelm von Archenholz and by Pierre Grosley and François de la

---

30. Mark Girouard, *Life in the English Country House* (New Haven CT, 1978), pp. 122–3, 136–43, 189, 219.

31. V.H.H. Green, 'The university and social life', in L.S. Sutherland and L.G. Mitchell, eds, *The History of the University of Oxford*, 8 vols (Oxford, 1984–94), V, pp. 322–7 and 330–1.

Rochefoucauld (and his tutor) when they visited England in the second half of the eighteenth century.[32] Surprised European visitors also noticed that Englishmen had replaced the embrace and the kiss with the handshake.[33]

These changes are strong indications that it was at this point that the gift of the friend's body lost the significance it had so long carried; but if they are symptomatic of that change having occurred, they are not its cause. At its end, the argument I have followed in this paper does lead to one possible explanation. I have suggested that the immediate social context for the gift of the friend's body in sixteenth- and seventeenth-century England was the greater extent to which in this society, in comparison to our own, the life of the body – in the daily cycle of working, eating and drinking, the bodily functions and sleeping – was carried on outside the family, in the sense of being carried on outside the marital home. I have argued that bodily intimacy was then enabled by this wider currency to become an instrument by which social relationships could be established and given meaning; and the good-humoured homoeroticism we sometimes see in the gift of the friend's body signalled the place of comforting security such relationships afforded in an insecure world.

These wider ties did not leave the family unaffected. They rather helped to embed it in relations of service and formal friendship that both made it porous to inspection and correspondingly supported. One expression of this was the practice in English society of adolescents leaving their parents' home to act as servants in households higher in the social scale, often with their parents then receiving children in similar circumstances from below.[34] Such a gift across social divisions curiously echoes the communal eating and drinking in the hall of a great house I described earlier: creating bonds of social cohesion at precisely the points at which the symbolic system emphasised social division. The inhabitants of seventeenth-century England lived, in effect, in a potential multiplicity of families, a fact that can be disguised today by the family

32. [Johann Wilhelm von Archenholz], *A Picture of England*, 2 vols (1789), I, p. 128. [Pierre Jean] Grosley, *A Tour to London*, trans. by Thomas Nugent, 2 vols (1772), I, p. 40. Jean Marchand, *A Frenchman in England 1784* (Cambridge, 1933), p. 25. Norman Scarfe, *Innocent Espionage* (Woodbridge, 1995), p. 199.

33. von Archenholz, *A Picture of England*, II, pp. 103–4. [Honoré Gabriel Riquetti, Comte de Mirabeau], *Mirabeau's Letters during his Residence in England*, 2 vols (1832), I, p. 189.

34. Grant McCracken, 'The exchange of children in Tudor England: an anthropological phenomenon in historical context', *JFH* 8 (1983), pp. 303–13.

defined as the group of mother, father and children now coinciding with other definitions such as presence in a common household.

By the end of the seventeenth century the historic transition was already underway in England in which the family – in the sense of the unit composed of parents and their children – detached itself from these wider ties. What replaced them were the ties of family solidarity between mother, father and children which have since come to be regarded almost exclusively as creating 'the family'.[35] This transformation placed a burden of social meaning on the heterosexual bond between husband and wife that before it had not been required to carry alone. Was that burden of meaning the reason why the gift of the body came to be acknowledged only as a sexual gift between men and women?[36]

That this may indeed be the explanation for the ending of the symbolic world I have described is reinforced by a fundamentally parallel phenomenon. Homosexual desire was not represented in this new conception of the sodomite as an alternative sexuality, a different but in some way logically symmetrical choice to heterosexuality. It was a perversion. The assumption is encapsulated in the title of a broadsheet published in 1707, containing a sensational account of the arrest of a group of sodomites: *The Women-Hater's Lamentation*.[37] An asymmetry as pointed as this gave these new conceptions of the sodomite an unspoken affinity with the burden of social organisation now placed on heterosexuality. The perversion of heterosexuality in the one appears as the evidence for the naturalness and inevitability of the other. It was the first step in that proliferation of 'perversions' that was only to multiply in the scientific culture of the eighteenth and nineteenth centuries.

These two phenomena are two sides of the same newly minted coin and together constitute a change fundamental enough to have torn apart the symbolic world I have described. I am inclined to think therefore that it is indeed here that the explanation lies for its ending. But whether or not I am right in suggesting this explanation, as the older meaning that had once adhered so powerfully to the desire for the body of the friend slipped finally away, the new sexual culture of eighteenth-century England was ready to provide

35. Jean-Louis Flandrin, *Familles: Parenté, Maison, Sexualité dans l'Ancienne Société*, trans. Richard Southern as *Families in Former Times* (Cambridge, 1979).

36. The material I discuss in this paper is in marked contrast to the need for the instrumentality of a fictional female viewer to articulate desire for the male body analysed by Karen Harvey in the eighteenth-century erotica discussed in her paper in this volume.

37. Anon, *The Women-Hater's Lamentation* (1707).

it with a new and radically abjected meaning. The world about it had changed, and the body of the friend was lost.[38]

38. *Transcription:* To assist the non-specialist reader, the quotations in this paper (whether from original or modern editions) are given with modern punctuation, spelling, and capitalisation, other than in the titles of books. I have expanded abbreviations, and I have not preserved italic type. Quotations not in English are given in translation. Where I have emended a misprint I have noted this. I have also noted where it is not immediately obvious that at issue is a different spelling rather than a different word and where I have adopted more familiar spellings of names than in the quotation.

CHAPTER FIVE

Homo Religiosus:
Masculinity and Religion in
the Long Eighteenth Century

JEREMY GREGORY

In 1673, Richard Allestree, regius professor of divinity at Oxford and provost of Eton, lamented his failure to convince 'the more impregnable, masculine part of the gentry' of the need to live a religious life, and he described those who neglected religion as 'our masculine atheists', echoing contemporary opinion that scoffers against religion were more likely to be men. This led him to place his hopes on what was widely perceived to be a surer link between femininity and religious piety. '[T]o speak an impartial Truth', he concluded, ''tis not to be denied, that the reputation of Religion is more kept up by women than men.'[1] In the light of Allestree's comments it might be thought that the two co-ordinates of this essay, 'masculinity' and 'religion', are rather ill-paired. Much recent eighteenth-century scholarship has implicitly agreed with his premise of a negative correlation between men and religion, and has suggested that men were in the vanguard of atheism, although few scholars have shared Allestree's assumption that this was a matter of concern.[2] Instead they have tended to celebrate this implicit association between masculinity and irreligious – perhaps even a-religious – attitudes. If religion is mentioned at all, it is what Randolph Trumbach has labelled the 'religion of libertinism', which,

1. [Richard Allestree], 'The Ladies Calling', in *The Works of the Learned and Pious Author of the Whole Duty of Man* (Oxford, 1726), pp. 25, vii–viii.
2. *Inter alia*, Robert P. Maccubin, ed., *'Tis Nature's Fault: Unauthorised Sexuality in the Enlightenment* (Cambridge, 1987); George S. Rousseau and Roy Porter, eds, *Sexual Underworlds of the Enlightenment* (Manchester, 1987); Peter Wagner, *Eros Revived: Erotica of the Enlightenment in England and America* (1988); M. Hunter and D. Wootton, eds, *Atheism from the Reformation to the Enlightenment* (Oxford, 1992); and David Berman, *A History of Atheism in Britain: From Hobbes to Russell* (1988).

apparently, was characterised by 'the new meaning attached to sexual relations between males'.[3] Acknowledgement of this negative association between masculinity and religion has been encouraged by the standpoint of most historians dealing with the topic. By and large they have taken an unabashedly 'modernist' tone, which has led them to concentrate on men as secular beings without any reference to religious considerations. For these historians, the interest of the period after 1660, and especially after 1700, is that it saw the origins of current-day gender definitions.[4] Trumbach, for example, has argued that 'the modern system of gender and sexual relations' emerged precisely in this period, when this-worldly hedonism and sexual gratification replaced outmoded Christian priorities. Furthermore, according to Anthony Fletcher, a whole new series of printed genres from about 1670, such as conduct books, medical literature, periodical literature, and the novel, were related to, and underpinned, these new gender relations, and their preoccupation with the here and now.[5]

While there may be something to say in support of all these suggestions, it seems clear that, although a new area for historical enquiry, the history of masculinity is fast developing a periodisation, which will force studies of manliness to ape the increasingly outmoded characterisations of more traditional political and social history. As England supposedly moved from a religious to a secular world, the 'godly man' of Stuart England is seen as being replaced by the 'polite man', the 'sentimental man' or the 'sexual man' of the Hanoverian period,[6] and interest lies in these new men and not

3. Randolph Trumbach, 'Erotic fantasy and male libertinism in enlightenment England', in Lynn Hunt, ed., *The Invention of Pornography: Obscenity and the Origins of Modernity, 1500–1800* (New York, 1993), p. 254. Trumbach's views can also be followed in his other work (see Further Reading in this volume, pp. 239–58). Others who stress the importance of homosexuality above all else in discussing eighteenth-century masculinity include R. Norton, *Mother Clap's Molly House: The Gay Subculture in England, 1700–1830* (1992).

4. Gill Perry and Michael Rossington, eds, *Femininity and Masculinity in Eighteenth-Century Art and Culture* (Manchester, 1994) does not mention religion. The secularising tendencies can be seen even for the period before 1660. Susan D. Amussen, '"The part of a Christian man": the cultural politics of manhood in early modern England', in S. Amussen and M. Kishlansky, eds, *Political Culture and Cultural Politics in Early Modern England. Essays Presented to David Underdown* (Manchester, 1995), despite the title, fails to explore the religious implications of masculinity.

5. Trumbach, 'Erotic fantasy', pp. 254–5; Anthony Fletcher, *Gender, Sex and Subordination in England, 1500–1800* (New Haven CT, 1995), p. 385. He claims, on p. 283, that in the late seventeenth century 'a new secular ideology of gender' emerged.

6. See Sears McGee, *The Godly Man in Stuart England: Anglicans, Puritans and the Two Tables, 1620–1670* (1976), which largely stops in 1660. For the 'polite man', see L. Klein, *Shaftesbury and the Culture of Politeness: Moral Discourses and Cultural Politics in*

in the older religious ideals which had governed men's lives and expectations in the past. Ironically, a project which began in an attempt to uncover varieties of masculinity and in challenging some of the assumptions of more conventional history, may end up in marginalising strands of masculine behaviour, as well as certain discourses of masculinity, from the historical record.

This chapter argues instead for the importance of studying the religious context of much of the prescriptive literature for male behaviour. Indeed what may be surprising in recent attempts to examine masculine behaviour in the long eighteenth century, and in the fashionable interest in the languages surrounding masculinity, is the almost wholesale neglect of the large number of religious tracts, sermons and pamphlets (written from across the whole range of the religious spectrum) explicitly concerned to fashion male attitudes within a religious context. Taken together, these publications are illustrative of the ways in which the new print culture not only bolstered up new possibilities for gender roles but could also be harnessed in support of more traditional priorities.[7] Of course, as a source for discussing masculinity, this material is slippery. Books with such promising-sounding titles as *The Whole Duty of Man* (first published in 1658 and reprinted most years during the late seventeenth and eighteenth centuries, making it one of the best-sellers of the period) were aimed at a generic humankind, rather than being gender specific.[8] Similarly, the promising-sounding sermon by George Whitefield delivered in 1750 and entitled 'The putting on the new man a certain mark of the real Christian', in which he proposed to 'explain what [St Paul] would have us to understand by the New Man', was in fact a plea that 'real religion' should

---

Early Eighteenth-Century England (Cambridge, 1994); for the 'sentimental man', see G.J. Barker-Benfield, *The Culture of Sensibility: Sex and Society in Eighteenth-Century England* (Chicago IL, 1992), John Mullan, *Sentiment and Sociability: The Language of Feeling in the Eighteenth Century* (Oxford, 1988), Janet Todd, *Sensibility: An Introduction* (London and New York, 1986), John Sheriff, *The Good-Natured Man. The Evolution of a Moral Ideal, 1660–1800* (Alabama, 1982), and Henry Mackenzie's popular novel, *The Man of Feeling* (1771); for the 'sexual man' see T. Hitchcock, *English Sexualities, 1700–1800* (Basingstoke, 1997), his 'Redefining sex in eighteenth-century England', *HWJ* 41 (1996), pp. 72–90, and P.G. Boucé, ed., *Sexuality in Eighteenth-Century Britain* (Manchester, 1982).

7. On the ways in which new cultural forms supported older priorities, see Jeremy Gregory, 'Anglicanism and the arts: religion, culture and politics, 1600–1800', in J. Black and J. Gregory, eds, *Culture, Politics and Society in Britain, 1660–1800* (Manchester, 1991), pp. 82–109.

8. One of the contenders for the authorship of this most popular book was Lady Dorothy Packington. It is now accepted that it was written by Richard Allestree.

replace 'nominal Christianity'.[9] This was something that transcended gender boundaries, although modern sensibilities should warn us that behind such 'sexist language' are important unspoken assumptions about the relationship between gender and religion.[10] However, there are hundreds of printed titles specifically and clearly directed to men. In shaping the religious male, these can be regarded to have begun with conduct books written for young men, often under the rather nebulous category of 'youths', and especially those youths living in London and the larger towns where it was deemed 'harder to live a religious life'.[11] These were considered to be the key group for those interested in fashioning correct male behaviour, since, because they were at a transitional stage, it was hoped to put them on the right path for the rest of their lives.[12] An example of the concern to mould the behaviour of young men is the Presbyterian Thomas Gouge's *The Young Man's Guide, Through the Wilderness of this World, to the Heavenly Cannan. Shewing him how to carry himself Christian-like in the Whole Course of his Life* (1685), reprinted several times during the eighteenth century, and which emphasised, in almost Weberian fashion, the link between hard work and godliness. Gouge exhorted young men to avoid 'drunkenness', 'wantonness', 'uncleanliness', 'filthy and obscene talk', looking at 'lascivious pictures', and going to the theatre, which he considered 'a decoy for the stews'.[13] A parallel Anglican tract was Josiah Woodward's *The Young Man's Monitor: shewing the great happiness of early piety, and the dreadful consequences of indulging youthful lusts* (12th edition by 1793).

Other publications which can be considered to have explored the relationship between religion and masculinity were admonitions to men in positions of power and authority, represented at their most lofty by sermons to or about kings. George Horne's 'The Christian King', preached in 1760, compared Christ and Charles I, and argued that all men should imitate Christ, 'particularly in the article of suffering patiently'. Samuel Chandler's *The Character of a Great and Good King full of Days, Riches and Honour* was delivered on

---

9. George Whitefield, *The Putting on the New Man a Certain Mark of the Real Christian. A Sermon Preached at the Tabernacle, on 5 January 1750* (1750), p. 8.

10. Dale Spender, *Man made Language* (1980) and Toril Moi, *Sexual/Textual Politics: Feminist Literary Theory* (1985).

11. James Fordyce, *Addresses to Young Men*, 2 vols (1777), II, p. 320.

12. On the importance of 'youth' see I.K. Ben-Amos, *Adolescence and Youth in Early Modern England* (1994) and Paul Griffiths, *Youth and Authority: Formative Experiences in England, 1560–1640* (Oxford, 1996).

13. Thomas Gouge, *Young Man's Guide*, p. 391.

the occasion of the death of George II.[14] This category also encom-passed sermons preached before (male) members of parliament, before (male) magistrates at the assizes, before (male) aldermen, and before (male) electors. Other categories of the genre include manuals for men in more private capacities as husbands and fathers.[15] There are also more work-related publications such as Richard Steele's *The Tradesman's Calling* (1684, and reprinted in 1776 and 1780), Josiah Woodward's *The Soldier's Monitor* (1705, dished out to Marlborough's armies, and which reached its 30th edition in 1802), and his *The Seaman's Monitor* (1700, 14th edition by 1799), which emphasised the importance of 'spiritual ejaculations'.[16] Further examples include Edward Welshman's *The Husband Man's Manual* (1694), the anonym-ous *The Duty of a Husbandman. Containing Rules and Directions how the Business of Husbandry may be Improv'd to a Spiritual Advantage* (1703), publications written for professional and institutional and male-dominated bodies such as visitation charges to clergy, sermons to the Sons of the Clergy, and sermons to bodies such as the Society for the Reformation of Manners. Some of these writings were class-specific, such as Thomas Gisborne's *Enquiry into the Duties of Men in the Higher and Middle Classes of Society in Great Britain, Resulting from their Respective Stations, Professions, and Employments* (1795), and, for a different section of society, John Manncock's *The Poor Man's Cat-echism: or the Christian Religion* (1752). This suggests that overarching categories such as masculinity need to be complicated by issues of class and status.[17] To a certain extent, of course, much of the advice offered here mirrored that in a complementary series of works addressed to women.[18] Nevertheless, it is possible to discern a

14. George Horne, 'The Christian King', *The Works of the Right Rev. George Horne,* ed. W. Jones, 6 vols (2nd edn, 1818), III, pp. 398–401; Samuel Chandler, *The Char-acter of a Great and Good King, full of Days, Riches and Honour. A Sermon Preached on the Occasion of the death of His Late Majesty, King George II* (1760).

15. For instance, Daniel Defoe's, *A New Family Instructor; in Familiar Discourses be-tween a Father and his Children, on the most essential points of the Christian Religion* (1727) and [Anon], *The Weaver's Garland; or a Christian's Patience. In twenty-seven Divine and Moral Lessons between a Despairing Husband and a Chearful Wife* (Worcester, 1765).

16. Josiah Woodward, *The Seaman's Monitor, wherein Particular Advice is given to Sea-Faring Men, with Reference to their Behaviour* (2nd edn, 1703), p. 23.

17. For a discussion of some of the theoretical debates about the relationship between theories of gender and theories of class, see J.W. Scott, *Gender and the Politics of History* (New York, 1988), and, with reference to the sixteenth and seven-teenth centuries, Susan Amussen, *An Ordered Society: Gender and Class in Early Modern England* (Oxford, 1988).

18. For a discussion of some of these, see Jeremy Gregory, 'Gender and the cler-ical profession in England, 1660–1850', in R.N. Swanson, ed., *Gender and the Christian Religion* (forthcoming).

number of particular ways in which these writers addressed the relationship between masculinity and religion. As Allestree himself acknowledged, 'the obligation to moral and Christian Vertues is in itself universal, and not confin'd to any sex', but he maintained that 'the all-wise Creator . . . hath put peculiar properties and inclinations into his creatures . . . and altho' in mankind, which differs not in species but in gender, the variety may seem less; yet there is still enough to found some diversity, either in the kind or degree of Duty'.[19]

In stressing the religious imperatives behind the tracts and pamphlets which aimed to direct male behaviour, I am not denying other, perhaps competing, but often complementary, discourses which existed in this period. But it is significant that the religious objectives most often promulgated in this period meshed easily with other ideals, whereas in other periods there was arguably more of a tension between religious and secular aims. G.R. Cragg once noted that 'seldom has the religious man seemed to be so happily at home in society as in eighteenth-century England', observing, however, that 'this kind of involvement with society encouraged worldliness',[20] a statement which seems to imply that religious ideals before the Evangelical revival were so watered down that there was little difference between religious and this-worldly aims. So, too, C.F. Allison has charted the reaction against the perceived growth of antinomianism in the mid-seventeenth century, which led to the 'rise of moralism' and, in his opinion, the lowering of the religious gold standard.[21] But Cragg and Allison's remarks might be viewed more positively; religious ideals in the eighteenth century encouraged a strong social involvement, not because religion had become too worldly, but because of the widely shared aim to sacralise and sanctify secular society, and to carry religious principles into the world. The household, work-place, school, political forum, and all scenes of everyday life were seen as the proper sites of Christian activity. Moreover, religious priorities could themselves change over time. If, as Sears McGee has argued, before 1660 the model of the godly man was a combative one, where leading a properly religious life was envisaged as a constant war between the world of the flesh and heaven, after 1660 theology can be seen to have modified its

19. Allestree, 'Ladies Calling', p. 1.
20. G.R. Cragg, 'The churchman', in J.L. Clifford, ed., *Man Versus Society in Eighteenth-Century Britain* (Cambridge, 1968), pp. 54, 59.
21. C.F. Allison, *The Rise of Moralism: The Proclamation of the Gospel from Hooker to Baxter* (1966).

priorities and to have developed the notion that a rational and benevolent God had created a universe in which earthly ends were desirable as well as heavenly bliss.[22] This is not to suggest that tensions between the fleshly and the heavenly spheres disappeared (Henry Sacheverell, for instance, told the Sons of the Clergy in 1713 that the religious life was a 'Christian warfare' where the godly man had continually to fight the good fight[23]), but rather it is to argue that religious priorities could be fulfilled by engaging with the world, rather than battling against it or withdrawing from it. This stress on engagement with the world, moreover, is surely not unrelated to the qualified Arminian triumph after 1660, which arguably made religious ideals the goal for all men (and women) and not just the religiously elect.[24] Many years ago, Norman Sykes urged us to think of the eighteenth century in terms not of secularisation, but rather of laicisation, where religious ideals and duties once reserved for the clergy were now to be pursued by all in society.[25] This might usefully help us in thinking about the ways in which religious ideals in the post-Reformation world could increasingly be placed on all men, and not only the clergy.

One way of gaining insight into the assumptions that governed expectations of men's behaviour is to examine contemporary texts (overwhelmingly by male writers) that sought to define the character of the ideal Christian man. Perhaps the most popular text to discuss the relationship between religion and masculinity was Richard Steele's *The Christian Hero. An Argument Proving that No Principles but those of Religion are Sufficient to Make a Great Man*, first published in 1701, reaching a 20th edition by 1820, and dedicated to Lord Cutts, the hero of the battle of Namur. Steele is usually regarded as one of the pioneers of the new bourgeois concern to demarcate gender roles, a project which was central to the creation of the new polite culture of the period, and as such his publications are often viewed

22. McGee, *Godly Man*, p. 43; G.R. Cragg, *From Puritanism to the Age of Reason: A Study of Changes in Religious Thought within the Church of England, 1660–1700* (Cambridge, 1950); R. Sher, *Church and University in the Scottish Enlightenment: The Moderate Literati of Edinburgh* (Princeton NJ, 1985); R. Porter, 'Enlightenment and pleasure', in R. Porter and M.M. Roberts, eds, *Pleasure in the Eighteenth Century* (Basingstoke, 1996), p. 3. See also the essay in the same volume by C.D. Williams, '"The luxury of doing good": benevolence, sensibility and the Royal Humane Society', pp. 77–107.

23. Henry Sacheverell, *A Sermon preach'd before the Sons of the Clergy . . . 10 December 1713* (1714), p. 30.

24. For a discussion of this, see John Spurr, *The Restoration Church of England, 1646–1689* (New Haven CT, 1991), pp. 314–17; 321–3.

25. Norman Sykes, *Church and State in England in the Eighteenth Century* (Cambridge, 1934), p. 379.

as crucial elements in fashioning modern secular ideals of gender.[26] Central to Steele's argument here, however, is the observation that, after surveying the fortunes of classical heroes – Caesar,
Cato, Brutus and Cassius, whose careers all ended in despondency
– religious faith is the only basis for the truly heroic man, sustain-
ing discipline, public responsibility and above all an 'extreme
magnanimity' and forgiveness which defined the highest ideal for
male behaviour.[27] Given that traditional ideals of manliness had
placed great stress on physical strength, hardiness, courage and
martial values, such an emphasis on forgiveness is an important
shift in priorities. Further, Steele stressed that the truly Christian
hero treated his enemies with moderation. He offered his readers
two models of Christian heroism, 'the two great Rivals who possess
the full Fame of the present Age', thinly disguised versions of William
III and Louis XIV. Both, according to Steele, can be placed within
a religious framework, but Louis is presented as the anti-hero who
aimed at 'an extensive undisputed Empire over his subjects', while
William is the true hero, who wanted his subjects' 'rational and vol-
untary Obedience'. Steele concluded: 'To one therefore religion
would be but a convenient Disguise, to the other a Vigorous motive
of Action'. In short, William had 'a quick sense of the distress
and miseries of mankind which he was born to redress'.[28] He was
presented as a Christian superman, troubleshooting problems as
they arose.

The theme of forgiveness and magnanimity as being the essential hallmark of a truly pious man was developed by James Fordyce
in his *Addresses to Young Men*, published in 1777. In a chapter entitled 'On a manly spirit as opposed to cowardice', Fordyce noted
that 'much as the Roman valour has been extolled, I cannot for my
part praise it so highly', and gave as what he considered to be an
example of true manly heroism, Edward the Black Prince, who had
treated his opponent, the King of France, benignly. 'This illustrious
young man had all his passions under his command; he was a
kingdom to himself; his mind was alike imperial and gentle; and
his whole life, stained with no dishonour, addressed with every
virtue, proved that his behaviour on this occasion was the result of
pure magnanimity.'[29] The ideals of masculinity envisaged here are

---

26. See A. Ross, ed., *Selections from The Tatler and The Spectator* (Harmondsworth,
1982); Klein, *Culture of Politeness*; Kathryn Shevelow, *Women and Print Culture: The
Construction of Femininity in the Early Periodical* (London and New York, 1989).
    27. Steele, *Christian Hero*, pp. 30, 72.   28. Ibid., pp. 87–92.
    29. Fordyce, *Addresses*, II, pp. 209–12.

interesting, encompassing as they do qualities of command (but of oneself rather than over others), balance (between being too imperious on the one hand and too gentle on the other), and living a virtuous life. Fordyce further observed that 'True Valour has nothing to do with any kind of bravery that is not guided by the light of reason, or excited by the calls of justice and humanity. With such instances of brutal or unrational resolution a real Christian has nothing to do.' But Fordyce was certain that this did not mean that a Christian man could not act vigorously, and cited biblical examples to back up his case, such as the men in the Old Testament who fought in the name of the Lord, the centurion mentioned in the gospels, and Cornelius, the soldier who was commended for his gifts of alms in Acts.[30] He also made the distinction between what he termed 'active' and 'passive' courage, favouring the passive variety:

> the courage of a mastiff can never merit much applause, on the same ground we give the palm of fortitude, or constancy in suffering, to those who, while they feel it in all of its sharpness, continue to bear it without repining or wearying . . . and this . . . affords for the most part a clearer evidence of the manly spirit we recommend, than the boldest deeds in the field, or in the breach.[31]

Fordyce also stressed the importance of 'modesty' and 'candour' in the ideal man, believing that these would be best practised 'by that youth who is careful to keep alive, in his own mind, a tender and uniform spirit of true religion, for this will teach him meakness, moderation, forbearance with others and diffidence in himself; it will teach him caution "not to judge that he be not judged"'. He concluded that 'there is nothing that constitutes so much to produce an independent mind, as being truly religious . . . [such men] will ardently wish all mercenary designs, and unmanly dissensions were as much as possible forgotten in the joint pursuit of one grand comprehensive object . . . the welfare of their country'.[32]

Associating true manliness with Christian principles in this way might be seen as backward-looking, and indeed several authors suggested that modern forms of masculine activity, and in particular the neglect of religious priorities, were indeed 'unmanly' and led to 'effeminacy'.[33] The connection between the perceived decline of

30. Ibid., pp. 216–17.   31. Ibid., p. 219.

32. Ibid., pp. 328–9, 332. He went on to claim that 'there is nothing that contributes so much as to produce an independent mind, as being truly religious'.

33. For a discussion of the meanings attached to effeminacy in the period, see P.J. Carter, 'Mollies, fops and men of feeling: aspects of male effeminacy and masculinity in Britain, *c.*1700–1780' (D.Phil. thesis, Oxford University, 1995).

religious morality and the rise of modern effeminacy was a recur-
ring trope throughout much eighteenth-century writing. John
Brown's *Estimate of the Manners and Principles of the Times* (1757–58)
was perhaps the most famous lament, where he blamed the weaken-
ing of religious commitment on the part of men for the growth of
effeminate behaviour. In Brown's view,

> show and pleasure [had become] the main objects of Pursuit: As
> the general Habit of refined Indulgence is strong, and the Habit of
> Induring is lost, As the general spirit of Religion, Honour and public
> Love are weakened or vanished; as these Manners are therefore left
> to their own Workings, uncontrolled by Principle; we may with truth
> and Candour conclude, that the ruling Character of the present
> times is that of a vain, luxurious, and selfish EFFEMINACY.[34]

In instances such as this the meaning of 'effeminacy' is slippery,
and should not be confused with present-day connotations. The
'effeminate male' in this literature was not associated overtly with
homosexuality so much as with vanity, decadence and luxury, all of
which might be seen as self-centred, in contrast with true manliness
which involved consideration for others.[35] In a similar vein, Fordyce
bemoaned the decay of public spirit, and the luxury, idleness, pride
and dissipation of the times, asserting that the 'chief spring of
these evils' was 'a growing disregard to the spirit and practice of
devotion' and a neglect of 'the living Forms of Truth and Virtue,
which have been admired by the wise, the pious, and the manly in
all ages'.[36] Absence of this spirit, according to Fordyce, made men
susceptible to vice which, interestingly, he depicted as female. Sustained by religion, however, the young man will be able to resist
such temptation. To support his views, Fordyce turned to history,
arguing that 'many of you know, that so long as Athens and Rome
retained the masculine spirit of their games and sports, the frugality and simplicity of their manners, their reverence for religion
. . . they continued to shine'.[37]

---

34. John Brown, *An Estimate of the Manners and Principles of the Times* (7th edn,
1758), pp. 66–7.
35. See Susan C. Shapiro, 'Yon plumed dandebrat: male "effeminacy" in English
satire and criticism', *Review of English Studies* 34 (1988), pp. 400–12, and Susan Staves,
'A few kind words for the fop', *Studies in English Literature, 1500–1900* 22 (1982),
pp. 413–28.
36. Fordyce, *Addresses*, II, p. 366. See too his essay, 'On a manly spirit as opposed to
effeminacy', ibid., p. 227, where he characterised effeminacy as 'selfish and vicious'.
37. Ibid., pp. 349–51, 321, 141.

Despite the apparently backward-looking and perhaps nostalgic link between masculinity and religion, other writers, surveying the sweep of human history, suggested that the Christian stress on benevolence and forgiveness was itself new, and unmanly. One year before Fordyce's publication, Edward Gibbon, in the notorious Chapters 15 and 16 of his *Decline and Fall of the Roman Empire* (1776–88), had criticised the degenerating effects of Christianity on manly Rome, later noting that 'the clergy successfully preached the doctrines of patience and pusillanimity; the active virtues of society were discouraged; and the last remains of military spirit were buried in the cloister'.[38] To counter criticisms such as these, Fordyce drew on reports from 'intelligent and experienced officers of the navy' to confirm that 'those of their people who had a sense of piety, commonly proved the most useful and steady in the moment of action'. He further suggested that courage and fortitude were things that all men should aim to demonstrate throughout their lives: 'to expect from the Almighty help or deliverance without any active endeavour . . . is not faith, but fanaticism, presumption and sloth united. It may be added that a manly and a Christian spirit lead to the same behaviour[:] . . . active benevolence'.[39]

Concerns about the relationship between religion and masculinity reached a peak during the 1790s, when the post-Gibbonian critique of the ways in which religious priorities had sapped manly vigour gained immediate resonance in the period of the French wars. The issue was especially marked in discussions of patriotism. The evangelical Thomas Gisborne's *Enquiry into the Duties of Men* (1795), for example, criticised the idea that 'the Christian religion does not inculcate patriotism in its followers', and argued instead that Christian virtues 'were all designed to enforce the principle from which alone true patriotism is derived, and from the reception of which it must necessarily result; namely, that those, whom any peculiar bond of union connects, are under peculiar obligations to mutual attachment'. Indeed he asserted that 'the whole period of Christ's ministry was a scene of patriotism, manifesting itself in enduring the most cruel usage from his own nation for the purposes of producing its happiness'. Thus, according to Gisborne, 'the greatest benefit which any man can render to his country, is to

38. Edward Gibbon, 'General observation on the fall of the Roman empire in the West' at the end of chapter 38, IV, in *The Decline and Fall of the Roman Empire*, ed. Christopher Dawson, 6 vols (1977), p. 106.
39. Fordyce, *Addresses*, II, pp. 224, 230.

contribute to the diffusion of religion and virtue, of science and learning . . . let the man who loves his country endeavour to render himself and his family a pattern of Christian virtue, of useful but unassuming knowledge, of modest and simple manners'.[40]

Statements such as these remind us that what is significant about the ideal type of the godly man as put forward by a number of religious writers in the eighteenth century is the stress on participation within society, rather than the religious alternative of abstaining or withdrawing from the world: the *vita activa* was held up as the model rather than the *vita contemplativa*.[41] By highlighting social action, and right conduct within the world, as being the hallmark of masculine religiosity, these writers allowed the godly man of the period to be linked with a public virtue long deemed manly. As the future clergyman William Johnson Temple observed in a letter to his friend James Boswell:

> The constitution of human nature plainly proves that we were born to do something more than speculate, and that a state of pure reflection is unnatural to man. It is not therefore he who thinks most, but he who is most active for the good of his country and of mankind, that merits the glorious character of a man of virtue.[42]

This concentration on right action and outward behaviour can, in large measure, be seen as a reaction to the religious upheavals of the mid-seventeenth century, which were widely blamed on misdirected inner spirituality and wrong-headed wranglings over theology.[43] It might also be suggested that this concern to relate religion and this-worldly activities had distinct links to the Christian humanism of the early modern period. Historians are so used to discussing late seventeenth- and eighteenth-century ideals in terms of 'civic

---

40. Thomas Gisborne, *Enquiry into the Duties of Men in the Higher and Middle Classes of Society in Great Britain, Resulting from their Respective Stations, Professional and Employments* (1795), pp. 110, 114, 117, 119.

41. The tension between the two can be seen throughout Christian history. For a medieval discussion of the different types of religious life see *The Cloud of Unknowing and Other Works*, translated and introduced by C. Wolters (1985), and G. Constable, 'Twelfth-century spirituality and the later middle ages', *Medieval and Renaissance Studies* 5 (1971), pp. 40–5. In some ways, my characterisation of the godly man in the eighteenth century has affinities with Weber's ideal type of the inner-worldly ascetic: H. Gerth and C. Wright Mills, eds, *From Max Weber: Essays in Sociology* (New York, 1946), pp. 324–8.

42. Temple to Boswell, 13 September 1763, in *The Correspondence of James Boswell and William Johnson Temple, 1756–1795*, ed. T. Crawford, 2 vols (Edinburgh, 1997), I, *1756–1777*, p. 67. I owe this reference to Philip Carter.

43. Fordyce, *Addresses*, p. 367.

humanism', that they have neglected the complementary package of Christian humanism, where the model of ideal behaviour was a Christian action man, who fulfilled the practical morality of the *philosophia Christi*.[44]

This emphasis on outward and public religiosity was partly because too great a concentration on inner and private religiosity was believed to have unwelcome results. Not only was this because the disorders of the civil war period were largely attributed to a misleading religiosity, increasingly seen as a product of madness, it was also because over-emotional religiosity (termed enthusiasm in the period) was associated with what were considered to be weak and irrational women, and on both counts this affronted the godly man.[45] To a certain extent the preference for public rather than private religiosity was also felt to be one of proof in religious matters: internal callings had so often proved to be false; on the other hand, public displays of religiosity could be seen and verified, and as such gave strong evidence of a truly religious life.[46] This is not to argue that the religious ideal in the period neglected the cultivation of inner spirituality altogether, or reduced religion to social conduct, as some contemporary evangelicals and later nineteenth-century detractors complained.[47] The point is that the religious male was not encouraged to dwell unduly on his inner spiritual feelings (which might be misguided) in a private and solitary manner, but rather to use them to some outward purpose, for the benefit of society. Even John Wesley, who was often a stern critic of much of the established

44. On civic humanism, see J.G.A. Pocock, *Politics, Language and Time: Essays in Political Thought and History* (New York, 1971), *The Machiavellian Moment* (Princeton NJ, 1975), *The Political Works of James Harrington* (Cambridge, 1977), and his '*The Machiavellian Moment* revisited: a study in history and ideology', *Journal of Modern History* LIII (1980), pp. 49–72. On Christian humanism, see Margo Todd, *Christian Humanism and the Puritan Social Order* (Cambridge, 1987). Although her analysis effectively ends in 1660, and is ostensibly linked to 'Puritanism', much of what she says can usefully be applied to the Church of England in the century and a half after the Restoration.

45. The shift in blaming misdirected religiosity on madness rather than on the devil can be traced in M. Heyd, *Be Sober and Reasonable: The Critique of Enthusiasm in the Seventeenth and Eighteenth Centuries* (1995); Ronald A. Knox, *Enthusiasm: A Chapter in the History of Religion, with Special Reference to the XVII and XVIII centuries* (New York and Oxford, 1950).

46. See McGee, *Godly Man*, p. 230; Knox, *Enthusiasm*.

47. This critique of the eighteenth-century Church can be found in the writings of Wesley, Evangelicals and Newman. But for some rehabilitation of the Church of England in the period, see the essays in, and especially the introduction to, J. Walsh, C. Haydon and S. Taylor, eds, *The Church of England c.1689– c.1833. From Toleration to Tractarianism* (Cambridge, 1993).

religion of the period, claimed that 'the Bible knows nothing about solitary religion'.[48]

What is also clear is that, in discussing appropriate forms of male conduct, these religiously orientated writers were not only backward-looking but, in certain cases, could actually challenge some of the traditional characteristics of acceptable masculine behaviour. In so doing they used religious priorities to justify what might be seen to be novel kinds of manliness, although in advocating these newer ideals they frequently returned to what they considered to be older and forgotten patterns of behaviour. In his *Gentleman's Calling* of 1660, Allestree, drawing perhaps on what some have seen as earlier 'Puritan' concerns, had worried about some of the most commonplace pastimes of the male elite, such as rural sports and hunting. He lamented their addiction to sport, noting that 'some make hawking and hunting their callings', and complained about the 'boorishness' of rural sports, anticipating later concerns to demarcate the polite and civilised man from the rustic unsophisticate.[49] Other religiously motivated writers voiced concerns about duelling. The duel had been central to the aristocratic code of the early modern period, embodying some of the fundamental attitudes of elite masculinity, such as the pursuit of honour and reputation, as well as a certain amount of military expertise. It had similarly featured in early modern religious imagery where the idea of the religious life as a duel with the devil featured in sermons such as Humphrey Sydenham's *The Christian Duell* (1634).[50] Eighteenth-century religious writers, however, were in the vanguard of the attack on such assumptions. Charles Moore, the incumbent of Boughton Blean, in a tract of 1790, attacked duelling as an affront to Christian principles, since it was a form of suicide. Others criticised duelling for being self-centred.[51] Arguably this decline in religious warfare

48. Quoted in Cragg, 'Churchman', p. 65.

49. There is now an extensive literature on Puritanism. The salient features can be traced in Patrick Collinson, *English Puritanism* (1983) and his *Godly People: Essays on English Protestantism and Puritanism* (1983). See also P. Lake, *Moderate Puritans and the Elizabethan Church* (Cambridge, 1982) and *Anglicans and Puritans? Presbyterianism and English Conformist Thought from Whitgift to Hooker* (1988); Allestree, *The Gentleman's Calling* (1660), pp. 104–5; Klein, *Culture of Politeness*.

50. Donna Andrew, 'The code of honour and its critics: the opposition to duelling in England, 1700–1850', *SH* 5 (1980), pp. 409–34, and V.G. Kiernan, *The Duel in European History: Honour and the Reign of the Aristocracy* (Oxford, 1988); Humphrey Sydenham, 'The Christian Duell, in two sermons. Ad magistratum. Preached at Taunton, 1634', in *Sermons upon Solemne Occasions*, 2 vols (1637), II, pp. 39–108.

51. Charles Moore, *A Full Inquiry into the Subject of Suicide. To which are Added (As Being Closely Connected with the Subject) Two Treatises on Duelling and Gaming*, 2 vols (1790); Carter, 'Mollies and fops', p. 235.

imagery was mirrored in a shift in ideals of masculinity, where the polite man of the eighteenth century replaced the martial hero of earlier periods. In using religious precedents in order to modernise masculine patterns of behaviour, Vicesimus Knox was able to link masculinity to the new sentimentalism of the 1770s in his essay 'On the Unmanliness of Shedding Tears', by justifying crying because 'Jesus wept': 'Hardness of heart, and insensibility of temper', he wrote, 'conceal themselves under the appellation of manly fortitude', but '[t]o shed tears on sorrowful occasions, is no mark of a weak understanding, but of that tenderness and susceptibility, as it is in the noblest distinction of human nature, is emphatically styled HUMANITY'.[52] Although Knox recognised that tears has been 'misused' by the 'weak' and 'artful', nevertheless he concluded that '[t]he lachrymal glands were intended by Providence for use, as much as a other part of the mechanism of the human frame'.[53] Knox also used religious considerations to condemn what he termed 'the boxing mania' of the period as bestial and an affront to truly manly behaviour: 'such a taste must proceed from gross ignorance of better and more manly pleasures', concluding that boxing was 'unworthy of a gentleman, unworthy of a good citizen, unworthy of a Christian, and unworthy of a man'.[54]

In drawing out their ideals of masculine behaviour, religious writers found it useful to point to role models for the godly man. Paradigmatic types for the religious male were complex, partly because the traditional link between piety and femininity meant that the religious male, and especially the clergy (as religious professionals), could be suspected for their personal associations with women (being accused either of being too like women, or accused of wicked practices in the confessional where they had undue influence over women). There was thus a clear need to find unimpeachable models. An obvious model was, of course, the archetypal Christian male Jesus himself. Jeremy Taylor's *The Life of Christ; or the Great Exemplar of Sanctity and Holy Life* (1649), reprinted several times throughout the late seventeenth and eighteenth centuries, and his *Holy Living* (1650) and *Holy Dying* (1651) articulated an interest in the life of Christ as a pattern for emulation, which differed from the conventional Protestant stress on seeing Christ in

52. Vicesimus Knox, *Winter Evenings; or Lucubrations on Life and Letters*, 2 vols (2nd edn, 1795), II, pp. 180–2.
53. Ibid.
54. Ibid., I, 'On the art which has lately been honoured with the name of pugilism', pp. 238–44.

purely soteriological terms.[55] Taylor's approach in using the life of
Christ as the religious role model became a favourite motif for later
commentators. In a sermon of 1694 John Sharp, the Archbishop of
York, told his listeners of 'our obligation to live as Christ lived'.[56]
Sharp neatly attempted to 'protestantise' Christ's behaviour, con-
trasting his lifestyle with that of the 'papists':

> He did not so spend his time in solitude and abstractions as to
> hinder the discharge of any of the works of his calling. On the con-
> trary, he lived more publicly, because of his frequent privacies. His
> retirements served for no other purpose, than to make him more
> active and vigorous in doing good when he came into company. He
> so managed his devotions towards God, that they were no obstruc-
> tions, but a great furtherance of the duties he owed unto men.[57]

Christ himself, according to Sharp, 'preferred acts of charity to
the exact observation of the Sabbath'. In sum, Christ's life 'was but
one continued illustrious expression of kindness and charity'.[58] Similarly, in 1728 Samuel Chandler, in his 'Doing Good Recommended
from the Example of Christ', noted 'the extensive usefulness of
[Christ's] life': 'And was ever life more usefully employed, ever
example more worthy our imitation? How can we better learn what
will please God, than from the example of God himself, when he
was manifest in our flesh . . .'.[59] Even Gibbon did not sneer at Jesus,
whom he considered, like Socrates, had 'lived and died for the
service of mankind'.[60]

The ideal of living like Christ also featured heavily in William
Law's concept of Christian perfection, which he developed in his
book of that name in 1726, where he maintained that the truly
religious man should strive to live up to Christ, and must take
literally Christ's command to be perfect. Law is usually seen as a
mystical writer, but his model of Christian perfection, which he
defined as 'the right performance of our necessary duties' and 'the
exercise of such holy tempers as are equally necessary and equally
practicable in all states of life', has a down-to-earth quality and
intimated that while it was of course impossible to emulate Christ

55. See McGee, *Godly Man*, pp. 107–10.

56. *The Works of the Most Reverend Dr John Sharp, late archbishop of York,* 7 vols
(1754), V, *Four Sermons on the Imitation of Christ,* p. 223.

57. Ibid., p. 271.   58. Ibid., pp. 273–4.

59. Samuel Chandler, *Doing Good recommended from the example of Christ. A sermon
preach'd for the benefit of the Charity School in Gravel-lane . . .* (1728), p. 1.

60. Quoted in Roy Porter, *Edward Gibbon. Making History* (1988), p. 121.

entirely, some move towards perfection was achievable.[61] Further examples of the way in which living like Christ was offered as an ideal for human emulation were the numerous editions of Thomas à Kempis's *Imitation of Christ* (over 100 during the eighteenth century).[62] By holding up the life of Christ as a role model, writers after 1660 were recognising the potential ways at least in which it was possible to follow Christ's example here on earth. In some ways this can be seen as a throw-back to pre-Reformation attitudes. If the original Protestant reformers had highlighted the enormous gulf between man and God, writers in the second century of the Reformation increasingly saw the possibilities for human achievement. This potential fits well with what some have considered to be the optimism of the eighteenth century, and helps to remind us that optimism – and the pursuit of happiness – should not be conceived in purely secular terms.[63] Sometimes this philosophical optimism, most notably leading to benevolence towards others, has been seen as a peculiarly latitudinarian sentiment. However, it can be demonstrated that this optimism was firmly rooted within mainstream Anglicanism.[64] Yet the possibility of imitating Christ produced its flip side: the problem of falling short of the ideal. Samuel Johnson, for example, who was also influenced by Law, showed in his sermons and private writings how aware he was of his own failings, and this could lead to self-doubt.[65] Paradoxically, a religious ideal which emphasised hope and potential could sustain a belief in despair.

In second place as an exemplar for the godly man was St Paul, called by Fordyce in his *Addresses to Young Men* 'the wise and manly

61. William Law, *A Practical Treatise upon Christian Perfection* (1726), introduction, p. 3. This anticipated many of the arguments found in his *A Serious Call to a Devout and Holy Life* (1728).

62. These included George Stanhope's version, which was issued in nineteen editions between 1698 and 1814, and Wesley's own translation, published in 1735, and still in print in the early nineteenth century.

63. See R. Newton Flew, *The Idea of Perfection in Christian Theology* (1934), pp. 244–51; McGee, *Godly Man*, pp. 107–8; J. Passmore, *The Perfectibility of Man* (1972); P. Quennell, *The Pursuit of Happiness* (1988); and D. Spadafora, *The Idea of Progress in Eighteenth-Century Britain* (New Haven CT, 1990).

64. R.S. Crane, 'Suggestions toward a genealogy of the "man of feeling"', *English Literary History* I (1934), pp. 205–30, and M.C. Jacob, *The Newtonians and the English Revolution, 1689–1720* (1976); Donald Greene, 'Latitudinarianism and sensibility: the genealogy of the "man of feeling" reconsidered', *Modern Philology* 75 (1977), pp. 159–83, and John Spurr, '"Latitudinarianism" and the Restoration Church', *HJ* 31 (1988), pp. 61–82.

65. M.J. Quinlan, *Samuel Johnson: A Layman's Religion* (Madison, 1964), p. 13. See also C. Chapin, *The Religious Thought of Samuel Johnson* (Ann Arbor MI, 1968) and C. Pierce, *The Religious Life of Samuel Johnson* (1983).

apostle'.[66] St Paul fulfilled the function of a role model in two ways. First, his own life could be admired as an example of manly conduct. Paul's conversion experience obviously appealed to those like George Whitefield who stressed the importance of a real and transforming conversion in shaping the truly religious male, and converts such as the former slave-trader John Newton saw his own conversion, on 21 March 1748 during a storm at sea, in Pauline terms.[67] And throughout his life, with its clear engagement with the world, Paul could be seen as the archetypal Christian man of action, and his worldly activities could be used as a stick to beat those who saw religious perfection in renouncing the world. Seeing Paul as the model for Christian manliness appealed to commentators from across the range of the religious spectrum. Nonconformists such as Isaac Watts and John Evans highlighted 'the example of St Paul, represented to ministers and to private Christians, out of the Acts of the Apostles, and his own divine letters' as a model for Christian behaviour. Likewise the Anglican John Lynch preached at Lambeth Palace in 1771 on 'St Paul's character . . . and his example recommended to his successors in the Church'.[68] Second, Paul's statements, as recorded in the Bible, offered a rich mine for later commentators who used Paul's words to defend certain ideals for the godly male. Henry Sacheverell, for example, used Paul to support the idea that the apostle took the marriage of clergy for granted 'for (as he excellently argues) if a man know not how to rule his own House, how shall he take care of the Church of God'.[69]

What is interesting in the choice of role models for true male religious behaviour is the ways in which they could transcend denominational and sectarian boundaries. English Protestant writers after 1660 drew freely on Roman Catholic models of spirituality. These

66. Fordyce, *Addresses*, II, p. 266.

67. Bruce Hindmarsh, *John Newton and the English Evangelical Tradition. Between the Conversions of Wesley and Wilberforce* (Oxford, 1996), p. 22.

68. *The Example of St Paul, Represented to Ministers and to Private Christians, out of the Acts of the Apostles, and his own Divine Letters . . . Recommended by the Rev. I Watts and Mr J. Evans* (1726); John Lynch, *St Paul's Character Considered, and his Example Recommended to his Successors in the Church. A Sermon preached in the Chapel at Lambeth . . .* (1771). See also John Fletcher, *The Portrait of St Paul; or, the True Model for Christians and Pastors. Translated From a French Manuscript of the late Rev. John William de la Flechere* (Shrewsbury, 1790).

69. Sacheverell, *Sermon . . . Sons of the Clergy*, p. 2 (quoting 1 Timothy v. 8). For another use of St Paul, see Samuel Chandler, *St Paul's Rules of Charity, and his manner of recommending it, considered in a sermon preach'd to the society for relieving the widows and orphans of Protestant Dissenting Ministers* (1749).

of course could be problematic, and, unless suitably doctored, associated the religious male with a suspect religiosity.[70] Nevertheless, the period saw the development of a whole genre of Catholic devotional works being suitably edited for Protestant eyes.[71] The seventeenth-century French nobleman Gaston de Renty seems to have held a particular fascination for late seventeenth- and eighteenth-century English Protestants, including John Wesley. In the light of my earlier comments, his popularity is not hard to explain. De Renty was well known for his charitable activities, and this appealed increasingly to a mind-set interested in action. And, as a nobleman, he was of interest to those who wished to convert the aristocracy as a way of influencing the rest of society.[72] It is interesting to note, too, that a significant proportion of these Catholic role models were laymen, reflecting deeply entrenched Protestant suspicions of Catholic clergy, who were roundly criticised for living apart from the world and not being men of action.[73] Church of England writers were similarly able to find approval for Nonconformist models. One of the most popular books of the entire period was John Bunyan's *Pilgrim's Progress*, appropriated (and perhaps deradicalised) by Anglicans.[74] Likewise, role models could transcend divisions within the Church of England. As possible paradigms for the godly man, Archbishop John Tillotson recommended reading William Hinde's life of the Puritan John Bruen, John Fell's life of the high-churchman Henry Hammond, and Cotton Mather's life of John Elliott.[75]

The ways in which religious role models could transcend differences not only within the Church of England, but also differences between Protestant groups and differences between Protestant and Catholic cultures, is, in part, representative of what seems to have been a typical eighteenth-century *rapprochement* between religious denominations. Arguably, what seemed increasingly more important was to join forces to combat the perceived decline in religious priorities and the rise of atheism, rather than indulging in the

---

70. Gregory, 'Gender and the clerical profession'.

71. Eamon Duffy, 'Wesley and the Counter-Reformation', in J. Garnett and C. Matthew, eds, *Revival and Religion since 1700. Essays for John Walsh* (London and Rio Grande, 1993), pp. 1–19.

72. Ibid., pp. 6–12.

73. Ibid., and Isabel Rivers, ' "Strangers and pilgrims": sources and patterns of methodist narrative', in J.C. Hilson, M.M.B. Jones and J.R. Watson, eds, *Augustan Worlds. Essays in Honour of A.R. Humphreys* (Leicester, 1978), pp. 195–6.

74. Gregory, 'Anglicanism and the arts', pp. 90–1.

75. Duffy, 'Wesley and the Counter-Reformation', p. 4.

religious in-fighting which had created such turmoil in the sixteenth and early seventeenth centuries.[76] In any case, material written for a specific denomination might be read by others outside it, which helped to break down denominational boundaries. Indeed one characteristic of the eighteenth-century godly man was that he was urged to avoid as much as possible religious disputes. Fordyce himself reminded his readers that true religion had 'nothing to do with the minute distinctions of sects, or the miserable disputes of bigots'.[77]

Nevertheless, despite the ways in which role models for the godly male could be easily transferred from one denomination to another, in times of crisis denominations accused their rivals of encouraging a debased masculinity. Church of England writers in particular used non-Anglican models to provide negative portraits of the anti-type. In Anglican propaganda, Catholics were counter models, being depicted as lechers, sodomites and deviants.[78] Monasteries were particularly condemned as being centres of debauchery and socially useless, harbouring parasites on society. Interestingly this negative literature has been noted by historians of sexuality, but they have tended to pick up on it as an example of the new pornography of the period, and have downplayed the religious implications.[79] Similarly, to Anglican eyes, Nonconformists could be seen as weak or effeminate, disturbing rather than supporting the social fabric. And the fact that both Catholic and Nonconformist groups appeared to have an appeal to women cast aspersions on the non-Anglican religious male.[80]

The role models of the religious male I have discussed were intended for laymen as well as for clergy. It has sometimes been said that the period degraded the religious professional, and witnessed the triumph of the laity in religious concerns.[81] What is clear is that after 1660 the religious professional had no specifically privileged role in religious matters: all men had a duty to fulfil the role of *homo religiosus*. Conversely clergy were expected to adopt certain aspects of a secular masculinity as part of the post-Reformation collapse of the division between the clergy and the laity. Sermons

76. W.J. Gregory, 'Archbishop, cathedral and parish: the diocese of Canterbury, 1660–1805' (D.Phil. thesis, Oxford University, 1993), ch. 5.

77. Fordyce, *Addresses*, II, p. 321.

78. Gregory, 'Gender and the clerical profession'.

79. Wagner, *Eros Revived*, pp. 47–86.

80. Gregory, 'Gender and the clerical profession'.

81. Claire Cross, *Church and People, 1450–1660* (1976); Peter Clark, *English Provincial Society from the Reformation to the Revolution: Religion, Politics and Society in Kent* (Hassocks, 1977).

preached before the Corporation of the Sons of the Clergy emphasised the crucial social role of the clergy and the entire Corporation was viewed as a defence of Protestant attacks on celibacy as the ideal for the religious male. Glocester Ridley, for instance, reminded his audience in 1757 of pre-Reformation England where a 'papal militia of monks and friars were . . . hands subtracted from the labour that was due to the public', and he stressed the benefits of the Reformation in allowing a married clergy: it helped the rise of population and contributed to national strength.[82]

It is of course possible to argue that, despite the use of adjectives such as 'manly', these role models of ideal religious conduct were meant to be exemplars for women as well as for men, being directed to all Christians irrespective of gender. But what is surely significant is that these role models for Christians are almost overwhelmingly male, in part reflecting the post-Reformation demoting of Mary and female saints as religious patterns.[83] In the seventeenth and eighteenth centuries religious role models, although often supposed to transcend gender boundaries, were in fact predominantly masculine. This connection between Christian precepts and masculine exemplars thus not only had implications for the relationship between masculinity and religion, but it arguably affected women, for whom religious role models were sparse. And those women who were held up as models did so by transcending their femininity, providing examples of ungendered behaviour.[84]

Most of what I have so far outlined could be classified as part of a prescriptive literature which indicated how men should behave, rather than describing how they actually behaved. It can fairly be suggested that one reason behind the writing of the sermons, tracts and pamphlets I have been discussing is that men in practice were not in fact acting out their role as *homo religiosus*, and they needed to be constantly urged to do so. We might also want to extend the nature of the material which highlighted the ideal Christian man, ranging from Richardson's *Sir Charles Grandison* (1753–54) to Handel's *Messiah* (1746) and Benjamin West's *Death of Wolfe* (1771),

82. Glocester Ridley, *A Sermon preached before the sons of the Clergy* (1757), pp. 8ff.
83. Marina Warner, *Alone of All Her Sex: The Myth and the Cult of the Virgin Mary* (1976).
84. Old Testament women such as Deborah, Rachel and Sarah were problematic models: D. Valenze, *Prophetic Sons and Daughters: Female Preaching and Popular Religion in Industrial England* (Princeton NJ, 1985), pp. 36–7. According to Phyllis Mack, Quaker women modelled themselves on the 'aggressive, male Old Testament heroes': *Visionary Women: Ecstatic Prophecy in Seventeenth-Century England* (Berkeley CA, 1992), p. 136.

to indicate that a whole range of cultural forms (and indeed some of the newer forms such as the novel and the oratorio) were used to spread religious role models and were not evidence of secular preoccupations. *Grandison* is a particularly significant exploration of Christian manliness. Both Elizabeth Carter, the bluestocking and daughter of the rector of Deal, and Catherine Talbot, who lived in the household of Thomas Secker, Bishop of Oxford, advised Richardson on his treatment of the theme of the Christian hero, and within the novel the stress is on the role of the Christian man within society, who works for the good of society as a whole.[85] Yet this prescriptive literature needs to be read not merely as a reaction to bad practice, or as simply idealistic wishful thinking. The Preface to the 1726 edition of *The Whole Duty of Man*, for example, declared that 'it may be esteem'd as a particular recommendation of what is here deliver'd, that it was practice before it was speculation . . . *The Whole Duty of Man* had its first and most correct edition in life and practice.'[86] Further links between precept and practice can be seen in the funeral sermon dedicated to the godly man where the speaker took the opportunity to use evidence of real life exemplary behaviour to disseminate this model to a wider audience.[87] Evidence of the ideal pious man can also be found in funeral monuments where encomiums stressing the deceased's virtues would be a constant reminder of ideal behaviour.[88]

And of course 'real life examples' of the religiously motivated man can be easily discovered, as instances of some men who self-fashioned their behaviour along the prescribed lines. We can point to the religious societies (both in their Anglican and later evangelical forms) and the Societies for the Reformation of Manners which seem to have had some success in translating the ideals into reality.[89] There is also a growing list of exemplary bishops and clergy, whose

85. Gregory, 'Anglicanism and the arts', pp. 83–95. See also George Lillo's hit play of 1735: *The Christian Hero: a Tragedy*. For a literary depiction of the anti-hero, see Matthew Lewis' gothic novel, *The Monk* (1795), which contained (although perhaps to a heightened extent) Protestant views of Catholic depravities.

86. *Whole Duty of Man*, preface.

87. For example, S. Chandler, *Christ the Pattern of the Christian's Future Glory. A Sermon occasioned by the death of the late Reverend Mr George Smyth*, and also [Anon], *The Triumphant Christian: or Faith's Victory over Death and the Grave. Exemplified in the Last Experience and Dying words of a Private Gentleman* (3rd edn, 1754).

88. K. Esdaile, *English Church Monuments, 1530–1840* (1946).

89. S. Burtt, *Virtue Transformed. Political Argument in England, 1688–1740* (Cambridge, 1992) and J. Innes, 'Politics and morals. The Reformation of Manners movement in later eighteenth-century England', in E. Hellmuth, ed., *The Transformation of Political Culture: England and Germany in the later Eighteenth Century* (Oxford, 1990), pp. 57–118.

biographies emphasised their charitable giving, their hospitality, and their involvement in the world, while also acknowledging their private frugality.[90] These published biographies are significant not because they necessarily accurately reflected the lifestyle of the cleric concerned, but because they indicate the standardised conventions of how the truly godly professional should behave. There are, too, a significant number of laymen who can also be fitted into this model of the religious male. These include figures such as the Duke of Newcastle, known for his scrupulous devotion;[91] Samuel Johnson, who believed that charity was the true cornerstone of Christianity, and who gave away earnings from publications to the poor;[92] William Legge, the second Earl of Dartmouth, who was mentioned as a possible original for Sir Charles Grandison;[93] Captain Thomas Coram, the founder of the Foundling Hospital;[94] Edward Colston (the high church Bristol benefactor);[95] John Kyrle (1637–1726), who regularly attended church, gave to the poor and hungry, and was the 'Man of Ross' commended for his religious virtues in Pope's *Epistle to Bathurst*;[96] and at a humbler level the diarist Thomas Turner who struggled to live a religious life in East Hoathly.[97]

Sears McGee has argued that in early Stuart England the godly man had used personal suffering as a drive to repentance. It is possible to suggest that in Hanoverian England this modulated into a concern with the suffering of others, rather than with one's own, and manifested itself most obviously in the interest in philanthropy which was such a feature of the period.[98] Edward Radcliffe, in

90. For examples of clerical biographies, see Thomas Birch's *Life of the Most Reverend John Tillotson* (1752), Beilby Porteus's 'Review of the Life of Archbishop Secker' in *The Works of Thomas Secker, LL.D, late Lord Archbishop of Canterbury* (1769), and the numerous clerical obituaries in the *Gentleman's Magazine.*
91. N. Sykes, *Church and State in England in the Eighteenth Century* (Cambridge, 1934), pp. 277–82, 437–9.
92. Quinlan, *Johnson*, pp. x, 109.
93. *DNB.*
94. *DNB.*
95. *DNB.* See also, *An Abstract of Several Publick Charities Given by Edward Colston, Esq, chiefly in his lifetime. Recommended to the imitation of the charitable reader, in a proportion to his abilities; and to excite him to give Glory to God, for conferring so much wealth on a man, whose heart was continually devising liberal things* (1721).
96. *DNB.* See H. Erskine-Hill, *The Social Milieu of Alexander Pope: Lives, Examples and Poetic Response* (New Haven, 1975), p. 33.
97. D. Vaisey, ed., *The Diary of Thomas Turner, 1754–65* (Oxford, 1984), *passim.*
98. McGee, *Godly Man*, p. 38; B.K. Gray, *A History of English Philanthropy* (1905); B. Rodgers, *Cloak of Charity: Studies in Eighteenth-Century Philanthropy* (1949); D. Owen, *English Philanthropy, 1660–1960* (1965); D. Andrew, *Philanthropy and Police: London Charity in the Eighteenth Century* (Princeton NJ, 1989). See also R. Goldberg, 'Charity sermons and the poor: a rhetoric of compassion', *The Age of Johnson* IV (1991), pp. 171–216.

stressing the importance of charity, maintained that 'befriending the poor and needy, is taking into our protection, and embracing in our arms the Son of God'.[99] Moreover, commentators observed that eighteenth-century charity differed from that in other periods and countries. Philip Bisse, for example, noted that

> the manner of disposing our Charity in this Age, is chiefly by ena-
> bling Corporations of many well-disposed and wealthy men, to be
> themselves the directors of what they give; and altho' they are
> empower'd to receive perpetual Endowments, yet is the Whole in
> trust for the Benefit of others, and no part of it to the Behalf of the
> Governours . . . a method in every part directly opposite to that, which
> Universally obtain'd among the Foundations of the Monastic Orders.[100]

And after surveying the charitable initiatives of the second half of the century (in particular those organisations founded by Messrs Hetherington, Coventry, Hanway, and Howard) Vicesimus Knox declared that 'Christian charity never shone greater than in this age'.[101] More generally perhaps, the move to charity and benevolence as being the hall-mark of the religious male suggests that we need to modify older interpretations of the Age of Benevolence. Many years ago W.K. Jordan linked the growth of philanthropy to a decline of religious priorities; for him a major consequence of the Reformation had been a marked decline in gifts to the Church and a corresponding rise in gifts to the poor, a shift which he interpreted as a move towards secularisation.[102] But, as urged by the writers of a large number of sermons, giving to the poor and needy was not at odds with religious priorities, but rather a fulfilment of them.[103] The link between religion and (predominantly male) charity can also be seen in the four paintings depicting biblical scenes given in 1746 by William Hogarth, Joseph Highmore, Francis Hayman and James Wills to the Foundling Hospital, in Hogarth's *The Story of the Pool of Bethesda* and *The Good Samaritan* (given to St

99. E. Radcliffe, *The Charitable man the best Oeconomist, Patriot and Christian* (1761), pp. 5, 14.

100. Philip Bisse, *A Sermon preach'd at the Anniversary Meeting of the Sons of the Clergy . . . 1708* (1709), p. 5.

101. Knox, *Winter Evenings*, II, p. 2. See also R.K. McClure, *Coram's Children: The London Foundling Hospital in the Eighteenth Century* (New Haven CT, 1981); J.S. Taylor, *Jonas Hanway, Founder of the Marine Society: Charity and Policy in Eighteenth-Century Britain* (1985); R. Morgan, 'Divine philanthropy: John Howard reconsidered', *History* 62 (1977), pp. 388–410.

102. W.K. Jordan, *Philanthropy in England, 1480–1660* (1959).

103. D. Andrew, 'Reading charity sermons: eighteenth-century Anglican solicitation and exhortation', *Journal of Ecclesiastical History* 43 (1992), pp. 581–91.

Bartholomew's Hospital in 1736) and in his *St Paul before Felix* (given to Lincoln's Inn in 1756). All these indicated the moral parallel between divine and human acts of charity, and can be regarded as demonstrating that true Christian qualities, such as charity, took faith and worship out of the churches into the scenes of human activity.[104]

The elective affinity between certain ideals of masculine behaviour and certain ideals of religious behaviour which I have discussed for the century and a half after 1660, such as the stress on involvement in the world, and the stress on this being an objective for all men and not merely for a group of religiously elect or professionally privileged men, helps us to understand more fully the religious and cultural impact of the Oxford Movement, which, with its emphasis on clericalism and on inward religious emotionalism, can be seen to have challenged some of the most entrenched assumptions about both religious and masculine behaviour.[105] In the period before the 1830s, the preferred religion was often associated with manliness, and the ideal man was frequently regarded in a religious light. Against this joint pairing of 'manly religion' and 'the religious male' was pitted the concept of effeminacy, which was used to counter both the religion and the men deemed to fall short of the ideal. Linking the ideal man with a religiosity which was judged by its social role confirms Philip Carter's suggestion that eighteenth-century understandings of masculinity were more concerned with the social rather than the sexual aspects of male behaviour.[106] But, of course, the religious male was envisaged not only as a social being, he was also a sexual one. The pious man imagined by this rhetoric was a member of a heterosexual family: he was certainly not celibate, nor, God forbid, did he indulge in the more lurid practices of his Catholic rival. In this discourse of religious manliness some important correlations emerge between masculinity and Protestantism which have implications for our understanding of

104. R. Paulson, *Hogarth: His Life, Art and Times*, 2 vols (New Haven CT, 1971); Gregory, 'Anglicanism and the arts', pp. 86–7.

105. This adds another dimension to Peter Nockles's critique of the Oxford Movement: *The Oxford Movement in Context. Anglican High Churchmanship, 1760–1857* (Cambridge, 1994). See also G. Faber, *Oxford Apostles. A Character Study of the Oxford Movement* (1933), and my 'Gender and the clerical profession'. Much of what I've identified as the dominant eighteenth-century attitudes towards religion and masculinity can be linked – with some changes – to nineteenth-century concepts of Christian manliness: see Norman Vance, *The Sinews of the Spirit: The Ideal of Christian Manliness in Victorian Literature and Religious Thought* (Cambridge, 1985); David Newsome, *Godliness and Good Learning: Four Studies on a Victorian Ideal* (1961); and D. E. Hall, ed., *Muscular Christianity: Embodying the Victorian Age* (Cambridge, 1994).

106. Carter, 'Male effeminacy', *passim*.

the ways in which national identity was perceived. Many of the attempts to delineate the true religious male either explicitly or implicitly drew on a contrast between eighteenth-century England and the situation in the medieval past or in contemporary continental Catholic countries. In both instances the religious male was portrayed as having acted as a parasite on society, and the development of a religious identity was seen to have been reserved for a specific caste of men. The nexus between Protestantism, masculinity and Englishness was forged, then, as part of a contrast between the vices of an effeminate continental Catholicism and the virtues of a healthy masculine Protestantism.[107] It was only in Protestant England, so the rhetoric ran, that the religious male could truly flourish; it was only in Protestant England that all men could aspire to be *homo religiosus.*

107. Linda Colley, *Britons, Forging the Nation, 1707–1837* (New Haven and London, 1992); Michèle Cohen, *Fashioning Masculinity: National Identity and Language in the Eighteenth Century* (1996).

CHAPTER SIX

James Boswell's Manliness[1]

PHILIP CARTER

In November 1764 James Boswell, then aged 24, reached Switzerland on the third stage of his European tour. It was seventeen months since he had been seen off from England by Samuel Johnson, in which time he had spent nearly a year in Holland studying law at Utrecht and toured a selection of German states, before moving on to Switzerland. Here, Boswell was eager to arrange an interview with another of his intellectual heroes, Jean-Jacques Rousseau, whose work he had recently discovered. The *philosophe* accepted the request for several meetings at which Boswell realised that, unlike his London literary acquaintants, Rousseau did not enjoy lengthy conversation. This left Boswell with a dilemma: how to tell his life story without causing offence? After their second meeting Boswell had the idea of writing a brief autobiographical essay. This 'Sketch of the early life of James Boswell' provided details of his upbringing and schooling, conduct in London and Holland, his early love and sex life, and his tendency towards melancholy. The pen portrait concluded with a brief summary and a question which Boswell hoped his great reader would answer: 'Sir, I have given you in haste an account of all the evil in my nature. I have told you of all of the good. Tell me, is it possible for me yet to make myself a man?'[2]

The question brought the 'Sketch' up to date, transforming it from a survey of the recent past to Boswell's present desire to be judged by Rousseau, and either declared a man, or informed how to achieve this status. However, for all the urgency of his request

---

1. I would like to thank Elaine Chalus, Joanna Innes and Sarah Knott for their comments on earlier versions of this chapter.
2. 'Sketch of the early life of James Boswell, written by himself for Jean-Jacques Rousseau, 5 December 1764', in Frederick A. Pottle, *James Boswell. The Earlier Years, 1740–1769* (1969), p. 6.

in December 1764 – his use of 'yet' implies time running out
– Boswell had actually been asking the same question over much
of the period covered by the 'Sketch'. Indeed, it is fair to say that
Boswell's bid to understand the theories and practices necessary 'to
make myself a man' is one of the major themes in his early writing.

This search for manliness is apparent in three other autobiographical sources which in more detail cover his early life, from his
education at Edinburgh and Glasgow Universities, to his decision
to come to London in November 1762 seeking a commission in the
Guards, and the start of his continental tour in the following year.
These three sources – comprising journals kept regularly from his
arrival in London, memoranda, and correspondence with friends
from university – reveal Boswell as a young man who was keen to
break free of his father's influence, and to be treated as an adult
in his own right.[3] Moving from youth to adulthood made Boswell
particularly sensitive to the subject of manliness, as is evident from
his frequent references to objects and people being manly or having manliness. In his London journal, for example, Boswell spoke
of the desirability of 'manly firmness', the attractiveness of 'manly
composure' and 'manly confidence', Dr Johnson's 'manly power
of versification', and of his own wish to 'be manly'. Likewise in
Holland, Boswell commented on the importance of 'manly conduct',
on the need to be 'manly and silent', and to think 'manly ideas'.[4]
On other occasions, he discussed men who had achieved such standards. About to depart for Holland, Boswell urged himself to improve
his conduct, or as he put it, to 'be like Chesterfield, manly', while
elsewhere he frequently referred to individuals – both actual and
imagined – who displayed admirable qualities as, amongst others,
the 'man of business', 'man of spirit' and 'man of consequence'.[5]

At times Boswell was pleased with his conduct and thought that
he deserved to be identified by one of these labels. But he was
equally aware of his failure to meet such standards on many other

3. Boswell's journal, kept throughout his adult life, has been published as part of
The Yale Editions of the Private Papers of James Boswell, 12 vols (1950–86). This chapter
looks at Boswell's understanding of manliness in the late 1750s and early 1760s.
These years are covered by Frederick A. Pottle, ed., *Boswell's London Journal, 1762–
1763* (1950), hereafter *BLJ; Boswell in Holland, 1763–1764* (1952), hereafter *BH;
Boswell on the Grand Tour: Germany and Switzerland, 1764* (1953), hereafter *GT*. Boswell's
daily memoranda, in which he planned his itinerary and reviewed his behaviour
during the previous 24 hours, are held at the Beinecke Library, Yale University.
They remain unpublished, although a number of extracts are reprinted in the above
volumes.
4. *BLJ*, pp. 82, 160, 270, 291, 272; *BH*, pp. 4, 28, 111, 166.
5. *BLJ*, pp. 78, 82, 199.

occasions. Instances of failure were also evaluated with reference to gender, unacceptable behaviour being deemed 'effeminate'.[6] In these situations, Boswell, all too aware of the dissonance between ideal and actual male behaviour, became concerned about his reputation. The result, for Boswell, was uncertainty and anxiety encapsulated in the question, 'can I make myself a man?', posed to himself, his friends, and in December 1764 to Rousseau. For the historian, Boswell's arduous and unresolved search for manhood provides texts that are rich in the language, theory and practice of manliness in the mid-eighteenth century.

Boswell's interest in manliness has not gone unnoticed. For example, studies have drawn attention to his fascination with, and admiration of, Captain Macheath, the highwayman and anti-hero of John Gay's *The Beggar's Opera* (1728). For Boswell, one of Macheath's most attractive features was his courage, clearly seen in his calm deportment as he awaited execution for robbery. Boswell's admiration for such behaviour is evident from his journal entry for 3 May 1763 in which he described a visit to Newgate gaol and his meeting with a real-life prisoner, Paul Lewis, on the day before his execution. Lewis was reported being in robust spirits, walking 'firmly and with a good air', for which action, amongst others, he was judged favourably as 'just a Macheath'.[7] In a recent article Michael Friedman has argued that Macheath and Lewis were admired because their courage corresponded with a key aspect of Boswell's understanding of 'manly conduct', forming one part of a concept of 'masculine *virtù* . . . so crucial to Boswell's self-esteem'.[8] This attachment to what was an essentially stoical definition of manliness certainly occurred at other points in the journals and memoranda. While in Holland Boswell wrote his 'Inviolable plan' – a glorified memorandum on 'how to form yourself into a man' – in which he stressed the stoical sentiments that 'everything may be endured' and 'to bear is the noble power of man'.[9]

In Boswell's estimation, both Macheath and Lewis served as exemplars of manly fortitude under the ultimate test, the threat of death. But his interest was always based on more than this coolness under pressure. Boswell's account of Lewis paid equal attention to the prisoner's dashing character, noting his fine clothes and manners. He was described as a 'genteel, spirited, young fellow'

---

6. See, for example, *BLJ*, p. 43; *BH*, p. 45. 7. *BLJ*, pp. 251–2.
8. Michael D. Friedman, '"He was just a Macheath": Boswell and *The Beggar's Opera*', in Paul J. Korshin, ed., *The Age of Johnson* 4 (New York NY, 1991), pp. 98, 102.
9. 'Inviolable plan. To be read over frequently, 16 Oct. 1763', in *BH*, pp. 375, 377.

and later as a 'handsome fellow'.[10] In part, therefore, it was Lewis's debonair and modish appearance that led Boswell to praise and equate him with the equally suave and attractive Captain Macheath. Indeed, when Boswell likened himself to Macheath it was in this role as a fashionable gallant. Thus during a visit to Covent Garden in the same month he befriended two young women, took them to a tavern, drank a pint of sherry and, before having sex with them, sang a ballad from *The Beggar's Opera* and 'thought myself a Macheath'.[11]

Boswell's appetite for sexual encounters is well known by anyone with even a cursory knowledge of the man. Second only to his celebrity as a biographer, Boswell's reputation as a fornicator has been firmly established by, amongst others, Lawrence Stone.[12] This conspicuous libido has also led Michael Friedman to argue that sexual appetite, again enshrined in the rakish figure of Macheath, formed the second fundamental part of Boswell's concept of 'masculine *virtù*'.

From these and other studies Boswell's understanding of manliness emerges as the adoption of one of two distinct personality types: the stoic and the rakish libertine. Both characteristics were certainly present in Boswell's early autobiographical writing. This said, it is less certain whether these two types were Boswell's only conception of manliness. In other words, when Boswell asked Rousseau if he could become a man, it seems unlikely that he wanted to be told only that he had the makings of someone able to face death with equanimity, or to attract female company with wine, tall stories and a song.

The limitations of viewing Boswell's manliness simply in terms of the stoic or rake are also apparent if we consider the social context in which Boswell sought to develop from child to adult, from boyhood to manhood, during the early 1760s. As a number of biographers have pointed out, Boswell did spend a remarkably large amount of time at public executions and pursuing sexual encounters. But the journals also show how these activities formed only one part of his life in London and had virtually no place in his Dutch routine. Rather, during the early 1760s Boswell was primarily

10. *BLJ*, pp. 251–2.   11. Ibid., p. 264.
12. Lawrence Stone, *Family, Sex and Marriage in England, 1500–1800* (1977), pp. 572–99. Boswell's journals have since proved a useful source for other historians of sexuality. See, amongst others, essays in G.S. Rousseau and Roy Porter, eds, *Sexual Underworlds of the Enlightenment* (Manchester, 1987); Roy Porter and Leslie Hall, *The Facts of Life: The Creation of Sexual Knowledge in Britain, 1650–1950* (London and New Haven CT, 1995).

seeking acceptance in urban polite society, initially by gaining a commission in the Guards and then, as his interest in this waned, by securing a place in a prestigious literary society centred on Samuel Johnson. Boswell's account of his daily life in Holland was similarly dominated by his legal studies and attempts to enter a polite society of clubs and social functions.

It was within this refined, intellectual environment that Boswell spent most of his time in the early 1760s, and it was with reference to this society that he made many of the comments on manliness noted above. In the remainder of this chapter I want to look in more detail at what Boswell meant when he spoke of the 'manly' behaviour of himself or of others. In the next two sections I argue that the early journals, memoranda and correspondence reveal two distinct but compatible modes of social behaviour that Boswell sought to develop in his bid to make himself a man. These styles of manliness – defined, first, in terms of dignity, economy and independence and, second, gentility, sympathy and sociability – recur in Boswell's discussion of idealised male types pieced together through his interaction with men on the street, and his talking and reading about manly conduct.

This examination is not intended to serve primarily as a biographical account of an admittedly fascinating character on whom much has recently been written. Rather, it is hoped that this case study highlights points of interest for our wider understanding of eighteenth-century manliness.[13] On one level, Boswell's autobiographical writings offer an insight into mid-century concepts of ideal manliness. But as the record of an actual individual who recorded his daily conduct with remarkable frankness, the journals and memoranda in particular also throw light on the experience of being a man, and the often tense relationship between representations and realities of manly conduct. Thus while willing to live up to a series of ideals, Boswell was also prepared to compromise or ignore such values when faced with the practicalities of daily life, most obviously life in a class-conscious society. The result – discussed in a final section on 'Boswell as blackguard' – saw him either tailoring his understanding of manliness to fit these pronounced class aspirations, or replacing his ideals with alternative concepts of

---

13. The candour of Boswell's journals has made him a valuable case study for a number of scholars. See Thomas Gilmore, 'James Boswell's drinking', *ECS* 24 (1991), pp. 337–58, which examines changing attitudes to alcoholism; Felicity A. Nussbaum, *The Autobiographical Subject: Gender and Ideology in Eighteenth-Century England* (Baltimore MD, 1989), ch. 5 looking at concepts of character formation; and Stone, who interprets Boswell's conduct as evidence of an emerging post-Puritan male libertinism, *Family, Sex and Marriage*, pp. 572–99.

manly behaviour defined according to dramatically different criteria. By highlighting the complexities contained within a case study, the chapter warns against what Olwen Hufton describes as 'the erection of the theoretical or "generic" woman and man . . . at the expense of, as far as one can discern, the experience of real people', including, we might add, the nuances of their gender identity.[14]

Boswell as 'man of dignity'

The journal entry for 4 August 1763, the day before Boswell left London for Holland, gives the impression that he was relieved to be departing a city full of temptations for a country and a lifestyle that held few such attractions. He was, he wrote, embarking on 'a less pleasurable but a more rational and lasting plan', as a result of which 'I shall be the happier for being abroad'. What he hoped for now was the strength of character to 'pursue my plan with steadiness that I may become a man of dignity'.[15] Clearly Boswell's assessment of his nine-month residence in London was not, on this occasion, particularly positive. The city's pleasures had, he believed, undermined his efforts to make himself a man, or to behave in a 'manly' fashion. Boswell certainly had good reason to view London as a source of potential corruption. His residence from November 1762 to August 1763 was not his first visit to the capital. An earlier stay in 1760 had ended in the humiliation befitting a child when, after falling into debt and dissolute company, Boswell had been recalled to Scotland by his disapproving father.[16]

To break free of his family's influence, Boswell knew that he had to rise above the temptations of city life, which required the 'steadiness' of a 'man of dignity'. The latter was a quality that Boswell detected in several male companions of whom he wrote favourably while in London. One was William Johnson Temple, a close friend from Edinburgh University who often instructed Boswell against reckless behaviour. In May 1763, for example, Boswell reported how his friend had 'talked to me seriously of getting out of a course of dissipation and rattling and acquiring regularity and reserve'.

14. Olwen Hufton, *The Prospect Before Her: A History of Women in Western Europe, 1500–1800* (1995), p. 5.
15. *BLJ*, p. 333.
16. On this complex and often troubled relationship see Felicity A. Nussbaum, 'Father and son in Boswell's *London Journal*', *PQ* 57 (1978), pp. 383–97; Susan Manning, 'Boswell's pleasure, the pleasures of Boswell', *BJE-CS* 20 (1997), pp. 17–32.

Temple himself had achieved the latter characteristics because he possessed rationality and intelligence, or 'good sense', as it was termed by Boswell and many other eighteenth-century commentators. Temple had 'so much good sense, good temper, and steadiness that he makes the best friend in the world' and was 'a character truly great'. Boswell detected similar qualities in other men. Charles Crookshanks, steward to his friend Lord Eglinton, was 'a very excellent fellow . . . honest, faithful and generous. He has very good sense.' Samuel Johnson mixed 'vivacity, solid good sense and knowledge', while earlier, in December 1762, Boswell had written positively about himself and his intention 'to follow the dictates of my own good sense'.[17]

Boswell valued sense because he believed that it facilitated sound judgement, and judgement was necessary to define and choose between the valuable and the trivial. His 'own good sense' functioned as a touchstone or 'monitor' as he put it, which allowed him to 'proceed consistently and resolutely'.[18] On other occasions, Boswell described this monitor as 'self-government', another important characteristic of the 'man of dignity', and again one that in periods of anxiety he was uncertain he possessed. In January 1763 his mood was upbeat. Commenting on how far he had matured since his first visit to London, he compared his 'ignorance at that time' with 'the knowledge and moderation and government of myself which I have now acquired'. Five months later he was less convinced: the memorandum for Sunday 19 June began with the call to 'attain self-government and please father'.[19] His capacity for ill-discipline was also troubling him when in October he wrote the 'Inviolable plan' in which he chastised himself for taking an unreasonable and unwarranted dislike to certain places and people. Such behaviour was irrational and hence unacceptable, being 'the sign of a weak and diseased mind'. Antipathies, he continued, did not 'move a man', though a 'hysteric lady or sickly peevish boy may be so swayed'.[20]

That one of the alternatives to the sensible man was a specific type of 'hysteric lady', rather than women in general, suggests that Boswell did not regard intelligence, rationality and sense as exclusively male attributes. Elsewhere, women such as Frances Sheridan, wife of the actor Thomas Sheridan, were described as 'very sensible and very clever', while his Dutch companion, Isabella de Zuylen,

17. *BLJ*, pp. 265, 213, 292, 82.   18. Ibid.
19. Ibid., pp. 141, 280.   20. 'Plan', in *BH*, p. 377.

was said to be 'so much above me in wit, knowledge and good sense'.[21] On one level, therefore, Boswell treated sense as a human quality that contributed to manliness not because it defined him as male but because it made him a better person. This said, elsewhere Boswell suggested that sense was still more common amongst men, hence his scepticism that women could be equally adept at scholarship. A letter from Temple commented on his friend's scorn for Catharine Macaulay's *History of England* (vol. 1, 1763), which both he and Boswell expected to be 'a panegyric on royalty and effeminate pleasure of a court' at the expense of 'a just encomium on virtue, frugality and publick spirit'. Temple agreed with Boswell that the idea of a female historian was in principle 'absurd enough' and that Boswell was right to 'laugh at a woman attempting to write a history of England'.[22] Similarly, Isabella de Zuylen's talents, while attractive, also troubled Boswell, who welcomed criticism of her abilities – reporting, for example, a friend's opinion that 'a man who has half her wit and knowledge may still be above her' – not least because it guaranteed what Boswell called 'the dignity of the male sex'.[23] As the 'Inviolable plan' made clear, dignity was also maintained by its juxtaposition to a second character, the boy or adolescent. In self-confident mood Boswell contrasted his own maturity with the failings of others, as in an entry for April 1763 when he criticised one of Temple's legal colleagues as 'a prig, a fop, an idler' whose 'manners are very opposite to ours'. For all his shortcomings the man was judged 'in the main a good enough lad', an assessment which implied that any faults were attributable to his youth.[24] However, the confidence which Boswell derived from this encounter was soon eroded by other incidents when age seemingly proved no guarantee against unacceptably juvenile and hence unmanly behaviour. A month before his move to Holland, for example, he wrote to Temple of his anxiety about leaving England, before chastising himself for being 'feeble-minded' and acting in a 'very effeminate and very young' manner.[25] Here, youth/effeminacy

21. *BLJ*, p. 54; *BH*, p. 230.

22. Boswell and Temple's opinion that, as a woman, Macaulay would be uncritical of court trivialities was especially misplaced given her radical credentials. Temple, having read the *History*, admitted to being 'agreeably disappointed, for I find her the very reverse of what I expected'. Temple to Boswell (7 Jan. 1764), in *The Correspondence of James Boswell and William Johnson Temple, 1756–1795*, ed. Thomas Crawford, 2 vols (Edinburgh and New Haven CT, 1997), I, p. 85.

23. *BH*, p. 230.   24. *BLJ*, p. 240.

25. Boswell to Temple (26, 28 July, 2 Sept. 1763), in Crawford, ed., *Correspondence*, pp. 54, 57, 65.

and adulthood/manhood emerged not as specific ages but as modes of expected conduct, definitions which perhaps explain the absence of any clear statement in the journal on the point at which manhood began.

On this, as on other occasions, Boswell saw greater resolve as the route to more acceptable conduct. Having complained to Temple, he wrote afterwards of his intention to 'pluck up manly resolution . . . and establish a proper character' and 'to summon up Resolution . . . [to] make myself a Man'.[26] Resolution and self-government were necessary for controlling episodes not only of emotional but also of material indulgence. Boswell's journals contain a number of warnings against being attracted to frivolous objects and entertainments. The entry for 2 January 1764 was typical in its instruction to be 'firm, on guard . . . manly and silent' by never being 'moved with trifles'.[27] Other essentially worthy pursuits also had to be practised in a responsible manner. Boswell commented frequently on the importance of temperance, and reiterated a message popular in eighteenth-century conduct literature when he spoke of the need always 'to keep the golden mean between stinginess and prodigality'. Such behaviour would, Boswell hoped, bring him closer to what he termed the 'man of economy', a 'character of worthy imitation . . . who with prudent attention knows when to save and when to spend, and acts accordingly'.[28] The antithesis to this idealised man of economy was the immoderate individual who later appeared in the shape of one Monsieur des Essar, a member of a Utrecht debating society who had offended Boswell by publicly correcting his French. The note for 31 March 1764 criticised des Essar for being 'a fop in learning', among whose many faults was the fact that he 'is extravagantly French'.[29]

What ultimately distinguished a man of dignity or economy from the foppish des Essar was the former's independence. For Boswell, sense, self-government and moderation facilitated freedom from the influence of others and formed a central component of the manly personality. This, Boswell admitted, had not always been his way. As he wrote on 13 December 1762, 'formerly I was directed by others. I took every man's advice . . . I was fond to have it', though he now preferred to 'keep my own counsel' and to 'act entirely on my own principles'. Boswell explained this change in terms of his becoming 'an independent man' – a status that allowed him to fulfil two aims crucial for his transition from youth to manhood.

26. Ibid., p. 65.   27. *BH*, p. 111.   28. *BLJ*, p. 186.   29. *BH*, p. 198.

Firstly, independence had allowed him to come to England against his family's wishes and, more importantly, to remain free of his father's influence, if not his financial assistance. Secondly, independence made it possible for Boswell to enter and succeed in London's polite literary society. Thus, in the same entry, he commented on his conversation with Thomas Sheridan, who as well as being an actor was a celebrated lecturer in elocution. Boswell offered a positive assessment of his conduct with this experienced public speaker. Sense and an independent mind gave him the 'conscious assurance that I was in the right', an assurance which allowed him to speak to Sheridan with what, significantly, he described as 'manly firmness'.[30]

Boswell as 'pretty man'

Boswell's positive self-image on this day owed much to his perceived capacity for moderation, independence and confidence – characteristics that he believed could make him a 'man of dignity'. But Boswell's conversation with Sheridan suggests other qualities that he thought important for making himself a man. This encounter was also pleasing because it demonstrated his ability to socialise, to exchange ideas, and to behave in a polite or genteel manner –attributes that Boswell considered integral to a second idealised male figure which he often termed the 'pretty man' or 'pretty gentleman'. Such qualities were clearly important to a young man hoping to achieve maturity in London, the place where, as Boswell put it, 'men and manners may be seen to the greatest advantage'.[31]

Boswell's interest in men's aptitude for polite social encounters is a particularly conspicuous theme in his early journals and correspondence. Positive descriptions of new male acquaintances included

30. *BLJ*, p. 82.
31. Ibid., p. 68. Boswell's positive use of 'pretty' was at odds with the predominant eighteenth-century application for men in terms such as 'pretty fellow' denoting a vain, trivial and foppish individual. See, for example, the anonymous essay, 'The memoirs of a young man of fashion', whose subject was 'capricious, extravagant, a fop . . . what gay circles of both sexes call a very pretty fellow', *London Magazine* 67 (1778), pp. 20–1. Boswell used the word 'pretty' and the phrases 'pretty man' and 'pretty gentleman' in respect of himself and others on a number of occasions: *BLJ*, p. 320; *BH*, pp. 166, 350; Crawford, ed., *Correspondence*, pp. 15, 42. Boswell's usage may have been a result of his Scottish upbringing, where the term continued to have positive connotations. If so, it is ironic that his Scottish legacy emerged in his labelling of men who possessed a level of refinement that he believed generally absent in Scotland.

frequent references to their refinement and gentility. Adam Smith, he told his friend John Johnston, was a 'most polite well-bred man'. Charles Douglas, Duke of Queensbury, was a man of the 'greatest politeness . . . the greatest humanity and gentleness of manners', while Norton Nicholls, whom Boswell met through William Temple, possessed 'an amiable disposition, a sweetness of manners, and an easy politeness that pleased me much'.[32] Alongside descriptions of these admirable figures, Boswell gave careful consideration to his own reputation for refinement. Journal entries made shortly after his arrival in London indicated how Boswell viewed politeness as central to his construction of a new self – a more mature figure than the juvenile youth who had visited the capital two years earlier. In the entry for 21 November 1762, for example, Boswell distinguished between his current 'composed genteel character' and the 'rattling uncultivated one which, for some time past, I have been fond of'. Maintaining this newly genteel self meant avoiding the often rowdy and uncivil society of some of his former Scottish acquaintances who gathered at the London house of an old Edinburgh friend, Lady Betty Macfarlane. On 16 January 1763 Boswell remarked that he had not called on Lady Betty for three nights 'as I wanted to have nothing but English ideas, and to be as manly as I possibly could'. A letter to Temple in the following year suggests he thought he had been largely successful, having 'conducted myself in a manly, & genteel manner' since his arrival in Holland.[33]

Refinement was evidently a key part of Boswell's understanding of what it took to become a man. But what did this mean in terms of day-to-day living? On one level, Boswell's definition of gentility was concerned with externalities such as appearance. When he recorded details of his dress, for example, it was often to mention that he had sported a 'genteel' frock coat or suit to attend a prestigious social gathering, giving him the air of a 'man of fashion', a term which, like 'pretty', Boswell used positively. Image and gentility also combined in more prosaic surroundings, such as on his visit to a London sword-smith, Mr Jeffreys. Realising that he had come out without money, Boswell sought to present himself in a manner that would allow him to obtain a sword on credit: 'I determined to make a trial of the civility of my fellow creatures, and what effect

32. Boswell to Johnston (11 Jan. 1760), in *The Correspondence of James Boswell and John Johnston of Grange*, ed. Ralph S. Walker (Edinburgh, 1966), p. 7; *BLJ*, pp. 63, 257.

33. *BLJ*, pp. 47, 145; Boswell to Temple (17 Apr. 1764), in Crawford, ed., *Correspondence*, p. 91.

my external appearance and address would have'. At first, Mr Jeffreys refused Boswell's proposal but relented after his customer had complimented him and 'bowed genteely'. On leaving, Boswell rather patronisingly warned Jeffreys against taking similar risks in future and was evidently satisfied as he recalled how the shopkeeper had dismissed his concern by claiming that 'we know our men', the end to an encounter that, in Boswell's opinion, was 'much to my honour'.[34]

Wearing fine clothes or bowing at an opportune moment was part of Boswell's perception of polite manliness. But gentility was also possible in a state of what he called 'undress', that is, amongst men devoid of the material trappings of refinement. In these instances, Boswell's definition was altogether more nuanced, politeness and 'prettiness' emerging as manifestations of virtuous character, rather than a display of fine dress or well-timed manners.

In this more sophisticated discussion, attention was drawn to two qualities characteristic of the truly 'pretty man'. The first required an individual to be sincere and easy, or relaxed, when in company. It was this which attracted Boswell to men like the actor West Digges, 'a pretty man [with] . . . most amiable dispositions', and Andrew Mitchell the British envoy to Berlin whom he described as 'a worthy and a very pretty man' being 'polite and easy'.[35] Adam Smith and Norton Nicholls possessed similar qualities. Nicholls was said to have 'an amiable disposition [and] . . . an easy politeness', while Smith was 'realy amiable', having 'nothing of that formal stiffness and pedantry which is too often found in professors'.[36] Boswell's assessment of his own social conduct often found him trying to imitate this style. Preparing for a trip to The Hague, he wrote of the need to 'have no affectation', and be 'an amiable pretty man'.[37] At the same time, he was aware that the bouts of melancholy he suffered in Holland were making it increasingly difficult to behave in a suitably sociable manner. Despondency made Boswell either a recluse or a dull companion, two forms of behaviour that he believed unbecoming in a man. The entry for 22 April 1764 noted how he had been 'dreary' when speaking with Archibald Maclaine, co-pastor at the English church at The Hague; in response, Boswell called on himself to 'rouse. Be Johnson . . . At all events, be *manly.*' The pep-talk continued in a slightly later memorandum in which

---

34. *BLJ,* p. 60.
35. Ibid., p. 76; Boswell to Johnston (10 Sept. 1764), in Walker ed., *Correspondence,* p. 132; *GT,* p. 25.
36. *BLJ,* p. 257; Walker, ed., *Correspondence,* p. 7.   37. *BH,* p. 92.

he again wrote of the need to 'get into a good humour, and be manly'.[38]

Refinement was, however, not just about being easy and sociable; genuine sociability had also to be regulated and fashioned towards productive and edifying ends. Thus, the second characteristic of the truly polite man was his ability to regulate and control his behaviour. Boswell as 'pretty man' sought to temper his relaxed and easy style in order to educate but not offend his audience. Unfortunately, this capacity for controlled social conduct also appeared to be lacking on a number of occasions. In a typical entry from January 1763, he complained of his being 'very hearty at dinner' and 'too ridiculous'. This, he knew, was neither true politeness, nor the route to respectable manhood; an audience was likely to 'applaud a man for it in company, but behind his back hold him very cheap'.[39]

As with many of Boswell's slip-ups, failure came after declarations of good intent. The previous month had seen him attempting to rectify his garrulous and jokey behaviour with a 'plan of studying polite reserved behaviour, which is the only way to keep up dignity of character'.[40] The importance of polite reserve also featured prominently in the Dutch journal, not least because it prevented him discussing his melancholy in public. On 10 February 1764, for example, he complained that his 'spirits were very low', but stressed the need to 'keep it to self' and to be 'more grave . . . and support it with manly dignity . . . At night be soft, polite, and guarded.' Such watchfulness was summed up by the French concept of *retenu*, or 'restraint', which Boswell discussed frequently in memoranda on this theme, either praising himself for being '*retenu* yet cheerful', or urging himself to do better in future, and writing on the need to 'swear *retenu* and [be] manly', or to use '*retenue* to accustom yourself to constant useful conversation, with mild and grave dignity'.[41]

This last point on behaviour during debate is worth dwelling on for a moment, since conversation was at the heart of Boswell's construction of 'pretty' or polite manliness. From the journals the good conversationalist emerges as a man – and Boswell's edifying conversations invariably took place in male company – who communicated according to the two tenets of manly politeness: sociability and reserve. These emerged in various ways during a meeting. Firstly, there was the need to think about one's performance, or style of delivery. This required putting others at their ease by being

---

38. Ibid., pp. 225, 247.   39. *BLJ*, p. 121.
40. Ibid., p. 61.   41. *BH*, pp. 140, 85, 227, 165.

relaxed and receptive, while being sufficiently in control to avoid intrusiveness, and, perhaps most importantly, to avoid dominating an exchange. Accordingly, in his account of 'the good, worthy, and respected man', Boswell stressed the need to be 'moderately reserved' in public and 'not to talk of yourself'. This was a view reiterated in the 'Inviolable plan', which highlighted the benefits of being 'excessively careful against rattling, though cheerful to listen to others'. The antithesis of the 'worthy' man was again the foppish des Essar, who used conversation as a vehicle for embarrassing obsequiousness and insensitive self-promotion. In Boswell's words, he was 'vain, he makes compliments. He gets bored, and his misery makes the rest of us ashamed of ours.'[42]

Control in conversation was also intended to regulate subject matter, steering the speaker away from matters trivial or personal towards more edifying issues. Secondly, therefore, polite men were expected to think about the content of their conversation. Boswell was again quick to censure himself and others when this did not occur. He was particularly scornful of the MP George Dempster, with whom he spent the evening of 20 July 1763. Dempster's attempts to defend republicanism were dismissed as 'sophistry', making him a 'feeble antagonist' and a 'very weak man'. Boswell, in contrast, was pleased with his performance, which appeared to have incorporated the various elements of successful discourse. 'I behaved extremely well tonight', he wrote, 'I was attentive, cheerful and manly.'[43]

If Dempster was poor company, and as a result 'weak', Samuel Johnson was someone who embodied many of the qualities Boswell thought important for the young man in polite society. The entry for 6 July 1763, for example, was especially fulsome in its praise of the 'stupendous Johnson' who embellished his mental powers with 'force of expression' and 'strokes of vivacity with solid good sense' to create a man 'highly instructive and highly entertaining'.[44] But for all his authority and eloquence, Johnson also had a reputation for less refined behaviour. On their first meeting Boswell wrote warmly of Johnson's intelligence but disapproved of his 'dreadful appearance', 'very slovenly' dress, 'uncouth voice' and his 'dogmatical roughness of manners'.[45] Boswell found these traits 'disagreeable' and contradictory to his often rather more genteel definition of the 'pretty gentleman', which, on these occasions, he found more suitably depicted by his second mentor in polite manliness, Joseph Addison.

42. Ibid., p. 24; 'Plan', in *BH*, p. 378; ibid., p. 198.
43. *BLT*, p. 316.   44. Ibid., pp. 291–2.   45. Ibid., p. 260.

Boswell's interest in Addison and his fictional *alter ego* Mr Spectator is, again, readily apparent from the journals and correspondence, especially those written in London. Boswell told Rousseau that he had first read the *Spectator* in Edinburgh aged eight.[46] Now in London in his early twenties the periodical proved a valuable guide in his cultivation of the responsible urbanity that its authors had promoted. Boswell clearly wanted to be seen as a man in the Addisonian mould, witnessed most obviously in numerous references to his reading the papers and his patronising of Mr Spectator's old haunts such as Child's coffee house. Less concrete but equally important evidence of the *Spectator*'s influence is discernible in the basic rules shaping Boswell's understanding of polite manliness. This model of male refinement, in which ease was tempered by self-control, drew directly on Addison and Richard Steele's refashioning of traditionally elite concepts of civic manliness in line with life in an increasingly pluralistic and commercial, urban society – reminding us that Boswell was just as eager to think himself a Mr Spectator as he was a Macheath.[47] It is worth noting that being Mr Spectator also demanded a capacity for sensitivity which Boswell was eager to develop, as suggested by his praise of Addison whose 'character in sentiment . . . I aim to realize'. Occasional references to acts of charity or being moved, in sympathy, to tears provide glimpses of Boswell not just as a 'man of feeling' but also as someone for whom Christian notions of benevolence were an important part of the manly identity.[48]

Boswell as 'blackguard'

Boswell's early journals, memoranda and correspondence reveal him as someone who recognised and applied the theory and language

---

46. 'Sketch', in Pottle, *James Boswell*, p. 2.

47. For Addison's contribution to the refining process see Lawrence E. Klein, 'Property and politeness in the early eighteenth-century Whig moralists. The case of *The Spectator*', in John Brewer and Susan Staves, eds, *Early Modern Conceptions of Property* (1995), and for the redefinition of manliness see Philip Carter, 'Men about town: representations of foppery and masculinity in early eighteenth-century urban society', in Hannah Barker and Elaine Chalus, eds, *Gender in Eighteenth-Century England. Roles, Representations and Responsibilities* (1997).

48. *BLJ*, p. 62. The importance of Christianity for definitions of manliness is discussed in Jeremy Gregory's chapter in this volume. Boswell's references to his frequent Bible readings often stimulated a sentimental response: the history of Joseph, for example, 'melted my heart and drew tears from my eyes'. Boswell himself used the term 'man of feeling' to describe Lord Eglinton in December 1762. *BLJ*, pp. 196, 67.

of manliness to evaluate aspects of his and others' lives; and, furthermore, as someone who saw this process of evaluation as central to the development of an adult identity. This chapter has so far sketched the various styles of manliness that Boswell was keen to develop, and some of the personality types that he was eager to impersonate. Manliness encompassed a range of attributes – sense, self-control, moderation, independence, refinement and sentiment – embodied in the idealised figures of the 'man of dignity', 'man of economy' and 'pretty man'. In these discussions, Boswell appears to consider manliness as a universal category for men, an ideal to which all were able to aspire, though in which not all men were equally competent, as his discussions of his own shortcomings reveal. But the journals also show that in reality Boswell's manliness was a subject complicated and contorted by other questions of identity, of which social status was perhaps the most pervasive. Boswell's bid for respectability, while closely bound up with being manly, was also infused with a snobbery that often problematised this category, blurring the line between manliness, a gendered identity, and the class-based identity of gentlemanliness.

This snobbery is apparent in Boswell's attitude to certain men beneath his own social station. However strongly he approved of the *Spectator* in theory, Boswell had little time for its potentially egalitarian interpretation of manliness where men engaged in cross-class socialising at male venues such as the coffee house. Boswell certainly sought a reputation for Spectatorial politeness with men of equal or higher social rank, but emphasised reserve for very different reasons with his social inferiors. One such individual was Thomas Terrie, from whom Boswell rented rooms in Downing Street. Though a 'jolly, civil man', Terrie's status was such that Boswell thought it best to 'be easy and chatty . . . yet to maintain a proper distance'. This distance was, however, difficult to enforce on account of Mr Terrie being 'rather too free', a familiarity that required Boswell to carry 'myself with reserve and something of state'.[49] Tensions between Boswell's understanding of manliness as social theory and as a class-conscious reality appeared not just in the need to guard against the presumptions of other lesser men. On a number of occasions Boswell worried about his own behaviour when it appeared as if he too was adopting the conduct of men further down the social scale. This was apparently a real problem, for a few days later Boswell found himself eating, drinking and singing in his landlord's company. Once sober, Boswell was mortified

49. *BLJ*, pp. 81, 54.

by his behaviour, claiming that he had 'let myself down too much', and had become 'a low being'.[50]

In one sense, Boswell treated his encounters with social inferiors as another opportunity to confirm, or in this case to lose, manly dignity in a city full of temptations. Boswell's self-criticism can be seen in part as a call for greater self-control and moderate conduct, even if the resulting concept of manliness was now limited to his own social group. However, we must not also overlook those occasions when Boswell freely participated in low behaviour: when he adopted the guise of the 'blackguard'. Though not as frequent as his accounts of the 'man of dignity' or 'pretty gentleman', Boswell's blackguard persona appears on several occasions in both the London and Dutch journals. The origin of the term is unclear, initially referring to menial servants, shoeblacks, soldiers or thieves. Mid-eighteenth-century definitions stressed base conduct in general rather than a specific profession; Johnson's *Dictionary of the English Language* (1755) defined blackguard as 'a cant term among the vulgar; by which is implied a dirty fellow of the meanest kind'. Boswell as 'blackguard' certainly worked on presenting a dirty and vulgar appearance. To celebrate the King's birthday in 1762 he 'resolved to be a black-guard' by dressing in his oldest suit worn when being powdered, dirty breeches, black stockings, a battered hat belonging to an army officer, and an 'old oaken stick' instead of his sword. Similar effort went into constructing a reputation for obnoxious and vulgar behaviour: roaring along the street, clattering his cane on the ground, and stopping at taverns to drink heavily.[51]

The 'blackguard' provides us with a new picture of Boswell willingly casting off many of the traits – sense, moderation, polite-ness and sentiment – that seemed to lie at the heart of his under-standing of manliness. Of course, in these moments Boswell saw his behaviour not as discarding manliness but replacing one class-specific understanding of manly conduct for a different, but equally class-related, definition. As a blackguard Boswell thought himself 'manly' because he appropriated a reputation for hardiness through manual labour, and for robust manners which a number of contem-poraries viewed as a healthy corrective to increasingly genteel and effeminate forms of male conduct.[52] Finally, and most obnoxiously,

---

50. Ibid., p. 95.   51. Ibid., p. 272.

52. The dramatist George Colman, for example, adopted the pseudonym 'Black-guard' in his praise of the 'manly wits' of the early eighteenth century and condemna-tion of the present 'frippery age' in which refinement was understood as 'a delicacy of manners that produces effeminacy'. *The Gentleman*, 2 (July 1775), reproduced in his *Prose on Several Occasions*, 3 vols (1787), I, p. 172.

Boswell thought himself manly because the blackguard persona allowed him to indulge his rapacious sexuality. On the evening of the King's birthday, he picked up and had sex with two young women while being refused by a third. The disappointment of this last encounter was evidently outweighed by his behaviour with the first woman, with whom he 'performed most manfully', and with the second, who he 'abused . . . in blackguard style', that is to say, raped.[53]

Conclusion

In the end it would appear that a discussion of Boswell's manliness leads back to an account of his sexual behaviour. Certainly, it is foolish to deny that Boswell considered sex an important part of his adult identity and his understanding of manliness, both as a universal and personal category. His belief that, in London, 'the ladies . . . have not the same advantages of indulging passion and whim and curiosity that men have', may well have been based on his and other men's ability to participate in a metropolitan sex industry that remained closed to his polite female acquaintances. While providing the means to distinguish between men and women in polite society, as well as to dominate those women with whom he had intercourse, sex was also a way of asserting superiority over other men. Reflecting on an evening of energetic love-making with the actress Mrs Louisa Lewis in January 1763, Boswell declared himself satisfied that 'this conquest [was] completed . . . with a manliness and prudence that pleased me very much'. Nor had his macho triumphalism diminished on the following day; taking tea with Mrs Lewis he mocked their table companion – 'one of the least men I ever saw' – before going on alone to a reception where he 'strutted up and down, considering myself as a valiant man who could satisfy a lady's loving desires five times a night'.[54]

Here I have suggested not that Boswell failed to link sex and manliness, but that he did not do so to the exclusion of other manifestations of manly behaviour. These occurred even at moments of overt sexuality. His comment on the 'manliness and prudence' of his seduction technique was, in part, an allusion to his self-control as a man of economy, the 'whole expense' of the conquest being 'just eighteen shillings'. Similarly when Boswell later contracted

53. *BLJ*, pp. 272–3. 54. *BLJ*, pp. 216, 140–2.

venereal disease from Lewis he was forced on confronting her to salvage his honour not with reference to his sexual prowess but with a display of self-control and reserved civility that would have impressed Mr Spectator and clearly pleased Boswell: 'I really behaved with a manly composure and polite dignity that could not fail to inspire an awe'.[55]

Both his sexual and social behaviour towards Lewis substantiate Felicity Nussbaum's assertion that Boswell's 'male "character" rests precariously on the power to maintain dominance over women'.[56] But, as we have seen, this male character was not defined just in opposition to women. Rather, the young Boswell's manliness was also precariously constructed with reference to other males; it was defined, on the one hand, in opposition to the immature youth or the frivolous adult, and, on the other, in imitation of a more worthy group located within urban polite society. In this literary environment of coffee house, bookshop and club, manly behaviour was defined less by sexual prowess than such qualities as self-command, independence, dignity and politeness, discussed in texts like the *Spectator* and displayed by role models such as Addison and Johnson, in whom Boswell detected an admirable synthesis of old styles of civic and newer modes of refined manliness.

On one level, therefore, Boswell's early autobiographical writings suggest the importance and pervasiveness of these well-established discourses of manliness, and as a result are evidence of a connection between the messages of prescriptive literature and young male readers. But the value of the case study is not just in setting out what ideals were to be emulated, but also how effectively these were either put into practice or complicated by others forms of social identification. Exposing the tensions between what people were told to do, what they attempted to do, and what they actually did, is something that women's history has been doing for a number of years, and is clearly an issue that histories of masculinity must confront.[57] This chapter has suggested that the young James Boswell is a good starting-point for this type of enquiry. Boswell's incredible capacity for self-confession reveals someone for whom manliness was an essential but also complex and fluid identity, configured

---

55. Ibid., p. 160.   56. Nussbaum, *Autobiographical Subject*, p. 115.

57. Amy Louise Erikson, *Women and Property in Early Modern England* (1993); Laura Gowing, *Domestic Dangers. Women, Words and Sex in Early Modern England* (Oxford, 1996). For a similar approach in the history of class identity see Margaret R. Hunt, *The Middling Sort. Commerce, Gender and the Family in England, 1680–1780* (Berkeley CA, 1996).

differently with respect to the sex, class and nationality of one's companion, and the geographical location and time of day when meetings took place. By and large, Boswell thought himself able to reconcile these multiple manly personae; the day after the notorious blackguard incident, for example, was spent back in polite coffee-house society with William Temple. Of course Boswell may have been exceptional in his ability to do this – the journals certainly reveal him to have been, at the same time, an exceptionally insensitive, arrogant, and vulnerable individual with sufficient wealth and leisure time to think about and engage in various styles of manhood. At the very least Boswell raises interesting questions about methodological approaches to men's history, providing us with a snapshot of the complexities of a manliness defined somewhere between intention and action, theory and practice. This said, the next crucial question – to what extent was James Boswell's manliness that of other men – still requires further research.

PART THREE

Violence

CHAPTER SEVEN

Reforming Male Manners: Public Insult and the Decline of Violence in London, 1660–1740[1]

ROBERT B. SHOEMAKER

Historians of crime, who have for some years been interested in the topic of 'women and crime', have only recently turned to the study of the male criminal *per se*. While in patterns of prosecuted crime men have historically been accused of involvement in a much wider range of offences than women, one feature of male criminality which stands out is their disproportionate involvement in crimes which involve interpersonal violence. Reflecting contemporary stereotypes that men were naturally more aggressive than women, studies of crime invariably find considerably higher levels of violence among men than women. Thus, for London between 1660 and 1725, men accounted for 75 per cent of the indicted assaults, and 81 per cent of the recognisances, which were specifically identified as violent at the Middlesex quarter sessions. Similarly, in his study of the neighbouring county of Surrey, John Beattie found that men accounted for 91 per cent of the defendants accused of homicide between 1660 and 1800.[2] It can be argued that such statistics reflect contemporary stereotypes, that because female violence was less conceivable it tended to be under-recorded, but such impressive differences between male and female experience cannot be explained away so easily. If we accept that men in this period *were* more likely to be violent, then not only do we need to discover why that was the

1. I would like to thank Faramerz Dabhoiwala and Tim Meldrum for their insightful comments on an early version of this piece; and Tim Hitchcock for his unwavering support and helpful editorial advice.

2. John Beattie, *Crime and the Courts in England 1660–1800* (Princeton NJ, 1986), p. 97. The figures for Middlesex derive from the research which led to my book, Robert B. Shoemaker, *Prosecution and Punishment: Petty Crime and the Law in London and Rural Middlesex, c.1660–1725* (Cambridge, 1991).

case, but we also need to explore the significance of the fact that over a period of several centuries the amount of violent crime recorded in England, and therefore the amount of violence men committed, declined substantially. The fact that such an important change could occur underlines the point that violence is not an inherently masculine trait; certain social patterns and definitions of masculinity encourage or discourage violence. In her contribution to this volume, Elizabeth Foyster has shown how prescriptive writers in the eighteenth century sought to problematise and control male anger and aggression. This chapter will investigate an aspect of the concurrent actual decline of violence in this period, the process by which men's violence on the streets of London was replaced by an alternative means of pursuing conflicts, the public insult.

When disturbed by the objectionable behaviour of others, men in this period could respond in various ways: by ignoring it, through litigation, through verbal insult, or through physical attack (the latter two strategies were often conducted in groups). One of the stereotypical gender differences in this period was that, in the words of Richard Allestree, 'a woman [has] ordinarily only that one weapon of the Tongue to offend with', while a man can attack with 'anger' and 'brawling'.[3] But in fact, in the century after the Restoration men, too, frequently pursued conflicts and attacked the honour of others through public insult. Such behaviour was remarkably similar to stereotypically female behaviour, however, and concerns about effeminacy contributed to the decline of the public insult in the late eighteenth century. Male defamation was more prominent in this period than either before or after, and as such it arguably constitutes an important stage in the long-term decline of male violence in England.

It is hardly surprising that such a change was most visible on the busy streets of the capital. With its rapidly growing population, expanding economy, and increasingly self-confident middle class, London was in the forefront of economic and social change in this period.[4] Metropolitan men faced particular challenges. In a population numerically dominated by women and where women played a

3. [Richard Allestree], *The Whole Duty of Man, Laid down in a plain and familiar way for the use of all, but especially the meanest reader* (1659; 1703 edn), p. 257. See also Joy Wiltenburg, *Disorderly Women and Female Power in the Street Literature of Early Modern England and Germany* (Charlottesville VA, 1992), pp. 106–9.

4. For London in this period, see P. Earle, *A City Full of People: Men and Women of London, 1650–1750* (1994); P. Earle, *Making of the English Middle Class: Business, Society and Family Life in London 1660–1730* (1989); L. Schwarz, *London in the Age of Industrialisation* (1992).

significant part in the city's flourishing public social life, middle-class and gentry male Londoners were exposed to a number of potentially feminising influences, not least new, 'polite' standards of behaviour.[5] In this context, men sought new ways of asserting their masculinity.

The decline of public violence in English history was a long-term process but the seventeenth and eighteenth centuries appear to have played a crucial role in this transition. In her recent study of English violence in the early seventeenth century, Susan Amussen argued that violence was endemic, whether exercised by the state in judicial punishments, by masters of households over their wives, children, servants and apprentices, or by men of relatively equal status in alehouse brawls or duels. Amussen concluded that violence was a 'key component of the "traditional" model of manhood'. Nonetheless, she notes that there were many forces in the early seventeenth century, including both Church and state, which sought to introduce a reformed model of manhood, in which 'violence was replaced by self-restraint and the recourse to the law'. In a similar study of violence focusing on the eighteenth century, Beattie also argued that 'violence was part of everyday life', but he argues that both violence and attitudes towards it began 'to change decisively after 1700, particularly . . . by the early decades of the nineteenth century'.[6]

Evidence of changing *attitudes* towards male violence can be found from the attempts to reform male manners in the early seventeenth century described by Amussen to the efforts to increase the judicial punishments for such behaviour in the late eighteenth and early nineteenth centuries.[7] Evidence of changing male *behaviour* also

5. No calculations of the sex-ratio of the London population exist for this period, but for compelling evidence that, largely as a result of large-scale immigration of women seeking posts as domestic servants, larger urban areas had more women than men, see David Souden, 'Migrants and the population structure of later seventeenth-century provincial cities and market towns', in P. Clark, ed., *The Transformation of English Provincial Towns 1600–1800* (1981), pp. 149–60. For women in London social life, see Robert B. Shoemaker, *Gender and Society in England 1650–1850: The Emergence of Separate Spheres?* (1998), pp. 277–9.

6. Susan Amussen, '"The part of a Christian man": the cultural politics of manhood in early modern England', in Susan Amussen and Mark Kishlansky, eds, *Political Culture and Cultural Politics in Early Modern England* (Manchester, 1995), pp. 220, 227; John Beattie, 'Violence and society in early-modern England', in Anthony Doob and Edward Greenspan, eds, *Perspectives in Criminal Law* (Aurora, Ontario, 1985), pp. 37, 41.

7. Peter King, 'Punishing assault: the transformation of attitudes in the English courts', *Journal of Interdisciplinary History* 27 (1996), pp. 43–74; Randall McGowen,

comes from a long period, but the century after the Restoration appears to have been crucial, particularly in London. The only reliable statistical measure of levels of violence concerns homicide, an offence which because of its serious nature (and the difficulty of disposing of a body) is likely to be reliably recorded. Although historians have traced a long-term decline in levels of homicide from the Middle Ages to the early twentieth century,[8] recent studies suggest that the period of this study witnessed one of the most dramatic declines of any period. The best evidence for London comes from Beattie, who found that the number of convictions for homicide in Surrey declined by 60 per cent between 1660 and 1760. Similarly, James Cockburn found that in the neighbouring county of Kent between 1680 and 1720 the number of homicides fell by half. Levels of homicide are of course not necessarily a reliable indicator of the frequency of other types of violence, but these statistics fit in with considerable other evidence, both judicial and literary, of the declining practice of violence in this period. Beattie also identified a decline in violent property crime in Surrey after 1700. As he concluded from his study of the criminal records, during this period 'men and women would seem to have become more controlled, less likely to strike out when annoyed or challenged, less likely to settle an argument or assert their will by recourse to a knife or their fists, a pistol or a sword. . . . men became more prepared to negotiate and talk out their differences.'[9]

Concurrently, there is evidence of growing popular and official intolerance of violence. In the early eighteenth century new arguments were advanced against duelling, and the brutality of hunting was subject to increasing criticism.[10] This period also witnessed the

---

'Punishing violence, sentencing crime', in Nancy Armstrong and Leonard Tennenhouse, eds, *The Violence of Representation: Literature and the History of Violence* (1989), pp. 140–56; Beattie, *Crime and the Courts*, pp. 88–9, 111.

8. Lawrence Stone, 'Interpersonal violence in English society', *P&P* 101 (1983), pp. 22–33, summarising T.R. Gurr, 'Historical trends in violent crime: a critical review of the evidence', *Crime and Justice: An Annual Review of Research* 3 (1981), pp. 295–353. Stone's article provoked a debate with J.A. Sharpe, in which Sharpe noted some of the problems of evidence and interpretation posed by Gurr's evidence and Stone's interpretation of it, but he concluded that the general trend outlined by Gurr and Stone 'seems to be broadly correct': 'The history of violence in England: some observations', *P&P* 108 (1985), pp. 206–24 (with response by Stone). These issues are also discussed in J.S. Cockburn, 'Patterns of violence in English society: homicide in Kent 1560–1985', *P&P* 130 (1991), pp. 70–106.

9. Beattie, *Crime and the Courts*, pp. 112, 162; Cockburn, 'Patterns of violence', p. 77.

10. Donna Andrew, 'The code of honour and its critics: the opposition to duelling in England, 1700–1850', *SH* 5 (1980), pp. 417–20; Anthony Fletcher, *Gender, Sex and Subordination in England 1500–1800* (New Haven CT, 1995), pp. 323, 328.

introduction or greater use of forms of criminal punishment which did not inflict violence on the convict. At the Middlesex sessions, there was a decline in the use of traditional 'shaming' punishments such as the stocks, the pillory, and public whipping for petty offenders, and greater use of houses of correction, where the violence that was used (whipping) was only one aspect of the punishment and was performed in private. Following the Transportation Act of 1718, felons were more likely to be transported than hanged.[11] Similarly, if the growing intolerance of wife-beating in the late seventeenth and early eighteenth century did not actually lead to a reduction in the practice, it seems to have made it less visible, especially among the middle class.[12] By mid-century, Methodists attacked the violent behaviour of all classes when they condemned duelling, animal-killing sports, drunkenness and fighting.[13] Although these changes did not remove violence from English life, they did reduce it, or at least make it less public. As such, they mark important shifts in attitudes and behaviour, in which men were increasingly expected to avoid the use (and threat) of physical force, which laid the ground for further significant shifts which took place later in the century.

At the same time, as Foyster argues, new standards of conduct were introduced for men, particularly those from the urban middle and upper classes, which placed a high value on restraint, civility and refined public conversation. As is evident in the writings of Anthony Ashley Cooper, third Earl of Shaftesbury, in periodicals such as the *Tatler* and the *Spectator* (edited by Joseph Addison and Richard Steele), in the increasingly popular conduct books, and later in sentimental novels, respectable men were increasingly expected to follow a code of behaviour, often termed 'politeness', which told them to reign in their emotions, follow the dictates of reason, and act with affability in social situations. Conversation, in this manner, came to be seen as an essential means of improving oneself, and was facilitated by the rise of institutions of public sociability such as coffee houses (popular in London by the late 1650s), and clubs and assemblies (popular from the 1690s). The *Tatler*, for example, was directed at the men who frequented coffee houses and the women who sat around tea tables, and it sought to define

11. Shoemaker, *Prosecution and Punishment*, pp. 161–3 and ch. 7; Beattie, *Crime and the Courts*, ch. 9.

12. Margaret Hunt, 'Wife beating, domesticity, and women's independence in eighteenth-century London', *G&H* 4 (1992), pp. 10–33; Wiltenburg, *Disorderly Women and Female Power*, ch. 6.

13. G.J. Barker-Benfield, *The Culture of Sensibility: Sex and Society in Eighteenth-Century Britain* (Chicago IL, 1992), pp. 75–6.

'tattle', or gossip, as a positive force for both men and women. This new understanding of masculinity has been seen as particularly suited to the increasingly important world of commerce and finance in London, and indeed these new institutions and publications were most popular there.[14] In a rapidly growing metropolis, filled with immigrants and permeated by new forms of wealth, men of all social classes needed new means of establishing and defending their honour, and of criticising, where necessary, the dishonourable actions of others. In particular, men engaged in business needed codes of behaviour which encouraged and regulated public conversation in order to make commercial transactions easier, resolve disputes, and facilitate economic and social exchanges between men of varying levels of status and wealth. Although this code of behaviour was intended very much for the upper middle class and gentry, its effects were not limited to those classes. A similar campaign to discipline the passions of men throughout English, and particularly London, society can be found in the Reformation of Manners campaign, launched in the 1690s, especially in its attack on male drunkenness.[15]

The new emphasis in prescriptions for male behaviour was thus on talk rather than action, and this was reflected in the growing popularity of the public insult among men, a type of behaviour which, while it would be condemned as uncivil by the ideologists of politeness, was arguably encouraged by their efforts to suppress violence and the new importance they gave to male conversation. As Susan Amussen suggests, slander, and litigation over slander, gave men a more 'respectable' means of resolving disputes than through a fight or duel. That defamation was an alternative to

14. Lawrence E. Klein, *Shaftesbury and the Culture of Politeness: Moral Discourse and Cultural Politics in Early Eighteenth-Century England* (Cambridge, 1994); Fletcher, *Gender, Sex and Subordination*, ch. 16; Steve Pincus, '"Coffee politicians does create": coffeehouses and Restoration political culture', *Journal of Modern History* 67 (1995), pp. 807–34; Kathryn Shevelow, *Women and Print Culture: The Construction of Femininity in the Early Periodical* (1989), pp. 94–8. Sentimental fiction, however, encouraged men to be more expressive of their feelings: Barker-Benfield, *The Culture of Sensibility*, ch. 5.

15. See, for example, [Josiah Woodward], *A Disswasive from the Sin of Drunkenness* (1711). For the Societies for the Reformation of Manners, see Robert B. Shoemaker, 'Reforming the City: the reformation of manners campaign in London, 1690–1738', in Lee Davison *et al.*, eds, *Stilling the Grumbling Hive: The Response to Social and Economic Problems in England, 1689–1750* (Stroud, 1992), pp. 99–120; D.W.R. Bahlman, *The Moral Revolution of 1688* (New Haven, 1957); T.C. Curtis and W.A. Speck, 'The Societies for the Reformation of Manners: a case study in the theory and practice of moral reform', *Literature and History* 3 (1976), pp. 45–57.

physical violence can be seen in a pamphlet in defence of coffee houses published in 1675, in which it was argued that if people were denied the 'freedom of words' they found in coffee houses, they would 'sooner . . . fall to their swords'.[16]

There are a number of reasons why historians of defamation have tended to pay insufficient attention to the fact that men regularly made public insults. They have been misled by the contemporary stereotype of slander as a feminine activity; they have focused almost entirely on the church court records, which only regularly document sexual insults, which were more likely to be made by women; and they have been more interested in the victims of insult (who were predominantly female) than those who made the insults.[17] Even in the church courts, however, where the only slanders which were admissible concerned moral offences, a substantial proportion of the people accused of defamation were male. Tim Meldrum demonstrated this in his study of the London consistory court: in two periods, between 1700 and 1710 and 1735 and 1745, he found that 37 per cent of the defendants were men.[18] Although the courts of quarter sessions arguably provide a more representative picture of public insults (since any behaviour which might lead to a breach of the peace, and thus any type of insult, could be reported), we find a similar proportion of men: in a sample of the Middlesex records from 1660 to 1740, which constitutes the core database used in this study, 42 per cent of those accused of defamation were men.[19] Despite contemporary stereotypes, defamation was not a preserve of the female tongue.

16. Amussen, 'The cultural politics of manhood', p. 226; 'A Dialogue Between Two Horses', December 1675, BL Add. Mss. 34362, fol. 41r (cited by Pincus, 'Coffeehouses and Restoration political culture', p. 832).

17. For this literature (not all of which embodies these sins and omissions), see Anna Clark, 'Whores and gossips: sexual reputation in London 1770–1825', in Arina Angerman *et al.*, eds, *Current Issues in Women's History* (1989), pp. 231–48; Laura Gowing, *Domestic Dangers: Women, Words and Sex in Early Modern London* (Oxford, 1996); Martin Ingram, *Church Courts, Sex and Marriage in England, 1570–1640* (Cambridge, 1987), ch. 10; Tim Meldrum, 'A women's court in London: defamation at the Bishop of London's consistory court, 1700–1745', *LJ* 19 (1994), pp. 1–20; Polly Morris, 'Defamation and sexual reputation in Somerset, 1733–1850' (Ph.D. thesis, University of Warwick, 1985); J.A. Sharpe, *Defamation and Sexual Slander in Early Modern England: The Church Courts at York*, Borthwick Papers 58 (York, 1980).

18. Meldrum, 'A women's court in London', p. 6.

19. This sample is based on an examination of the recognisances to appear at the August or September meeting of the Middlesex sessions every other year. Since the court met twelve times a year (including the Westminster sessions), this accounts for 1/24th, or roughly 4 per cent, of the approximately 135,000 recognisances issued during this period. LMA, MJ/SR/1217–2721 (1660–1739).

Nor was it a preserve of the lower classes, despite seventeenth-century stereotypes to that effect.[20] The satire on London life, *Hell Upon Earth: or, the Town in an Uproar* (1729), noted that men of all classes sought to improve their status through 'this vile impulse to slander'. Similarly, it has recently been argued that the coffee house, that important site of male gossip, was frequented by men (and women) of all social classes.[21] Although the quarter sessions evidence relating to social status is patchy, since many men were not identified by status or occupation, it is clear that men from all classes engaged in defamation. In 1683 the Middlesex grand jury complained that many of the indictments which were brought before it concerned disputes among the poor, and the 'offences arise from scolding, backbiting, and reproaching'.[22] The large number of defendants at quarter sessions who were unable to find sureties for their recognisances also suggests that many poor men defamed. But there was also a significant number of middle- to high-status defendants among the accused, accounting for half the defendants in the sample whose status or occupation was identified. These include two chandlers, a goldwiredrawer and five gentlemen. At the church courts, where litigation was much more costly, male litigants appear to have followed 'middling crafts or trades'.[23] Although some men of the 'polite' classes were thus not above making a public insult, for the most part those making insults were of a *somewhat* lower social standing. The public insult was a perverted form of the new gentlemanly concern with conversation, but it affected a much broader social spectrum.

As recorded in the church court and quarter sessions records, men made a variety of insults, some of which can be seen as arising out of older conceptions of masculinity, and some of which can be related to the new concerns of politeness. Evidence of the former can be seen in the fact that men were almost as likely as women to make sexual insults, calling a woman whore, common whore, murderous bitch and whore, and so on. In the quarter sessions records men were more likely than women, however, to make more specific accusations, which often involved bragging about their own exploits. John Daniel told Mary, the wife of Henry Jones, that she was

20. [R. Allestree], *The Ladies Calling, in Two Parts* (1673; 6th impression, Oxford, 1693), p. 50.

21. *Hell Upon Earth: or the Town in an Uproar* (1729), p. 17; Pincus, 'Coffeehouses and Restoration political culture', p. 814.

22. LMA, MJ/SBB/408, p. 47 (Oct. 1683).

23. Meldrum, 'A women's court in London', p. 7.

a 'common whore and . . . that he had often times layne with her and could when he pleased'.[24]

Needless to say men used different terms of abuse towards other men: rogue, knave and dog were the favourites. The first two could be used in sexual insults, but they were mostly used to address a different kind of dishonesty: dishonesty in terms of not keeping one's word. The most important context in which this was relevant in London at this time was of course in maintaining a man's credit in the world of trade. In a society without formal credit agencies, the security of most financial transactions depended upon a tradesman's word and his reputation for financial solvency. Richard Allestree noted that to men who 'subsist by dealings in the world, [a good name] is so necessary, that it may well be reckoned as the means of [his] livelihood'. Thus the insult that one was a 'perjured rogue' was particularly damaging. As Daniel Defoe put it, 'the credit of a tradesman . . . is the same thing in its nature as the virtue of a lady'.[25] A tradesman's reputation was established publicly and, since disputes over credit were bound to arise, we can see why so many shopkeepers were the targets of insults. We can also see why the victims of such insults brought their slanderers to court. William Dyer, for example, prosecuted Thomas Harris, his former apprentice, 'for endeavouring to take away his reputation and credit, thereby endangering the loss and ruin of his employment, by reporting that he had pawned his silver candlesticks and other plate and was ready to crack break and run away'.[26] Harris had probably suffered financially from Dyer's lack of probity and by making this accusation in public he not only achieved some revenge but he warned other tradesmen not to deal with Dyer, thereby updating the fund of popular knowledge about the reliability of potential trading partners. As recent research has shown, significant numbers of women, too, were involved in businesses in London at this time, and they too made insults on this issue, though not apparently as often. Defoe noted that, on the subject of attacking credit, women 'are sometimes fully even with the men, for ill usage, when they please to fall upon them in this nice article'.[27]

24. LMA, MJ/SR/1392, R. 142 (Aug. 1670).

25. Julian Hoppit, 'The use and abuse of credit in eighteenth-century England', in N. McKendrick and R.B. Outhwaite, eds, *Business Life and Public Policy* (Cambridge, 1986), pp. 64–5; [Allestree], *The Whole Duty of Man*, p. 246; Daniel Defoe, *The Complete English Tradesman* (1726; Gloucester, 1987), p. 134.

26. LMA, MJ/SR/1651, R. 173 (Sept. 1684).

27. Defoe implied that when women did this they were seeking revenge for 'slights' they had received: *Complete English Tradesman*, p. 138.

The use of insults to attack and defend commercial reputations was in a sense encouraged by the newer, more 'polite' version of masculinity emerging at this time. Nonetheless, scandalous words and physical violence were not mutually exclusive: half of the men who were bound over for defamatory words were also accused of committing some form of real or threatened violence. Only 13 per cent of the cases, however, include specific references to physical violence such as beating, bruising, and wounding (a further 13 per cent included threats of violence, and 24 per cent were labelled as assaults, a vague term which could mean anything from a verbal threat to a physical attack). Whether a dispute ended with fisticuffs or merely verbal insults must have depended on a number of factors, not least the participants' own understanding of what was appropriate male behaviour. There is some evidence in the quarter sessions records and elsewhere that men were increasingly object-ing when challenged to fight by other men: instead of fighting, they went to a justice of the peace and got their antagonist bound over to appear at quarter sessions. Thus one yeoman was bound over for reviling and abusing a gentleman 'calling him knave and challenging him to fight in the field'.[28] Another example of this new intolerance of fighting comes from a newspaper account from 1719, describing a type of quarrel which frequently erupted in London's narrow streets, between two gentlemen whose coaches were unable to pass one another in a street near the Strand. When the gentlemen drew their swords, the paper reports, 'the mob very contrary to their modern practice, interposed and prevented mis-chief'; the gentlemen 'were soon seemingly friends, and parted'.[29]

It is not clear whether men were making more public insults in this period, or that such insults were simply attracting more atten-tion than they had in the past due to the decline of violence and the new importance accorded to male conversation. According to the court records, the number of insults does not appear to have changed. For a number of reasons, however, these records provide only a partial picture. We have seen that in the church courts men accounted for 37 per cent of the defendants for slander in London in the first half of the eighteenth century, a figure which is remark-ably similar to Laura Gowing's figure of 41 per cent for the same court between 1572 and 1640.[30] Yet, as argued earlier, the church

---

28. LMA, MJ/SR/1472, R. 66 (Sept. 1674). See also MJ/SR/1434, R. 162 (Sept. 1672); MJ/SR/2762, R. 166 and 183 (August 1741).

29. *Weekly Journal: or Saturday's Post* (5 Dec. 1719).

30. Meldrum, 'A women's court in London', p. 6; Gowing, *Domestic Dangers*, p. 37.

court evidence is limited, because only one type of insult, on sexual matters, was commonly prosecuted in these courts.

While the quarter sessions records include a broader range and larger number of insults, they suffer from a different problem. Defamation was not an indictable offence, and is only recorded in recognisances, bonds to appear at sessions to answer a complaint. A high proportion of recognisances, however, do not identify the nature of the dispute. A defamation case could be simply recorded as a recognisance 'to keep the peace', or the offending behaviour could be labelled an 'assault', without providing any indication that an insult had taken place. And even where it is noted that the defendant was guilty of 'scandalous words', the specific insulting words or any violence that was used were not consistently recorded. The level of detail recorded very much depended on the individual inclinations of justices of the peace (or their clerks), and some were much more conscientious than others. Three justices, for example, were responsible for more than half of the cases during an apparent outbreak of defamation in urban Middlesex in the early 1670s.[31] If my 4 per cent sample of the Middlesex sessions records is representative, an average of approximately 14 men per year were bound over by the justices for defamation in suburban London; although the court's jurisdiction covered approximately two-thirds of the population of the metropolis, it did not include the City of London and Southwark.[32] In any case, given the fact that only a fraction of such behaviour is likely to have been reported to justices, the number of men actually making insults was no doubt very much higher.

Ultimately, the limitations of the court records mean that they cannot provide us with an accurate picture of chronological change. Another type of source, social commentary and conduct books, does provide evidence of an increase in male defamation in this period, or at least of greater awareness and concern being expressed over the extent of this behaviour. In his treatise on the 'ten sins of the tongue', published in 1663, William Gearing wrote that 'if ever men's tongue's were set on fire with hell, it is in this age: and if profaneness, slanders [etc.] were taken out of men's words, how

31. The justices were Charles Pitfield, Josiah Ricroft and Peter Sabbs.

32. The sampling method is outlined in note 19 above. Since a 4 per cent sample found an average of 0.56 cases per year, multiplying by 25 results in the estimate of 14 cases per year. In 1680 the Middlesex sessions had jurisdiction over about 60 per cent of the population of the metropolis, and due to the rapid growth of the suburbs this proportion increased over the course of this period: Shoemaker, *Prosecution and Punishment*, pp. 16–17.

few would remain'. Similarly, a pamphlet entitled *A Check to an Ungoverned Tongue* (1705) stated that 'calling foul names . . . is grown so very common among us, that . . . it is looked at as part of the accomplishment of a Gentleman to be able to do it blustringly, and with fluency and variety'. Although complaints about the growth of insult in this literature seem to have been concentrated in the first half of our period, later examples can also be found: in 1743 one commentator complained that the 'contagion' of slander was 'spreading even among men . . . even among men of literature and understanding'.[33]

That public insult had become fashionable for men in this period can also be seen from its link with two of the new passions of the late seventeenth and early eighteenth centuries: party politics and coffee houses. According to the Reformation of Manners polemicist Josiah Woodward, the passion for insult at this time was fuelled by the vehemence of party conflict. As he put it, a 'great cause' of defamation is 'that people of a party in any matter appertaining to Church or state esteem it as a commendable piece of service to their cause, to bespatter their opposites right or wrong'.[34] Party conflict of course also led to violence between the 1680s and the 1720s, but the party system ultimately had the effect of disciplining the conduct of political disputes. Political arguments frequently took place at that fashionable new centre of refined urban sociability, the coffee house. The conventional greeting in coffee houses was 'what news?', and while much of what was discussed was political, there was plenty of opportunity to spread gossip and slander as well. In 1726 Defoe suggested that coffee houses served the same function for men that the tea table served for ladies: as places devoted to the spread of scandal, where in the words of Defoe, 'the characters of all kinds of persons and professions are handled in the most merciless manner [and] reproach triumphs'.[35] Some complained that the disease spread to the printed word as well, particularly the newspapers, which were so often read in coffee houses

33. William Gearing, *A Bridle for the Tongue; or a Treatise of Ten Sins of the Tongue* (1663), preface; *A Check to an Ungoverned Tongue* (1705), p. 28; *The Ladies Cabinet, or a Companion for the Toilet* (1743), p. 15.

34. Josiah Woodward, *The Baseness and Perniciousness of the Sin of Slandering and Backbiting* (3rd edn, 1729), pp. 16–17. See also Edward Fowler, *The Great Wickedness, and Mischievous Effects of Slandering* (1685); Thomas Frank, *A Letter to a Member of Parliament in the North: Concerning Scandal and Defamation* (1732), p. 7.

35. Pincus, 'Coffeehouses and Restoration political culture', pp. 819–20; Defoe, *Complete English Tradesman*, pp. 133–4.

and which were also becoming increasingly popular in this period. The print medium offered plenty of opportunities for launching verbal attacks on the reputations of others. In 1732 Thomas Frank complained that 'in most of the papers published' there was a 'spirit of envy, scandal and detraction run through them, pointing either at whole communities, or particular persons'.[36] Through its importance in attacking (and establishing) credit and reputation, male public insult was also, as we have seen, encouraged by another new great passion of the age – trade.

But as this pamphlet literature suggests, male insult was the subject of much criticism, paradoxically as part of the same literary attempts to civilise male behaviour which contributed to the decline in violence and the rise in politeness, attempts whose goal has been characterised by G.J. Barker-Benfield as a 'reformation of male manners'. Some of the earliest criticisms of male defamation came in the context of the first formal Reformation of Manners societies (1690–1738), whose writers characterised defamation as a male problem, which was linked with other failings of the tongue, such as profane swearing and cursing, blasphemy, lying, flattery and backbiting. The public insult was thus viewed as part of the general wave of irreligiosity which was thought to be spreading through English society in the late seventeenth and early eighteenth centuries.[37]

Much of the concern about the apparent outbreak of male defaming at this time, however, derived from the fact that authors were worried that men were taking up a female vice, and that in the process gender boundaries were dissolving. As Richard Allestree wrote in 1674, 'I know we use to call this talkativeness a feminine vice . . . [but] 'tis possible [now] to go into masculine company where 'twill be as hard to edge in a word, as at a female gossiping. . . . as to this particular of defaming, both sexes seem to be at a vye: and I think he were a very critical judge, that could determine between them.' By engaging in slander men were adopting female traits, and becoming 'unmanly'. In pamphlets like *A Check to an Ungoverned Tongue* (1705), men were warned that to defame was in effect to declare 'plainly that you are slaves to your own passions', a fault of

---

36. Frank, *A Letter to a Member of Parliament in the North*, p. 7. On the growth of newspapers, see Jeremy Black, *The English Press in the Eighteenth Century* (1986).

37. Barker-Benfield, *Culture of Sensibility*, p. 56; Woodward, *Baseness and Perniciousness of the Sin of Slandering and Backbiting*.

course normally ascribed to women. And the *Ladies Cabinet* argued in 1743 that men were adopting this vice 'owing to an effeminate emulation of the fair [sex], to court their esteem'.[38]

The increased attention focused on male public insult in this period thus raised the worrying possibility that men were becoming effeminate. This is indicative of a wider problem raised by the rise of politeness and the reformation of male manners. As Lawrence Klein has noted, politeness required men to converse with women, in order both to force men 'to abandon qualities they reserved for discourse among themselves' including aggression, and to allow them to acquire new skills in 'the pursuit of pleasure, ease and liberty, a sense of humour, the constant framing of learning by the standard of sociability'. Yet as Michèle Cohen and Philip Carter have pointed out, writers expressed concern that men's tongues should not thereby become undisciplined, and lose 'sight of classically "manly" values such as heroism, sense and hardiness'. Those who did were often labelled 'fops'. Thus men who frequented the mixed-sex environment of coffee houses were parodied as being emasculated by their female company, their absence from traditional masculine recreations, and by the desiccating nature of the drink itself, which purportedly rendered them impotent. Similar concerns were later expressed about sentimental literature, since the attempt to make men more attentive to feeling and sentiment self-evidently threatened to render them effeminate.[39]

With regard to defamation, concerns about the blurring of gender difference were not without foundation, for there were many similarities between patterns of male and female public insult. Whereas Laura Gowing has identified fundamental gender differences in the language of defamation in late sixteenth- and early seventeenth-century London, there are some important similarities in the insults made by men and women which were prosecuted a century later.[40] The detailed descriptions of incidents in which

---

38. [R. Allestree], *The Government of the Tongue* (1674; Oxford, 1702), pp. 72–3, 123. *Check to an Ungoverned Tongue*, p. 31; *The Ladies Cabinet*, p. 15.

39. Lawrence E. Klein, 'Gender, conversation and the public sphere in early eighteenth-century England', in J. Still and M. Worton, eds, *Textuality and Sexuality: Reading Theories and Practices* (Manchester, 1993), p. 108; Michèle Cohen, *Fashioning Masculinity: National Identity and Language in the Eighteenth Century* (1996), ch. 2; Philip Carter, 'Men about town: representations of foppery and masculinity in early eighteenth-century urban society', in H. Barker and E. Chalus, eds, *Gender in Eighteenth-Century England* (1997), p. 53; Pincus, 'Coffeehouses and Restoration political culture', pp. 823–4; Barker-Benfield, *Culture of Sensibility*, ch. 3.

40. Gowing, *Domestic Dangers*, ch. 3.

defamatory words were voiced by men in this period have all the characteristics of a stereotypical female gossip session, with male defamers standing in doorways or kitchens, with plenty of women, as well as men, in the audience.[41] A closer analysis of the language and gestures used by the sexes does reveal some important differences. As we have seen, in sexual insults, both men and women used the term whore, but men made more specific accusations, often citing their own exploits. While women made more sexual insults, men's insults tended to cover a wider range of alleged malfeasance, including business dealings. Men were also more likely to combine violence with insult. Yet for the most part these are differences of degree rather than kind, and it is clear that in their defamatory activities men *were* engaging in actions commonly performed by women.

If gender differences were to be maintained, how, then, were men supposed to defend their own honour, and attack the dishonourable activities of others? In earlier times this had often been done through violence, and a late example of this approach comes from a pamphlet written in 1709, when men were told by Henry Hooton that it was more 'manful' to attack a man with a sword than 'basely' to defame him in public. By the 1740s, however, authors were arguing that men should simply forgive or ignore those who insulted them, rather than respond with violence or litigation, since a man's honour was not as harmed by malicious tongues as a woman's. The Christian argument that both men and women should be judged by inner standards of virtue rather than in public was not new in the mid-eighteenth century, but it was used more often in criticising defamation. In 1745 the conduct book *The New Whole Duty of Man* posed the question, 'suppose a man should give me the lie, or call me names, or abuse me with reproachful language'. It responded by pronouncing that 'mercy requires me to remit and forgive the fault, and not to strike and wound him, nor rigidly by a vexatious suit at law to exact the hurt of the offender for such trifling offences as do me no harm'. The same did not apply to women, however. An essay on marriage published two years later, which noted 'how much more nice [i.e. precarious] the honour of a woman is, than a man', argued that 'a man cannot be dishonoured but by reason,

---

41. For example, see LMA, London Consistory Court, DL/C/255, ff. 136, 417–34, 455, 465 (1714–15).

but the opportunity is enough to defame a woman'.[42] Since the public defence of honour and reputation was associated with women, it was argued that men needed to abandon notions that their self-worth depended on the opinions of others. In 1753 an allegorical story was published in the *Gentleman's Magazine* with the moral that honour should no longer be determined by opinion, by which it had 'always been kept', but by 'the regions of immortality, to which they will at length be conducted in time'.[43] In the second half of the eighteenth century the very definition of honour as based on public reputation, in which one's sense of worth depended on the opinions of others, was called into question by Evangelical writers and the critics of duelling, as standards of male behaviour which emphasised inner virtue and character were more frequently articulated. By this point sexual conduct had become far less important than it had been in the seventeenth century in shaping men's reputations (hence insults on this topic lost their force). A greater distinction was now made between men's private and public behaviour, and the former was no longer deemed suitable subject matter for discussion in public.[44] In a number of ways public insult therefore lost its relevance for men.

It is unclear how quickly this led to a decline in male public insult. A sample of the London consistory court records between 1780 and 1825 found that men accounted for 'more than half' of the defendants accused of defamation. Yet the number of cases brought before the court had fallen to a fraction of the level they were at in the first half of the eighteenth century; this was part of a long-term decline in defamation litigation in the church courts (involving both men and women) from the seventeenth to the early nineteenth centuries. Concurrently, the social status of the litigants had apparently declined: only a quarter of the plaintiffs were middle class, and more than half of the cases came from the

42. Henry Hooton, *A Bridle for the Tongue: or Some Practical Discourses* (1709), p. 36; *The New Whole Duty of Man* (1745), p. 308; *The Art of Governing a Wife, with Rules for Batchelors* (1747), p. 14.

43. *Gentlemen's Magazine* 23 (June 1753), p. 273, summarising an article which appeared in the *Adventurer* no. 61 (5 June 1753).

44. John Tosh, *A Man's Place: Masculinity and the Middle-Class Home in Victorian England* (London and New Haven, forthcoming 1999), ch. 5; Faramerz Dabhoiwala, 'The construction of honour, reputation and status in late seventeenth- and early eighteenth-century England', *TRHS* 6th ser., VI (1996), pp. 212–13. This shift is also evident in the changing ideological grounds for attacks on duelling between the early and late eighteenth century: Andrews, 'The code of honour and its critics', pp. 417–22.

working-class East End of London.[45] It is possible that by this time middle- and upper-class men rarely engaged in public insults, while the new attitudes towards male honour took more time to reach the lower classes (or were not intended to do so), but further research is clearly necessary on this issue.

The century after the Restoration was an important transitional period in the reform of male behaviour, in which the new attention given to male public insult formed an important stage in the long-term decline of violence. This is at least what happened in London, which, with its rapidly evolving social and economic structure, was no doubt precocious in this respect; the pattern of change in other parts of the country was probably different. London was at the forefront of developments which encouraged male defamation: the 'rage' of party conflict; the growth of trade; the popularity of coffee houses, periodicals, and newspapers; and the rise of the literature of politeness, which was particularly concerned to promote conversation and develop new standards of behaviour for this increasingly dynamic urban setting. As this last point suggests, London was also the place where critiques, not only of violence, but also of insult, were most likely to develop.

Men of all classes had always engaged in defamation, but the decline (but not disappearance) of violence, together with the new attention paid to male conversation, both encouraged male public insult and made it the subject of unprecedented criticism. Ultimately, this scrutiny led to its decline as it became a victim of the same efforts to civilise male manners, as well as concerns about effeminacy. When criticising others and responding to attacks on their honour, men, especially respectable men, appear to have moved in the seventeenth century from violence to defamation and then, in the mid-eighteenth century, from defamation to inaction and a new concern with inner virtue. This is admittedly a crude description of a much more complex pattern of change, since violence and defamation coexisted for a much longer period than this model suggests, but it does give us a clearer idea of the overall process by which men became less violent. It shows us that the changes in male behaviour usually described as 'the civilising process' were not imposed from above by the state or ruling class (as suggested by Norbert Elias), but arose instead out of the culture, patterns of

45. Clark, 'Whores and gossips', pp. 239–40.

sociability, and commercial transactions of the respectable middling sort in London (though they were not confined to that class).[46] It also demonstrates that changes in male behaviour had the potential to undermine gender differences, thereby precipitating renewed efforts to redefine masculinity. New patterns of male behaviour developed in opposition not only to older conceptions of masculinity, but also to prevailing ideas of the feminine.

46. Norbert Elias, *The Civilizing Process: The History of Manners* (1939; Oxford, 1978). For a similar critique of Elias, for a slightly earlier period, see Steve Hindle, 'The keeping of the public peace', in Paul Griffiths *et al.*, eds, *The Experience of Authority in Early Modern England* (Basingstoke, 1996), pp. 237–8.

CHAPTER EIGHT

Boys will be Boys? Manhood and Aggression, 1660–1800[1]

ELIZABETH FOYSTER

'Being a clear moonlight night I was engaged with other Boys in a mockfight. We had wooden swords and pistols, and were drawn up on each side the street, but on a sudden all our sport was spoiled by the appearance of a troop of two of real soldiers upon the Bridge entering the Town with their swords drawn.' So the eighteenth-century Nonconformist minister James Clegg recalled his childhood.[2] Such displays of youthful male behaviour were common in early modern England. 'Anything that looks like Fighting, is delicious to an Englishman', wrote one French visitor in 1719, after observing how large crowds gathered in the London streets to watch boys fighting.[3] Showing or boasting of physical bravado could play an important part in a boy's transition to adulthood. As adults, when aggression was exercised through physical violence, brawls outside alehouses or duels between gentlemen could serve as means for men to settle disputes and establish status.[4] Aggressive language and behaviour could also be employed by some men to maintain their superior position in the household over women and servants. Models of male aggression from which boys could learn were plentiful. As

1. I would like to thank Keith Bartlett, Anthony Fletcher, Jeremy Gregory, David Turner and especially Helen Berry for their helpful comments and suggestions on this chapter.
2. H. Kirke, ed., *Extracts from the Diary and Autobiography of the Reverend James Clegg* (London, 1899), p. 19.
3. H. Misson, *Memoirs and Observations in his Travels over England* (London, 1719), p. 304.
4. For examples of brawls see J.M. Beattie, *Crime and the Courts in England 1660–1800* (Princeton, 1986), pp. 91–4, S.D. Amussen, 'Punishment, discipline, and power: the social meanings of violence in early modern England', *JBS* 34 (1995), pp. 1–34; for duelling see V.G. Kiernan, *The Duel in European History: Honour and the Reign of the Aristocracy* (Oxford, 1988) and D.T. Andrew, 'The code of honour and its critics: the opposition to duelling in England, 1700–1850', *SH* 5, 3 (1980), pp. 409–34.

well as witnessing patterns of behaviour from their fathers, masters
and other male adults, boys could draw upon examples of male
heroes in popular literature, and learn the hard way from fights in
the playground and in the streets with other boys.[5]

This chapter will look at one particular way in which male
aggression was problematised in the period 1660–1800. Of course,
contemporaries had always recognised that when employed inap-
propriately or excessively, male aggression could be harmful and
destructive to the social order.[6] But by looking at a range of printed
literature, including conduct books, sermons, handbooks for
educationalists, and periodicals, this chapter will show how in this
period there were new understandings of what lay behind the male
propensity for aggression. Anger was the emotion which caught
these writers' attention, and was constructed as a specifically *male*
issue or concern. While it was recognised that there were degrees
of anger so that not all anger was aggressive, and that all aggression
could not be attributed to anger, the writers of these literatures
attempted to place limits on the occasions when men could overtly
express their anger as aggression to others. Writing at a time when
sociability was of key importance to middle-class manhood, their
message may have been particularly pertinent. By training boys
to exercise self-control over their anger, and express it without
physical aggression to others, the eighteenth-century authors of
prescriptive literature believed that they had found one solution to
containing male violence.[7]

Physical strength was an obvious characteristic which distinguished
men from women, and could be used to justify male superiority over
women. But boys' bodies were weak and needed to be strengthened.
While James Nelson in his 1756 *Essay on the Government of Children*
believed that John Locke's directions to make holes in boys shoes to
let in water, and give them hard beds, 'probably are never followed',
many who wrote on the upbringing of boys continued to suggest

---

5. For popular literature see M. Spufford, *Small Books and Pleasant Histories* (Cambridge, 1981), pp. 225–32, and I.K. Ben-Amos, *Adolescence and Youth in Early Modern
England* (London, 1994), pp. 23–5; for examples of boys' experiences of fights at
school, see A. Fletcher, *Gender, Sex and Subordination in England 1500–1800* (London,
1995), pp. 308–9.

6. Amussen, 'Punishment'; M. Hunt, 'Wife beating, domesticity and women's independence in eighteenth-century London', *G&H* 4, 1 (1992), pp. 10–33; E. Foyster,
'Male honour, social control and wife beating in late Stuart England', *TRHS* VI (1996),
pp. 215–24.

7. For modern-day thinking on the distinction between anger, aggression and violence see J.R. Averill, *Anger and Aggression: An Essay on Emotion* (New York, 1982).

ways of training them to endure physical hardships.[8] George Chapman, a master of Dumfries school in the 1770s, advised that 'to suffer pain with a manly spirit' was a useful lesson to teach boys. As well as engaging in sports such as riding and fencing, children should be made 'more robust' by subjecting them to country air and cold baths.[9] The Nonconformist minister Isaac Watts believed that while physical education was particularly important for those destined for the manual trades, all boys would benefit from some physical training, advising parents to give serious consideration to the sports and physical diversion of their sons.[10] Other conduct literature gave similar advice, always warning of the excessive fondness of mothers which encouraged them to indulge their sons with physical comforts, only to 'prolong the feebleness of childhood'.[11] Evidence of parents putting this advice into practice is not difficult to find. Adam Martindale was one father who could not contain his pride when he remembered the precocious strength of his two-year-old son: 'he was a beautiful child, and very manly and courageous', he wrote in 1663.[12] 'Consider what your boys must undergo before they arrive at manhood, and I am sure you will agree with me that it is not wise to bring them up too tenderly', Thomas Fremantle advised his wife Elizabeth Wynn in 1803.[13]

One of the intended purposes of this physical education was that it would ease the parents' or teachers' task of training the mind. The health of the body and the mind, as Chapman explained, were closely related. 'The body, when softened by indolence, or mistaken tenderness, enfeebles the mind . . . when pampered and weakened by luxury . . . it subjects the mind to wants not its own, and excites

8. J. Locke, *Some Thoughts Concerning Education*, ed. J.W. and J.S. Yolton (Oxford, 1989), pp. 86, 98; J. Nelson, *An Essay on the Government of Children*, 2nd edn (London, 1756), pp. 127–31.

9. G. Chapman, *A Treatise on Education* (Edinburgh, 1773), pp. 130–1, 134–5.

10. I. Watts, *A Discourse on the Education of Children and Youth* (London, 1809), pp. 331, 364–6.

11. Chapman, *A Treatise*, pp. 129–30; for more on the fears of indulgent mothers see M.R. Hunt, *The Middling Sort: Commerce, Gender and the Family in England, 1680–1780* (Berkeley CA, 1996), p. 113; for other examples of conduct literature which encouraged physical exercise for boys see F. Osborne, *Advice to a Son* (Oxford, 1656) in L.B. Wright, ed., *Advice to a Son: Precepts of Lord Burghley, Sir Walter Raleigh, and Francis Osborne* (Ithaca NY, 1962), p. 50; F. Brokesby, *Directions to Young Students in the University* (1701), pp. 25–6.

12. As cited in M. Abbott, *Life Cycles in England 1560–1720: Cradle to Grave* (1996), p. 56; for other seventeenth-century examples see Fletcher, *Gender, Sex and Subordination*, p. 87.

13. As cited in L. Pollock, *A Lasting Relationship: Parents and Children Over Three Centuries* (London, 1987), p. 105.

those passions which are the enemies of happiness and of life'.[14] Just as boys' bodies were physically under-developed, so in their youth the reason which should govern their thinking was weak. Men had 'the larger share of Reason bestow'd upon them', and this justified the 'inequality in the sexes', explained the first Marquis of Halifax to his daughter in 1688.[15] During the early Enlightenment the importance of reason for manhood was particularly pertinent. But until the age of 21, and particularly from birth until the age of seven, a boy's reason and judgement were feeble, argued Nelson, and 'the Passions alone are their Guides'.[16] Physically and mentally weak, it was during youth that manhood was at its most fragile stage in the life-cycle, and male claims to superiority over women least sustainable. It was the passions which could undermine manhood at this age, and it was the passion of anger which was most threatening to men.

Anger was an 'unruly Passion', preached Lancelot Blackburne in July 1694, which by subverting a man's reason robbed 'a Man of the best part of himself'.[17] Anger is a vice which 'throws a Man into the utmost Disorder', and 'is a kind of Drunkenness, which seizes our Minds, and disturbs our Reason by Fumes more intoxicating than those of wine', warned the author of the 1742 *Moral Instructions for Youth*.[18] It was particularly troublesome in children and young men, since, as one writer put it, 'youth is naturally full of Fire . . . as now their Judgement is weak', and another labelled anger as 'this disorder of nature in youth'.[19] Anger so endangered a man's reason that it was often referred to as a 'short madness'.[20] Indeed, anger was so akin to madness in contemporary thinking that furious rage was a behaviour which was frequently used to diagnose insanity in this period.[21] 'Raving madness' was the name given to one of the

14. Chapman, *A Treatise*, pp. 6–7; P.J. Carter, 'Mollies, fops and men of feeling: aspects of male effeminacy and masculinity in Britain, c.1700–1780' (D.Phil. thesis, Oxford University, 1995), pp. 214–18.

15. As cited in V. Jones, ed., *Women in the Eighteenth Century: Constructions of Femininity* (London, 1990), p. 18.

16. Nelson, *An Essay*, pp. 16, 36, 150–1, 156–7, 176, 247.

17. L. Blackburne, *The Unreasonableness of Anger* (London, 1694), pp. 4–5, 13.

18. P. Sylvestre du Four, *Moral Instructions for Youth* (London, 1742), pp. 37, 39; J. Fawcett, *An Essay on Anger* (Leeds, 1787), p. 73 made a similar comparison.

19. Nelson, *An Essay*, p. 247; Watts, *A Discourse*, p. 339; see also the *Spectator* No. 408 (18 June 1712), p. 58; Ben-Amos, *Adolescence*, pp. 16–19.

20. See, for example, S.A., *A Sermon Proving, Slowness to Anger, The Truest Gallantry* (London, 1713), p. 10; Sylvestre du Four, *Moral Instructions*, p. 37; Fawcett, *An Essay*, p. 34; *Gentleman's Magazine*, II (1732), p. 949.

21. M. MacDonald, *Mystical Bedlam: Madness, Anxiety, and Healing in Seventeenth-Century England* (Cambridge, 1983), p. 140; A. Ingram, *The Madhouse of Language: Writing and Reading Madness in the Eighteenth Century* (London, 1991), pp. 26, 145.

two huge stone statues (both male figures) which in the late seventeenth century were constructed and mounted to loom over the entrance gates of Bethlem Hospital at Moorefields.[22] 'The furious man rages like a wild bull in a net', wrote John Fawcett, who, with his reason 'beclouded', is from a man 'transformed into a brute, or rather into a fiend and fury . . . He is now only a fit companion for Devils.' Resembling 'madmen and devils', anger was so serious that it had the power to make those who expressed it 'unworthy' of 'the name of a man' and unable to claim 'the character of a Christian'.[23] Deprived of his reason, an angry man was prone to both aggressive language and behaviour. When a man angrily responded to slurs on his reputation, 'he breaks out into loud and passionate clamours, into hasty threats, and bitter revilings'. Such behaviour was so unmanly that it betrayed 'his impotence, by the very means he would appear formidable', thought Blackburne.[24] A man governed by his anger was a 'frightful and odious spectacle' who attacked those who should have been most dear to him. 'He abuses the wife of his bosom. He flies upon the children of his own body, with the rage of a lion or tiger. He spares not his dearest and most valuable friends', Fawcett observed.[25]

Remarkably, despite the many medical advances which were occurring around them, most notably in this context the work begun by Thomas Willis in the 1660s on the nervous system, understandings of how anger was caused barely changed in these writings over 200 years.[26] Explanations rooted in Galenic physiology which laid emphasis on the heat of bodily humours, rather than on the importance of the brain and nerves in governing emotion, remained dominant. The minister John Downame in 1609 thought that anger was an 'affection' which resulted when 'the blood about the heart' was heated.[27] When another minister preached a sermon more than a hundred years later in 1713, he also taught that anger set 'the Blood on boiling' in the breast.[28] By the time Fawcett came to write his treatise in 1787, the word 'passion' was more commonly used than 'affection' to describe anger, but humoural understandings of

22. I am grateful to Allan Ingram for bringing the statues to my attention.
23. Fawcett, *An Essay*, pp. 34–5, 37, 76.
24. Blackburne, *The Unreasonableness*, p. 9.   25. Fawcett, *An Essay*, p. 36.
26. G.J. Barker-Benfield, *The Culture of Sensibility: Sex and Society in Eighteenth-Century Britain* (Chicago, 1992), ch. 1; R. Martensen, 'The transformation of Eve: women's bodies, medicine and culture in early modern England', in R. Porter and M. Teich, eds, *Sexual Knowledge, Sexual Science: The History of Attitudes to Sexuality* (Cambridge, 1994), pp. 114–16.
27. J. Downame, *A Treatise of Anger* (London, 1609), p. 3.
28. S.A., *A Sermon Proving*, p. 13.

the body still proved resilient. He explained that passions such as anger were 'mental exertions in conjunction with the ferments of the blood', and again referred to the heart 'boiling with anger', and releasing fumes which then suffocated the mind of reason.[29] This physiological phenomenon could have a dramatic effect on a man's physical appearance as well as his mental health. 'It renders the countenance sometimes red and fiery, sometimes pale and wan. It flames or scowls in the eyes; it wrinkles the brow; it enlarges the nostrils, and makes them heave . . . and sometimes it causes a tremor through all the limbs', Fawcett wrote.[30] Some men were thought to be born more 'hot and choleric' than others, and so were naturally more disposed to anger.[31] The propensity to anger could even be inherited, running 'in the blood from father to son'.[32]

Whereas medical understandings of anger remained fairly static, there were other changes across the seventeenth and eighteenth centuries in how anger was conceptualised. First, as Carol and Peter Stearns have pointed out in their seminal work on anger in nineteenth- and twentieth-century America, it was in the eighteenth century that the language for referring to and reproving an emotion like anger initially came into use. Whereas 'emotional ills commonly occurred as a vague melancholia' in the seventeenth century, epitomised by Robert Burton's 1621 colossal volume *The Anatomy of Melancholy*, which described a huge range of mental and physical symptoms and behaviours, by the eighteenth century emotions like anger were receiving separate treatment. With the multiplication of texts on anger and a clearer focus came a new vocabulary, with words such as 'tantrum' first being employed to describe critically an outburst of anger by an adult.[33]

A second, and crucially important difference which this eighteenth-century literature encompassed was that anger became

29. Fawcett, *An Essay*, pp. 15, 108.

30. Fawcett, *An Essay*, p. 10; see also, Downame, *A Treatise*, pp. 53–4; T. Nourse, *A Discourse upon the Nature and Faculties of Man* (London, 1686), pp. 149, 151; L. Jordanova, *Sexual Visions: Images of Gender in Science and Medicine between the Eighteenth and Twentieth Centuries* (Madison WI, 1989), p. 26.

31. S.A., *A Sermon Proving*, pp. 8–9; Fawcett, *An Essay*, p. 14.

32. Fawcett, *An Essay*, p. 16.

33. C.Z. Stearns and P.N. Stearns, *Anger: The Struggle of Emotional Control in America's History* (Chicago, 1986), chs 1–2; other important work by P.N. Stearns includes 'Men, boys and anger in American society, 1860–1940', in J.A. Mangan and J. Walvin, eds, *Manliness and Morality: Middle-Class Masculinity in Britain and America, 1800–1940* (Manchester, 1987), and 'Girls, boys and emotions: redefinitions and historical change', *JAH* 80 (1993), pp. 36–74; *OED* 'tantrum' (1714), it is interesting that this first reference is in relation to a woman.

a phenomenon which was increasingly related to men. In the late sixteenth and early seventeenth centuries anger had been a passion associated with women because of their lesser powers of reason. Sir Francis Bacon in 1597 thought anger reigned in 'children, women, old folks, sick folks', and William Gouge believed that 'women by reason of the weakness of their judgement are for the most part most violent' in their passions.[34] Downame in 1609 labelled one type of anger caused by discontent with 'domestical matters' as peculiarly 'the fault of women, or at least a womanish fault'.[35] By the late seventeenth century, as Fenela Childs has noted in her extensive survey of courtesy literature, criticism of the display of anger was far more likely to be directed against men.[36] This took humoural understandings of the body to their logical conclusion since men were believed to be hotter than women, and hence different temperaments from the sexes could be expected.[37] Joseph Addison, in a 1711 edition of the *Spectator*, thought angry disputation a 'male vice', which was 'altogether repugnant to the Softness' which was so 'endearing' and 'natural' to the 'Fair Sex'.[38] It became so against a woman's nature to be angry, that by the time Chapman wrote his 1773 *Treatise on Education*, he labelled 'sweetness of temper' as 'most ornamental' to the female sex.[39]

So at a time when women were understood to have highly sensitive nervous systems, and therefore might be expected to be more emotionally volatile, in terms of anger women came to be seen as less passionate than men.[40] By insisting that a passion such as anger, however mildly expressed, could play no part in the construction of femininity, this prescriptive literature contributed to developing contemporary notions of gender difference. Women's delicate nerves were instead thought to make them more sensitive to the anger of others, at the same time as they gave women a new moral

34. Sir Francis Bacon, *The Essays, or Councils, Civil and Moral* (London, 1718), p. 150; W. Gouge, *Of Domestical Duties* (London, 1622), p. 385.
35. Downame, *A Treatise*, pp. 28–9.
36. F.A. Childs, 'Prescriptions for manners in English courtesy literature, 1690–1760, and their social implications' (D.Phil. thesis, Oxford University, 1984), pp. 176–8, 249.
37. T. Laqueur, *Making Sex: Body and Gender from the Greeks to Freud* (Cambridge MA, 1990), pp. 28, 36, 40, 103, 108, 112.
38. 'Male and female roles', *Spectator* No. 57 (5 May 1711), as cited in A. Ross, ed., *Selections from The Tatler and The Spectator* (Harmondsworth, 1982), p. 252.
39. Chapman, *A Treatise*, p. 98.
40. For women and sensibility see Jordanova, *Sexual Visions*, p. 28; Barker-Benfield, *The Culture of Sensibility*, ch. 1; for women and anger see Averill, *Anger and Aggression*, p. 281.

authority.[41] Women, it was believed, 'were formed to temper Mankind, and soothe them into Tenderness and Compassion',[42] and, as John Gregory wrote in 1774, were 'designed to soften our hearts and polish our manners'.[43] The complementarity of the gender roles was repeatedly emphasised: 'we are made of differing Tempers, that our Defects may the better be mutually supplied', thought the first Marquis of Halifax.[44] Hence, as John Essex wrote in 1722, it was vital that young women learnt to 'first Bridle the Tongue, and seal up your Lips' before they were married.[45] For in marriage it was women's duty to reform their husbands by their own virtue and example.[46] Angry voices could now only be expected to be heard from a certain class of woman. As Webster explained, it was 'a Fishwoman at Billingsgate' who was most likely to display an angry spirit.[47] It was 'below a gentlewoman' to argue, thought the *Tatler*, and 'absolutely intolerable' in 'a lady of genteel education', wrote another.[48] For women of this social status, anger could endanger a woman's femininity precisely because it had become such a male attribute. This general shift of interest and concern away from female anger may even be reflected in the law courts, as compared with the so-called 'crisis' of scolding women of the early seventeenth century, prosecutions against angry women in the eighteenth century were becoming 'something of a curiosity'.[49] As we have seen, the disassociation of anger with femaleness was so complete by this later period that when men became excessively angry they risked slipping into bestiality rather than femininity.[50]

41. Barker-Benfield, *The Culture of Sensibility*, pp. xxvii, 26–7.
42. 'Male and female roles', p. 252.
43. As cited in Jones, ed., *Women in the Eighteenth Century*, p. 45; for this theme see also Hunt, *The Middling Sort*, p. 70.
44. As cited in Jones, ed., *Women in the Eighteenth Century*, p. 18.
45. As cited in M. Cohen, *Fashioning Masculinity: National Identity and Language in the Eighteenth Century* (London, 1996), p. 33.
46. Fletcher, *Gender, Sex and Subordination*, pp. 387, 396–7.
47. W. Webster, *A Casuistical Essay on Anger and Forgiveness* (London, 1750), p. 17.
48. As cited in Childs, 'Prescriptions for manners', p. 249.
49. M. Ingram, ' "Scolding women cucked or washed": a crisis in gender relations in early modern England?', in J. Kermode and G. Walker, eds, *Women, Crime and the Courts in Early Modern England* (London, 1994), p. 52; for the early seventeenth-century prosecutions against scolds see also D.E. Underdown, 'The taming of the scold: the enforcement of patriarchal authority in early modern England', in A. Fletcher and J. Stevenson, eds, *Order and Disorder in Early Modern England* (Cambridge, 1985), pp. 116–36.
50. I am grateful to John Tosh for originally making this point to me; see also Childs, 'Prescriptions for manners', p. 180, who notes that when condemned by writers anger is the only emotion which does not make a man 'womanish'.

A third change was that by the eighteenth century it was firmly believed that it was possible, and indeed desirable, for men to learn to control their anger. So whereas the cause of anger was seen as a humoural dysfunction within the body, it was thought feasible for the mind to be trained to contain anger. Since it was a natural passion, and some argued God-given, eradication of all anger was impossible.[51] But by teaching men to put their superior reason to good use, men could learn to exert mental control over their bodies, releasing anger and behaving aggressively only in appropriate circumstances. Locke was probably one of the most important proponents of the idea that manliness could be a matter of socialisation. 'Of all the men we meet with', he explained, 'nine parts of ten are what they are, Good and Evil, useful or not, by their Education. 'Tis that which makes the great Difference in Mankind.'[52] As William Webster explained in his 1750 essay, unlike other 'sensations which arise solely from the Body', like those caused by hunger or thirst, it was 'in our Power' to 'suppress', set 'bounds', and 'regulate' those which were triggered by anger.[53]

There was thought to be no better time to begin these lessons of self-control than in childhood. 'Children should be instructed in the art of self-government', suggested Watts in his treatise on education, who also believed that children should 'learn to keep the lower powers of nature under the command of their reason'. Such 'lower powers of nature' included the passion of anger, which 'above all', Watts thought children should govern. 'Show them how unreasonable and unmanly a thing it is to take fire at every little provocation', he wrote.[54] Male aggression here is understood to be as much the result of nurture as nature. It was vital that parents should 'conquer and regulate' their children's passions because otherwise they would grow and strengthen with disastrous consequences. 'The general indulgence of Parents to their Children in gratifying their Unreasonable Humours . . . disturbs the Oeconomy of the Family, and every Day, perhaps every Hour, throws the House into Disorder', Nelson warned.[55] By refusing to let them always have their will, by temperance parents could 'nourish' their children's bodies, and allow reason to gather force.[56] Teaching young men to present

51. In 1694 the *Athenian Mercury* argued that along with love and fear, anger was a 'necessary passion' since why else 'would God have implanted them in the minds of men?', XV, no. 20. I am grateful to Helen Berry for this reference.

52. Locke, *Some Thoughts*, p. 83.   53. Webster, *A Casuistical Essay*, p. 28.

54. Watts, *A Discourse*, pp. 332, 338.   55. Nelson, *An Essay*, pp. 22, 199–200.

56. Chapman, *A Treatise*, pp. 6, 22–3.

at the very least a visual appearance of equanimity was all important. 'Make yourself absolute master . . . of your temper and your countenance – so far, at least, as that no visible change do appear in either, whatever you may feel inwardly', the fourth Earl of Chesterfield wrote to his son.[57] Chapman went as far as to advise parents that 'when they happen to see any person in a passion', they should represent that person to their child 'as labouring under a shocking distemper, and greatly to be pitied'. If their son himself was 'rebellious', 'passionate', or 'disorderly', then parents should treat him 'as an invalid' and 'confine him to his chamber'.[58] Above all else, parents, and in particular fathers, should ensure that they did not discipline their sons when they themselves were 'choleric'.[59] If fathers were seen by their children being angry then 'we should candidly acknowledge, that we have been off our guard, and unhappily caught the infection', Chapman thought.[60]

An angry disposition was a disease which once caught in childhood was difficult to eradicate. Contemporaries believed that the 'sources' of the 'outrages which disturb the peace of society' could be traced back to how individuals had been treated when they were in their childhood. A boy who was allowed to indulge in his anger was likely to become an angry adult.[61] Once in adulthood the management of the passions became the sole responsibility of the man himself. 'We are not to submit to anger as our master, but to govern it as our servant', Fawcett taught.[62] But anger was a passion which could take a man 'a considerable exertion of self-command to restrain even for a single moment', wrote Adam Smith. Achievement of that self-control, however, could earn a man admiration and even magnanimity.[63] 'Nothing betrays a great mind so much, as suppressing these hasty emotions of anger', wrote Solomon Winlove in his 1781 *Moral Lectures*.[64] As married men, 'to preserve due authority in our families' is perhaps 'as difficult a branch of duty as any assigned us by Providence', thought Fawcett, but 'the great secret of family government lies in maintaining . . . resentment of disorder

57. As cited in Childs, 'Prescriptions for manners', p. 177.

58. Chapman, *A Treatise*, pp. 161–2.

59. Nelson, *An Essay*, pp. 164–7; Fawcett, *An Essay*, pp. 140–1.

60. Chapman, *A Treatise*, p. 162.

61. Chapman, *A Treatise*, pp. 22–3; see also the fate of the 'fiery' youth who was 'treated with indulgence' as a child in Fawcett, *An Essay*, p. 142.

62. Fawcett, *An Essay*, p. 11.

63. A. Smith, *The Theory of Moral Sentiments* (Basil, 1793), II, pp. 84–6; see also Nourse, *A Discourse*, p. 157.

64. S. Winlove, *Moral Lectures* (1781), pp. 12–13.

without rash anger'. Any expression of anger which was more forceful than this resentment could risk convincing inferiors that 'we are so far from being fit to govern others, that we are unable to govern ourselves'. In a nutshell, self-government was a prerequisite if men were to govern others.[65] 'The Angry Affection, which all Men know to be just like the Wind', Daniel Burgess taught in 1698, 'being moderate carries the Ship, but being tempestuous drowns it.'[66]

Of course, there was nothing particularly original about teaching men to exercise self-control over their emotions. Puritan conduct book writers of the early seventeenth century had long argued that men, especially when disciplining their wives, should withhold their words and hands until the heat of their anger had abated.[67] What was perhaps more innovative about the eighteenth-century writers was their approach. It was their intention, following Locke's example, that such self-government should be taught from childhood in a systematic and organised way. The incorporation of equanimity as a male virtue within the larger eighteenth-century campaign to reform male manners also gave it added value and importance. For this was a 'civil' or 'polite' age in which social qualities defined manhood. There was a burgeoning urban-based middle class hungry to consume advice on which manners were appropriate for company. Periodicals such as the *Tatler*, the *Spectator*, and the *Gentleman's Magazine* ensured that ideas about polite behaviour reached this audience.[68] Politeness, as one contemporary defined it, was 'a dextrous management of our Words and Actions'. It was what 'gives each Thought, Word, Act a proper Grace, And binds each Passion

65. Fawcett, *An Essay*, pp. 22, 29–30, 103.

66. D. Burgess, *Hastiness unto Anger Described and Disgraced* (London, 1698), pp. 3–4.

67. I am grateful to Alexandra Shepard for raising this point and for allowing me to read a chapter on this subject from her thesis, 'Meanings of manhood in early modern England, with special reference to Cambridge c.1560–1640' (Ph.D. thesis, Cambridge University, forthcoming).

68. A.C. Bryson, 'Concepts of civility in England c.1560–1685' (D.Phil. thesis, Oxford University, 1984); Childs, 'Prescriptions for manners'; L. Klein, 'The third earl of Shaftesbury and the progress of politeness', *E-CS* 18 (1984–85), pp. 186–214, *Shaftesbury and the Culture of Politeness: Moral Discourse and Cultural Politics in Early Eighteenth-Century England* (Cambridge, 1994), especially the Introduction, and 'Politeness for plebes: consumption and social identity in early eighteenth-century England', in A. Bermingham and J. Brewer, eds, *The Consumption of Culture 1600–1800: Image, Object, Text* (London, 1995), pp. 362–82; Carter, 'Mollies', and 'Men about town: representations of foppery and masculinity in early eighteenth-century urban society', in H. Barker and E. Chalus, eds, *Gender in Eighteenth-Century England* (London, 1997), pp. 31–57; for the middle class see P. Earle, *The Making of the English Middle Class: Business, Society and Family Life in London, 1660–1730* (London, 1989); and Hunt, *The Middling Sort*.

to its proper Place', so that man was 'mild and sociable to Man', thought the playwright James Miller. Anger, which impeded all social interaction, could be presented as the very antithesis of this ideal of 'self-management and self-presentation'.[69] Self-government, as Philip Carter shows in this volume, was vital to James Boswell's attempts to be seen as a 'man of dignity'.[70] In a period when it could take more than simply landed wealth to gain gentry status, manners became the defining feature of the gentleman.[71] The art of polite conversation, 'motivated by natural goodwill' and 'concerned with avoiding offence', was crucial to the self-fashioning of the gentleman.[72] For those who aspired to be regarded as gentlemen, angry behaviour was to be avoided at all costs. According to these treatises, true gentility was about avoiding the vices of the traditional social elite which had been occasioned by anger, such as duelling and adherence to false honour codes.[73] But it was also concerned with distinction from the 'rude and uncultivated Vulgar, whose undisciplined passions, thro' Indulgence, have more Ferocity than Beasts'.[74] As William Darrell wrote in 1713, although anger 'may become the Shippers of Wapping or the Oyster-Woman at Billingsgate, yet it suits not well the Breeding of Gentlemen'.[75] Control of anger had become a sign of class and social distinction.

Eighteenth-century ideas about male anger and self-government had the potential to appeal to a large audience, but we can question how far that potential was realised. From the 1740s a 'culture of sensibility' promoted alternative codes of behaviour for men by arguing for emotional release and display rather than self-control and reserve. Male readers of eighteenth-century novels were encouraged to share in the emotions of 'the man of feeling', who felt compassion, anxiety and grief, and was unafraid to express such sentiments openly.[76] Sentiment became a 'tool of piety' for the

---

69. Klein, 'The third earl', p. 190; J. Miller, *Of Politeness* (London, 1738), p. 4.

70. P. Carter, 'James Boswell's manliness', in this volume.

71. For a good discussion of the contemporary debates about what made a gentleman, see P. Corfield, 'The democratic history of the English gentleman', *HT* 42 (1992), pp. 40–7; see also Childs, 'Prescriptions for manners', pp. 236–7.

72. Carter, 'Men about town', pp. 49–50; Cohen, *Fashioning Masculinity*.

73. See, for example, T.S., *A Dissertation Concerning the Evil Nature and Fatal Consequence of Immoderate Anger and Revenge* (London, 1725); Nelson, *An Essay*, pp. 245–7; Fawcett, *An Essay*, pp. 55–61, 107.

74. Webster, *A Casuistical Essay*, pp. 29–30; see also p. 17.

75. As cited in Childs, 'Prescriptions for manners', p. 178.

76. J. Todd, *Sensibility: An Introduction* (London, 1986); Barker-Benfield, *The Culture of Sensibility*, pp. 247–50.

evangelical revival, since the timing of the rise of Methodism coincided with that of the 'cult of sensibility'.[77] Many Methodist ministers reacted against 'the coldness and formality' of Anglicanism and sought a faith which was more 'affectionate', 'experiential' and heart-felt.[78] Their preaching methods and styles, as well as their composition and encouragement of the singing of rousing hymns, could provoke extraordinary displays of emotion. William Grimshaw of Haworth noted the amazing 'weeping, roaring and agonies' amongst his parishioners after 'our dear Lord was pleased to visit my parish'.[79] It is within this culture that men were also being taught to restrain the expression of another emotion, anger. Debates about how to manage a passion such as anger which could have undesirable and aggressive consequences reveal the tensions for manhood which were inherent in the culture of sensibility. Ministers often gave conflicting messages about anger. Some argued that there were circumstances when anger was just and righteous. Just as God was angry with the wicked, 'a Good Man may be Angry' when he witnesses others breaking God's commandments, preached one minister in 1713.[80] But others argued for Christian forgiveness, that anger was sinful, and John Wesley even went so far in his notes on the Old Testament as to imply that anger was an unchristian and Jewish emotion.[81] The dissenter and prolific author Isaac Watts personifies the contradictions which underlay such teaching. One of the founders of 'affectionate religion', he also wrote in his *Discourse on the Education of Children and Youth* (1753) on the importance of teaching children to govern their passions. Watts and later evangelicals defended themselves against their critics' accusations of 'enthusiasm' by arguing that they sought to promote a faith which was based on the three pillars of experience, scripture and reason. But the popular impression of evangelism, bolstered by its enemies, that the revival was solely concerned with 'affectionate' religion,

77. P. Langford, *A Polite and Commercial People: England 1727–1783* (Oxford, 1989), p. 467; Barker-Benfield, *The Culture of Sensibility*, pp. xxvi, 71.

78. J. Walsh, 'Origins of evangelical revival', in G.V. Bennett and J.D. Walsh, eds, *Essays in Modern English Church History in Memory of Norman Sykes* (London, 1966), p. 148; I. Rivers, *Reason, Grace, and Sentiment: A Study of the Language of Religion and Ethics in England 1660–1780* vol. 1 *Whichcote to Wesley* (Cambridge, 1991); Barker-Benfield, *The Culture of Sensibility*, pp. 71–4.

79. As cited in Langford, *A Polite and Commercial People*, p. 278.

80. S.A., *A Sermon Proving*, pp. 13, 26; see also Fawcett, *An Essay*, pp. 7–9, ch. II.

81. G.S. Clapper, *John Wesley on Religious Affections: His View on Experience and Emotion and their Role in the Christian Life and Theology* (London, 1989), pp. 37–9, 122, 155.

was stubbornly resilient.[82] Confusion remained; one writer to the *Gentleman's Magazine* in 1764 lamented that many men 'pretend to justify anger, which they give way to on every trifling occasion' from their misreading of the scriptures.[83]

Anger was to be a troublesome emotion for the most important of thinkers in the rise of sensibility. The third Earl of Shaftesbury (1671–1713), called by some 'the father of sentimental ethics', fought hard to overcome his own 'Hottspurr Inclination'.[84] Attempting to find a middle ground, many of the writers on anger were anxious to show that although they advocated restraint, they did not believe that men should be insensible to the actions of those around them.[85] The virtues of courage and fortitude were still exalted, and writers warned that men should not avoid expressing anger simply out of fear. If fear was all that was preventing a man from being angry, then 'the meanness of the motive takes away all the nobleness of the restraint', Smith thought.[86] Courage was defined as 'a Firmness of Spirit' which allowed men 'to encounter every Danger when necessary; and to demean ourselves in a proper Manner under Trouble, Pain, and Disappointment'.[87] This courage could require moral as well as physical fortitude.[88] 'The passions are the principles of human actions', the *Spectator* reported in 1712, so 'we must endeavour to manage them so as to retain their vigour, yet keep them under strict command'.[89] Men should therefore be spirited, but also show that their reason was in control of the actions of their bodies by showing restraint, and by managing anger with decorum. Then, thought the writers, anger was most likely to have greatest effect. It was learning how to harness anger so that it could be a constructive rather than destructive force for manhood which was most difficult.

Boys born in this period, especially from the middling sorts, entered a world which held conflicting codes of conduct for their gender. On the one hand, boys' parents and teachers encouraged them to nurture their physical strength. On the other, boys were expected to display this strength only in a regulated environment

82. Rivers, *Reason, Grace, and Sentiment*, pp. 167–93, 208; Langford, *A Polite and Commercial People*, p. 278.

83. *Gentleman's Magazine* XXXIV (1764), p. 313.

84. Barker-Benfield, *The Culture of Sensibility*, pp. 105, 111.

85. Webster, *A Casuistical Essay*, p. 42; S.A., *A Sermon Proving*, p. 8; Smith, *The Theory*, I, p. 49.

86. Smith, *The Theory*, II, p. 89.   87. Nelson, *An Essay*, pp. 196–7.

88. Locke, *Some Thoughts*, pp. 175–6; Carter, 'Mollies', pp. 221–3.

89. *Spectator* No. 408 (18 June 1712), p. 58.

such as on a sports field. As adults, men were expected to distinguish between just and unjust anger, and to exercise their superior reason in their use of strength. Anger could serve a useful function in maintaining a man's dominant position in his household, but only if expressed moderately and with restraint. Outside the home, directed male aggression could be channelled to preserve national security, as Linda Colley has shown British culture has 'largely defined itself through fighting', but even soldiers were trained in self-discipline and self-control.[90] In civil life, conduct book writers argued that nurturing male physical strength was not the same as encouraging male aggression, and that if the mind was trained to exert control over the passions, then unnecessary violence could be avoided. In the eighteenth century, arguments in support of manly self-control and governance were given an unprecedented force when they became the desirable characteristics of the 'polite' or 'civil' gentleman. But unease that such control of the passions could render men insensible and inactive soon became apparent. The contemporary stereotype of the 'fop' was a man who was so excessively devoted to politeness that he had surrendered all the traditionally manly virtues of hardiness, courage and strength. He was popularly portrayed as a physically feeble young man.[91] The 'cult of sensibility' ensured that debates about the role of the passions in the construction of manliness continued. Within this culture of sensibility men were encouraged to express their emotions, but the question of how and when men could express an emotion such as anger remained a sticking point and was largely unresolved.

This chapter has concentrated on a survey of prescriptive literature written for men, rather than the actual experience of men who were angry or who were aggressive towards others. But it seems probable that the subtleties of the arguments of this literature, as well as the contradictory messages which it relayed, may have eluded or at least confused many men. Alternatively, as Philip Carter's study of Boswell in this volume convincingly argues, some men may have been able to adopt or reject the different 'styles of manliness' which prescriptive literature promoted, as and when appropriate.[92] Nevertheless, traditional stories of male bravado and courage, apparently untouched by the changing world of male values in which they were read and heard, remained popular throughout the

90. See, for example, *The Military Mentor* (London, 1804), I, Letter XXIV 'On Anger', pp. 270–2; L. Colley, *Britons: Forging the Nation 1707–1837* (1992), p. 9.
91. Carter, 'Men about town', pp. 52–5.
92. Carter, 'James Boswell's manliness', in this volume.

eighteenth century. For the world 'accounts the Greatest Hectors, to be the Truest Heroes; and such as restrain and Bridle their Passions, to be no more than Timorous Sneaks, void of all True Spirit and Bravery', one writer on anger lamented.[93] In 1804 a writer to the *Gentleman's Magazine* bemoaned the fact that 'most men still set a due value upon anger, and show by their practice that it is one of those passions which is in no danger of becoming paralytic for want of exercise or air'.[94] The testing of manliness by youthful displays of aggression was so deeply engrained in popular culture, that it could establish a pattern of behaviour for later life which was difficult to counter. This was a popular culture which even extended some toleration for male anger into the law courts. Although words spoken in anger constituted defamation in law, those who killed another 'in the heat of passion' could be con-victed for manslaughter rather than murder, and so escape the hangman's noose. Husbands who beat their wives when they were in a rage continued throughout this period to exercise the argu-ment of 'just provocation' in their defence.[95] It was perhaps only from the mid-nineteenth century that the ideas advanced in this period concerning emotional self-control reached their full frui-tion as neo-stoicism became a dominant ideal of manhood. By this period the undesirable consequences of male anger had also been more firmly placed at the door of the lower classes, as, for example, marital violence was labelled increasingly as a vice of the slums.[96] Focusing on anger, writers between 1660 and 1800 had found a link between manhood and aggression, but their notions of how that link could be broken were underdeveloped and premature. As the title of this chapter suggests, it has always been far easier to be complacent about male aggression than it is to understand or control.

93. S.A., *A Sermon*, p. 3.   94. *Gentleman's Magazine* LXXIV, I (1804), p. 301.

95. H. C[onset], *The Practice of the Spiritual or Ecclesiastical Courts* (London, 1685), p. 335; T.S., *A Dissertation*, pp. 46, 51–5, 86; Beattie, *Crime*, pp. 77–80, 87, 91; Foyster, 'Male honour', pp. 223–4.

96. See, for example, Hunt, 'Wife beating', pp. 25–8.

PART FOUR

Sexuality

CHAPTER NINE

'Nothing is so secret but shall be revealed':[1] The Scandalous Life of Robert Foulkes

DAVID TURNER

Within the closely knit rural communities of later seventeenth-century England, rumour was a powerful and potentially devastating weapon. Its effects became clearly visible in the south Shropshire village of Stanton Lacy during the summer of 1676 when relations between the vicar, Robert Foulkes, and his parishioners were put under serious strain as stories of the minister's sexual proclivities began to circulate around the parish and further afield. The spotlight of village opinion was turned upon Foulkes's familiarity with a spinster, Anne Atkinson, on whom it was suspected he had fathered a bastard child which she had delivered secretly. These claims were investigated by Herbert Croft, Bishop of Hereford, who admonished Foulkes to abstain from Atkinson's company, apart from in church or else chaperoned by 'three or foure persons of good credditt and reputation'.[2] But rather than restoring harmony, the bishop's intervention served both to trigger a protracted series of law suits in the consistory court of Hereford and to intensify rumour about the vicar's behaviour. 'The scandal of it became so publick', Foulkes later recalled, that 'it burst out with that violence, like water long dammed up' and became 'vox populi; the Neighbourhood rings and ecchoes again with it'.[3]

1. Robert Foulkes, *An Alarme for Sinners* (1679), p. 8. I am grateful to Martin Ingram, Tim Hitchcock, Michèle Cohen and Dinah Winch for commenting on earlier drafts of this chapter.
2. Hereford Record Office [hereafter HRO], HD4/25 Libel against Robert Foulkes, 1/8/1676; HD4/26 Personal Answers of Robert Foulkes, 22/5/1677. Unless stated otherwise all references from Hereford Diocesan manuscripts are unfoliated and refer to the consistory court case *Office* v. *Foulkes*.
3. Foulkes, *Alarme for Sinners*, p. 6.

By January 1679, the adultery of Robert Foulkes and Anne Atkinson had become a 'spectacle to the world', when Foulkes was indicted and subsequently executed for the murder of their second illegitimate offspring.[4] Even by contemporary standards the case was particularly shocking. The details of Foulkes's 'Vicious Life and Ignominious Death' were debated in a series of printed pamphlets including, most vividly, an autobiographical sermon published under the title *An Alarme for Sinners*.[5] It was not simply the horror or the tragedy of the events that caught the public's attention; the timing of the scandal, during a period of heightened fear that the Church's enemies were gaining in strength, gave the story of an adulterous, infanticidal Anglican minister added political potency.[6] Moreover, although details of the infanticide remain sketchy, Foulkes's involvement in a felony normally associated with 'lewd women' raised contemporary speculation about his motives and a more general discussion about the nature and implications of male sexual agency.[7] Some years later, narratives of Foulkes's life were used in the campaign for the Reformation of Manners to challenge the assumptions of the sexual double standard and to remind men of the dangers of their lusts.[8]

4. Ibid., p. 3. Foulkes and Atkinson had fled to London some months previously and it was here that the murder trial and execution took place: Metropolitan Record Office, MJ/SR 1556 Middlesex Sessions Roll, 15/1/1679; Anthony Wood, *Athenae Oxonienses*, ed. Philip Bliss, 5 vols (1817), III, p. 1195.

5. See also *The Execution of Mr. Rob. Foulks* (1679); *A True and Perfect Relation of the Tryal and Condemnation, Execution and Last Speech of that Unfortunate Gentleman Mr. Robert Foulks* (1679); *The Shropshire Amazement* (n.d. *c*.1708?).

6. On the broader political context (which neglects to mention this case) see John Spurr, *The Restoration Church of England, 1646–1689* (New Haven CT and London, 1991), ch. 2.

7. On infanticide as a crime associated with women, see 21 Jac. I *c*.27; John Beattie, 'The criminality of women in eighteenth-century England', *JSH* 8, 4 (1975), pp. 80–116; John Beattie, *Crime and the Courts in England 1660–1800* (Oxford, 1986), pp. 113–24; Peter C. Hoffer and N.E.H. Hull, *Murdering Mothers: Infanticide in England and New England 1558–1803* (New York and London, 1984); Mark Jackson, *New-born Child Murder: Women, Illegitimacy and the Courts in Eighteenth-Century England* (Manchester, 1996); Keith Wrightson, 'Infanticide in earlier seventeenth-century England', *LPS* 15 (1975), pp. 10–22. Another case of infanticide involving a minister is discussed in Peter Lake, '"A Charitable Christian Hatred": The godly and their enemies in the 1630s', in Christopher Durston and Jacqueline Eales, eds, *The Culture of English Puritanism, 1560–1700* (Basingstoke, 1996), pp. 145–83.

8. See, for instance, *The Wonders of Free-Grace* (1690), pp. 37–52; *The Athenian Mercury* iv/16 (Saturday 21 November 1691); *The Hazard of a Death-Bed-Repentance* (1708), p. 19. These sources, all published by John Dunton, are discussed further in my forthcoming doctoral thesis, 'Representations of adultery in England *c*.1660–*c*.1740: a study of changing perceptions of marital infidelity in conduct literature, drama, trial publications and the records of the court of Arches'.

With its interaction of the universal, the local and the personal, the case of Robert Foulkes offers several fascinating points of entry into the world of sexual scandal in later seventeenth-century England from a fresh masculine perspective. In this chapter I wish to look beyond the printed narratives to examine the moment when the vicar's adultery first became the subject of suspicion and rumour in his parish. By probing the mass of legal documentation generated by the disputes between Foulkes and his parishioners, it becomes possible to reconstruct in colourful detail the social context in which the behaviour of Robert Foulkes came to be assessed as scandalous, and to access the channels of oral communication through which rumour was transmitted in Stanton Lacy and its environs. In doing so, this chapter will challenge a number of recent assumptions in historical writing on reputation and on the role of gossip and rumour in local society. Historians of many cultures are now realising the importance of honour and reputation as integral components of social relations. Providing a nexus between a sense of personal dignity and the perception of one's character and actions in the eyes of others, these concepts, though abstract and sometimes elusive, have been viewed as particularly useful in the assessment of gender and social status.[9] Typically, historians of early modern England have tended to view sexual reputation as a far more central concern for women than for men. Consequently, a gendered model of reputation has emerged which has obscured the moments when a man's extra-marital sexual relations could arouse disapproval and be regarded as shameful. The durability of this model, combined with a set of literary stereotypes, has also led to the assumption that the informal brokering of sexual reputation through gossip and rumour has predominantly been the activity of women. What is particularly striking about this case study is that it shows men operating in roles customarily viewed as pertaining to

9. The literature on these themes is now voluminous. Anthropological approaches are summarised in Frank Henderson Stewart, *Honour* (Chicago, 1994), pp. 1–29. For recent historical surveys see the collection of essays 'Honour and reputation in early modern England' *TRHS* 6th ser., VI (1996). On sexual reputation see Susan Amussen, *An Ordered Society: Gender and Class in Early Modern England* (Oxford, 1988); Anthony Fletcher, *Gender, Sex and Subordination in England 1500–1800* (New Haven CT and London, 1995); Elizabeth Foyster, 'The concept of male honour in seventeenth-century England' (Ph.D. thesis, Durham University, 1996); Martin Ingram, *Church Courts, Sex and Marriage in England, 1570–1640* (Cambridge, 1987), ch. 10; Laura Gowing, *Domestic Dangers: Women, Words and Sex in Early Modern London* (Oxford, 1996); Lyndal Roper, *Oedipus and the Devil: Witchcraft, Sexuality and Religion in Early Modern Europe* (1994), ch. 3; J.A. Sharpe, *Defamation and Sexual Slander in Early Modern England: The Church Courts at York*, Borthwick Papers 58 (York, 1980).

women: as the subjects and spreaders of sexual rumours. Although as a clergyman any sexual impropriety by Robert Foulkes was bound to attract public disapproval, as the case unfolded the sexual reputations of a number of local men were also placed under the spotlight. Thus, by relocating men in roles from which historians have tended to exclude them, this chapter seeks to broaden our understanding of the politics of reputation in early modern society, and will suggest ways in which questions of sexuality and gender might infuse men's relationships of authority with other men.

The principle that men and women bore equal culpability for extramarital sex was consistently reiterated in sermons and conduct literature throughout the early modern period. In the Christian moral framework that underpinned these writings, and which provided the rationale behind the judicial regulation of sexual mores, the inherent sinfulness of sexual immorality made it dishonourable in both sexes at all levels of society.[10] In practice, however, there has been an overwhelming tendency to view contemporary attitudes to male and female unchastity in more or less oppositional terms, and to use these distinctions as a cornerstone of gender difference in early modern English society.

In part this paradigm results from the tendency of many studies of sexual reputation to draw their conclusions from sources in which female sexual conduct is most clearly at issue. The concern with the transfer of property through legitimate inheritance in gentry advice literature, for instance, set great store by the chastity of wives and daughters on which the 'honour of families' was said to rest, and provided the formal basis for the sexual 'double standard'.[11] Moreover, stereotypes of voracious female sexuality pervaded seventeenth-century proverbs, ballads and other literary sources, making the sexual construction of female reputation immediately visible, belying 'any contention of an equal culpability for sexual sin'.[12]

10. Keith Thomas, 'The double standard', *JHI* XX (1959), pp. 195–216, esp. pp. 203–4; F. Dabhoiwala, 'The construction of honour, reputation and status in late seventeenth- and early eighteenth-century England', *TRHS* 6th ser., VI (1996), p. 204.

11. George Savile, Marquis of Halifax, 'The Lady's New-year's Gift: Or, Advice to a Daughter' (1688) in *The Works of George Savile Marquis of Halifax*, ed. Mark N. Brown, 3 vols (Oxford, 1989), II, p. 372; Thomas, 'The double standard', pp. 210–11.

12. Gowing, *Domestic Dangers*, p. 2; Susan Amussen, 'The gendering of popular culture in early modern England', in Tim Harris ed., *Popular Culture in England, c.1500–1850* (Basingstoke, 1995), pp. 48–68; Joy Wiltenburg, *Disorderly Women and Female Power in the Street Literature of Early Modern England and Germany* (Charlottesville VA and London, 1992).

Support for a gendered model of sexual reputation has also been derived from the records of defamation litigation in the church courts. The higher proportion of married women defending themselves against sexual slanders throughout the seventeenth and early eighteenth centuries, most markedly in London, has been taken as evidence for the centrality of sexual probity to female reputation.[13] While historians of defamation largely concur that for both men and women reputation had sexual components, male and female sexual slanders have been viewed with differing seriousness, even as 'incompatible' or 'incommensurable'.[14] Insults directed at men have been regarded as less concrete and consequently less powerful than those aimed at women. Hence while male insults such as 'whoremaster', 'rogue' or 'knave' might imply dishonourable sexual practices, they are seen as lacking the symbolic power of the corresponding female insult 'whore', with the effect that, as Laura Gowing has argued, 'sexual honour was imagined entirely through women'.[15] In striking contrast, men occasionally appear in the records of defamation positively revelling in their notoriety, 'boasting' or 'bragging' of their conquests in a manner that supposedly confirmed their security in the sexual system.[16]

The tendency to play down or disregard the importance of sexual probity to men is also evident from the conception of male honour as an altogether more active and 'public' code of behaviour discrete from more 'private' morality, as outlined in the classic account of honour by Mervyn James.[17] Consequently, while sexual behaviour was central to a woman's reputation, male reputation, by contrast, was based on a more complex amalgam of non-sexual attributes,

13. Laura Gowing, 'Gender and the language of insult in early modern London', *HWJ* 35 (1993), pp. 1–21; Tim Meldrum, 'A women's court in London: defamation at the Bishop of London's consistory court, 1700–1745', *LJ* 19, 1 (1994), pp. 1–20; Amussen, *Ordered Society*, p. 102. See also Sharpe, *Defamation and Sexual Slander*; Ingram, *Church Courts*, ch. 10.

14. Gowing, 'Gender and the language of insult', p. 3; but cf. Martin Ingram's earlier findings that the double standard was more 'a matter of degree' than 'absolute dichotomy between the ways in which male and female reputations were regarded', *Church Courts*, p. 303.

15. Laura Gowing, 'Language, power and the law: women's slander litigation in early modern London', in Jenny Kermode and Garthine Walker, eds, *Women, Crime and the Courts in Early Modern England* (1994), p. 30. See also Amussen, *Ordered Society*, pp. 102–3.

16. Gowing, 'Gender and the language of insult', p. 7; Meldrum, 'Women's court', pp. 10–11. Of course, boasting could equally reflect sexual insecurity: Foyster, 'Concept of male honour', p. 70.

17. Mervyn James, *English Politics and the Concept of Honour*, *P&P* Supplement 3 (Oxford, 1978), p. 28.

such as physical strength and courage, trustworthiness and economic competence, office-holding, professional status and the exercise of authority.[18] However, a number of recent studies have challenged James's model to argue that in some cases a man's public esteem could indeed be damaged by supposedly more 'private' or domestic matters, thus making redundant a rigid distinction between separate spheres of male honour.[19] Research has shown that in a society which saw household government as a microcosm of wider political order, an important component of a man's standing in the wider honour community was to demonstrate mastery of his wife and household subordinates. A man's sexual reputation, it has been argued, was therefore most readily harmed by being made a cuckold by his wife's adultery. While popular images of cuckoldry could link it to poor sexual performance, the shame of cuckoldry chiefly attached itself not to a man's own sexual activity, but to the failure to control that of his wife. While the imaginative appeal of cuckoldry in a range of contemporary literary sources is undeniable, it may in fact underestimate the extent to which a man's sexual immorality might contribute to his sexual dishonour.[20]

Our perception of male sexual licence has been further influenced by the emergence of a powerful stereotype of 'libertine' masculinity in England after the Restoration. This religiously and sexually unorthodox code of behaviour, receiving its fullest expression in the stage-comedies of the 1670s, celebrated a virile model of manhood in which debauchery was made consistent with virtue and whoring was declared a means by which a man could actually enhance his reputation among his peers.[21] Although in practice libertinism

18. Fletcher, *Gender, Sex and Subordination*, pp. 104–5, 126–53; Garthine Walker, 'Expanding the boundaries of female honour in early modern England', *TRHS* 6th ser., VI (1996), p. 235.

19. Foyster, 'Concept of male honour', pp. 5–6 and *passim*; Richard Cust, 'Honour and politics in early Stuart England: the case of Beaumont v. Hastings', *P&P* 149 (1995), pp. 57–94; Cynthia Herrup, ' "To pluck bright honour from the pale faced moon": gender and honour in the Castlehaven story', *TRHS* 6th ser., VI (1996), pp. 137–59; Felicity Heal, 'Reputation and honour in court and country: Lady Elizabeth Russell and Sir Thomas Hoby', *TRHS* 6th ser., VI (1996), pp. 161–78. See also Adam Fox, 'Ballads, libels and popular ridicule in Jacobean England', *P&P* 145 (1994), pp. 47–83.

20. Amussen, *Ordered Society*, ch. 2; Elizabeth Foyster, 'A laughing matter? Marital discord and gender control in seventeenth-century England', *RH* 4, 1 (1993), pp. 5–21 and 'Concept of male honour', pp. 77–87, ch. 5 *passim*.

21. James Grantham Turner, 'The properties of libertinism', in Robert P. Maccubin ed., *'Tis Nature's Fault: Unauthorised Sexuality during the Enlightenment* (Cambridge, 1987), pp. 75–87; Dabhoiwala, 'Construction of honour', pp. 205–6. For examples see David Turner, 'Rakes, libertines and sexual honour in Restoration England, 1660–1700' (MA thesis, Durham University, 1994), ch. 2.

attracted few committed adherents, the stereotype still remains an untested model of male sexuality in the 'long' eighteenth century, deflecting attention from its potentially more negative public consequences.[22]

Together these factors have given rise to an oppositional model of reputation that is in many ways symptomatic of what John Tosh has termed the 'profound dualism in Western thought' (including historical scholarship) that has disregarded the range of male experiences in the past or lumped them together as part of an undifferentiated patriarchy.[23] Whether wittingly or not, this model tends to reify responses to male and female behaviour which may obscure the extent to which reputation for both men and women depended on rank, occupational group and social status, or may have become more or less serious in different social contexts, or at different stages of the life-cycle.[24] A good deal more needs to be learnt about the local settings and systems of power relations in which the reputations of individual men and women were formed, in which insults and sexual slanders acquired their force. Just as the use of a broader set of sources might, as Garthine Walker has suggested, enable us to 'expand the boundaries of female honour' to include broader criteria than sexual conduct, so we need to deepen our understanding of sexual reputation to appreciate more fully the circumstances in which a man's own sexual activities could be used to discredit him in the wider community.[25] The religious injunction to chastity could provide a powerful category of social judgement and was a code of behaviour that all men had to negotiate.[26] The real issue to be addressed, therefore, is not whether sexual conduct was a component of male reputation *per se*, but to contextualise how, at specific moments, male sexual behaviour could become an issue of concern, and the processes through which it became 'scandalous'.

22. See, for instance, Lawrence Stone, 'Libertine sexuality in post-Restoration England: group sex and flagellation among the middling sort in Norwich in 1706–7', *JHS* 2, 4 (1992), pp. 511–26; cf. Tim Hitchcock, *English Sexualities, 1700–1800* (Basingstoke, 1997), pp. 21–2.

23. John Tosh, 'What should historians do with masculinity? Reflections on nineteenth-century Britain', *HWJ* 38 (1994), p. 180.

24. These criticisms are elaborated in Dabhoiwala, 'Construction of honour', *passim*. On the importance of age in the assessment of reputation see Paul Griffiths, *Youth and Authority: Formative Experiences in England, 1560–1640* (Oxford, 1996), pp. 100–2.

25. Walker, 'Expanding the boundaries', *passim*.

26. Susan Amussen, '"The part of a Christian man": the cultural politics of manhood in early modern England', in Susan Amussen and Mark Kishlansky, eds, *Political Culture and Cultural Politics in Early Modern England: Essays Presented to David Underdown* (Manchester, 1995), p. 217.

One of the ways in which this might be achieved is by examining the range of discourses and communicative interactions through which behaviour and character were evaluated in different social settings. A well-established anthropological literature has stressed the importance of gossip and rumour as informal means of disseminating information and brokering reputations in small-scale communities.[27] Despite a similarity of purpose, important conceptual distinctions have been drawn between 'gossip', often defined as informal talk about persons or events familiar to the speaker and hearers which was not necessarily malicious or untrue, and 'rumour', unauthenticated information spread on a wider scale, frequently scandalous in content. Nevertheless, it is often difficult or even inappropriate for historians to draw such fine distinctions from the written sources available.[28] Historical treatments of gossip in early modern England, especially that concerning sexual reputation, have primarily viewed it as a female activity. This is in part a consequence of the oppositional model discussed above, but also derives from a wealth of literary stereotypes which sought to denigrate female communication as slanderous and trivial, making 'gossip' the unique signifier of female speech and 'scandal' the defining subject of female discourse. The power of the tongue as woman's principal weapon was enshrined in popular images of scolds, shrews and 'gossips'.[29] Analyses of gossip and rumour as tools of the dispossessed in recent articles by Steve Hindle and Bernard Capp have demonstrated a more positive role of gossip in forming an outlet of resistance for the victims of patriarchal society, with gossip serving

27. Max Gluckman, 'Gossip and scandal', *CA* 4 (1963), pp. 307–316; Robert Paine, 'What is gossip about? An alternative hypothesis', *Man* n.s. 2, 2 (1967), pp. 278–85; Peter Wilson, 'Filcher of good names: an enquiry into anthropology and gossip', *Man* n.s. 9, 1 (1974), pp. 93–102; Sarah Engle Merry, 'Rethinking gossip and scandal', in Donald Black, ed., *Toward a General Theory of Social Control, Volume 1: Fundamentals* (New York, 1984), pp. 271–302.

28. Merry, 'Rethinking', p. 275; Ralph Rosnow and Gary Fine, *Rumor and Gossip: The Social Psychology of Hearsay* (New York, 1976); Dagmar Freist, *Governed by Opinion: Politics, Religion and the Dynamics of Communication in Stuart London 1637–1645* (London and New York, 1997), pp. 211–12, 255–77; Steve Hindle, 'The shaming of Margaret Knowsley: gossip, gender and the experience of authority in early modern England', *CC* 9, 3 (1994), p. 392; Chris Wickham, *Gossip and Resistance Among the Medieval Peasantry*, Inaugural Lecture (Birmingham, 1995), pp. 11–12.

29. Freist, *Governed by Opinion*, pp. 278–98; Martin Ingram, '"Scolding women cucked or washed": a crisis in gender relations in early modern England?', in Kermode and Walker, eds, *Women, Crime and the Courts*, pp. 48–80; Wiltenburg, *Disorderly Women*, p. 97; Claire Brant, 'Speaking of women: scandal and the law in the mid-eighteenth century', in Claire Brant and Diane Purkiss, eds, *Women, Texts and Histories 1575–1760* (London and New York, 1992), pp. 242–70.

more generally, in Hindle's words, as a 'repository of a specifically female social memory'. However, although it is recognised that men as well as women could show an interest in spreading tales about their neighbours, it has been assumed that male speech of this sort was necessarily seen as more rational and pertaining to social control.[30]

Many of these assumptions, however, rest on a rather partial reading of the available evidence. First, attention to rumour as a 'weapon of the weak' ignores the possibility that such communication could be most devastatingly used by the powerful, by the patriarchs themselves. More generally, attacks on loquacious women need to be seen in the context of much broader discussion in conduct literature which proscribed the seeking out and spreading of slanderous tales by men as well as by women. By the later seventeenth century, although the 'gossip' was increasingly represented as a woman, related figures such as the 'backbiter' and the 'tale-bearer' could be personified in advice literature as men. This perhaps reflected a growing recognition on the part of conduct writers that men as much as women could be talkative and slanderous in their speech, as Robert Shoemaker also argues in his contribution to this volume. 'Go into Masculine company', observed Richard Allestree in 1674, and 'twill be as hard to edge in a word, as at a Female Gossiping'. As to the spreading of scandalous rumours, 'both the sexes seem to be at a vye: and I think he were a very Critical Judge, that could determine between them'.[31]

The desirability of investigating and publishing the faults of one's neighbour was the subject of much debate and finely drawn distinction in contemporary thought. On the one hand, a good deal of surveillance that today we might mistake for voyeurism was legally sanctioned as evidence in cases of adultery at the church courts. Equally 'common fame' of adultery arising from the 'voice of just and honest men living in the neighbourhood' was an acceptable

---

30. Bernard Capp, 'Separate domains? Women and authority in early modern England', in Paul Griffiths *et al.*, eds, *The Experience of Authority in Early Modern England* (Basingstoke, 1996), pp. 117–45; Hindle, 'Shaming of Margaret Knowsley', p. 408. See also Deborah Jones, 'Gossip: notes on women's oral culture', in Deborah Cameron, ed., *The Feminist Critique of Language: A Reader* (1990), pp. 242–50; James C. Scott, *Domination and the Arts of Resistance: Hidden Transcripts* (New Haven CT and London, 1990), pp. 142–4 and *passim.*

31. Alexander Rysman, 'How the "Gossip" became a woman', *Journal of Communication* 27, 1 (1977), pp. 176–80; cf. *A Bridle for the Tongue: Or, the Trial and Condemnation of Whispering-Backbiter* (1700); *The Management of the Tongue* (1706), pp. 120–3. Richard Allestree, *The Government of the Tongue* (Oxford, 1674), p. 73.

mode of proof in the church courts, which may have given some legal credibility to justified suspicions.[32] Conduct writers, on the other hand, warned that although it was necessary for a man to admonish his neighbour for his sins, to discuss those ills in public breached the proper norms of charity and neighbourliness. Actively to seek out the vices of others furthermore risked 'curiosity' in men and women, a passion whose excitement threatened envy, malice and emulation.[33] From conduct literature at least, it is by no means clear that men's speech about sexual impropriety was necessarily considered more rational than women's. This becomes most apparent when gossip and rumour are placed in their social context, to which it is now necessary to turn.

Reconstructing the scandalous life of Robert Foulkes through the records of the consistory court of Hereford invariably raises problems of interpretation. First there is the practical difficulty of piecing together a story told in over 30 witness statements taken over the space of two years, some of which directly contradict one another. Second, the interest of legal officers in distinguishing 'common fame', the voice of the just, from the malicious whisperings of disaffected persons, means that we learn most about the content and spread of rumour from the records of litigation when its motives were contested.[34] Consequently, the surviving evidence highlights the role of rumour as a means of damaging the reputation of others, possibly at the expense of recording speech about illicit sexuality that was more neutral or even approving.[35] These cautionary remarks notwithstanding, legal records do at least permit an insight into the circumstances or kinds of behaviour that might be considered 'scandalous', and some of the possible uses of sexual rumours in village discourse.

Robert Foulkes was presented to the consistory court in August 1676 in a private prosecution promoted in the name of one of his parishioners, Francis Hutchinson.[36] He faced a complex set of

---

32. John Ayliffe, *Parergon Juris Canonici Anglicani* (1726), pp. 51, 277.

33. Allestree, *Government of the Tongue*, section VI, 'Of Uncharitable Truth'; Isaac Barrow, *Several Sermons Against Evil Speaking* (1678), sermon IX; *The Universal Monitor: Or, a General Dictionary of Moral and Divine Precepts* (1702), p. 203.

34. Ayliffe, *Parergon*, pp. 275–8; Ingram, *Church Courts*, pp. 242–4, 328.

35. For some richly documented examples of how different genres of speech could interact in daily conversation, see Freist, *Governed by Opinion*, pp. 255–77.

36. Hutchinson might have been persuaded to promote the case because he had no previous history of disputes with the vicar. See HRO, HD4/26 Articles of Exception brought by Robert Foulkes, 26/2/1678.

charges in which sexual immorality was bound up with litigiousness, physical and verbal violence, and a catalogue of professional misdemeanours, such as the failure to conduct services at the appointed times, and the neglect of pastoral duties such as administering to the sick and catechising the young.[37] The case dragged on inconclusively until the autumn of 1678, with witnesses being called for both sides. A tandem prosecution was brought against Foulkes's suspected lover, Anne Atkinson, for fornication and for bearing a bastard child, but again the evidence brought against her proved largely insufficient.[38]

At first glance, the dispute between Robert Foulkes and his parishioners appears to fit into a broader pattern of lay–clerical conflict occurring in later seventeenth-century England. Historians have viewed these altercations primarily as expressions of the religious expectations of the laity in the face of the professional incompetence or moral laxity of the clergy.[39] Much less attention, however, has been given to the ways in which such disputes could also give voice to a much broader panoply of tensions and local rivalries in which questions of social status and professional authority might become intricately bound up with sexual reputation. As with other cases involving powerful local figures that reached the courts, community opinion was often factionalised, with each side making use of rumour and gossip to damage the reputation of the other.[40] To understand the potency of sexual rumour in this case, therefore, it is first necessary to examine more closely the social relations of those involved, and the particular set of local circumstances that allowed gossip and rumour to thrive.

What must be stressed from the outset is that the social perception of the adultery of Robert Foulkes and Anne Atkinson was intimately bound up with their position in village life. Robert Foulkes was born in 1633 and from 1652 to around 1656 he was educated at

---

37. HRO, HD4/25 Libel against Robert Foulkes, 1/8/1676.

38. HRO, HD4/1 Box 40 Acts of Office (Archdeaconry of Ludlow) f. 77. On the fate of Anne Atkinson see Bodleian Library, MS Tanner 35 ff. 159r–159v, 171r.

39. Martin Ingram, 'From reformation to religious toleration: popular religious cultures in England, 1540–1690', in Harris ed., *Popular Culture*, pp. 95–123; Henry Lancaster, 'Nonconformity and Anglican dissent in Restoration Wiltshire, 1660–1689' (Ph.D. thesis, Bristol University, 1995), ch. 11; Donald Spaeth, 'Common prayer? Popular observance of the Anglican liturgy in Restoration Wiltshire', in S.J. Wright, ed., *Parish, Church and People: Local Studies in Lay Religion, 1350–1750* (1988), pp. 125–51; Spurr, *Restoration Church*, ch. 4.

40. David Rollison, *The Local Origins of Modern Society: Gloucestershire 1500–1800* (1992), p. 206.

Christ Church, Oxford. In September 1657 he married Isabella, daughter of Thomas Colbatch, rector of Ludlow, by whom he would have four children between 1665 and 1672. His marriage to Isabella marked his integration into a closely knit social network of south Shropshire clergy. In 1660 he was presented to the living of Stanton Lacy by the church's patron and eminent local landowner, William Earl of Craven.[41]

In *An Alarme for Sinners*, Foulkes characterised the period from his induction to the revelation of his adultery in 1676 as a time when he was 'beloved of my Parishioners, and respected in my Neighbourhood'.[42] Nevertheless, while Stanton Lacy lacked the tensions between Anglicanism and Dissent endemic to some areas after the Restoration, relations between the vicar and his parishioners were far from harmonious during this period.[43] Foulkes's career was blighted by recurrent hostilities with his neighbours that stemmed from the ambiguous circumstances of his social status. On the one hand, some sources referred to Foulkes as a 'gentleman' and his social standing was certainly enhanced by his function, his education and by his connections with local clergy and gentry families.[44] However, like all clergymen of this period, his livelihood was to a large extent dependent on the goodwill of his parishioners through the payment of tithes.[45] From the late 1660s Foulkes was involved in promoting an aggressive series of legal actions in both the ecclesiastical and secular courts against certain parishioners for the withholding of payments.[46] Foulkes was unafraid to use the threat of litigation, even if it brought him into direct conflict with parish office-holders, such as his churchwarden Richard Chearme with whom he seemed to be in perpetual conflict.[47] Such disputes brought into question not only rights to material goods – quite often they also served to highlight the cultural gulf between Foulkes and some of

41. *Shropshire Parish Registers: Hereford Diocese, Stanton Lacy* (printed transcript, n.d.), pp. 49, 67, 71, 73, 75; Joseph Foster, ed., *Alumni Oxonienses: The Members of the University of Oxford, 1500–1714*, 4 vols (Oxford, 1891), II, p. 522; Wood, *Athenae Oxonienses*, III, p. 1195.

42. Foulkes, *Alarme for Sinners*, p. 5.

43. Surviving evidence suggests that Nonconformity was relatively weak across south Shropshire. The survey of 1676 reported 400 conforming Anglicans, no Protestant dissenters and four 'papists' in Stanton Lacy: Anne Whiteman, ed., *The Compton Census of 1676: A Critical Edition* (1986), p. 255.

44. *The Execution of Mr Rob. Foulks*, p. 5; *A True and Perfect Relation*, p. 3.

45. Spurr, *Restoration Church*, pp. 181, 196.

46. Shropshire Records and Research Centre, MS 320/6 Estate book of Thomas Powys 1665–1670, p. 25.

47. See the court papers filed in HRO, HD4/25 *Foulkes* v. *Chearme*.

his parishioners when he brought the authority of written evidence to bear against the custom and oral tradition of the illiterate.[48]

The moral authority of the pulpit could also be used by Foulkes to factionalise village opinion by exposing wrong-doing and inciting parishioners to take legal action against their neighbours. Since religious observance was closely associated with status and identity in this period, these humiliating public interventions could damage the reputation of potentially powerful men in the community.[49] On one occasion, for instance, Foulkes urged his parishioners to present Richard Hopton senior to the petty sessions for supposedly embezzling £10 while performing his duties as churchwarden in 1672.[50] Such interventions brought into sharp relief the limits of the vicar's authority: on the one hand he clearly felt a moral right to reveal misdemeanours, on the other hand his opponents could accuse him of breaching norms of charitable living. The moral authority of the clergy was double-edged, encapsulated in the image of the minister as the 'people's looking glass', a spiritual and moral exemplar, but also subject to the closest scrutiny and surveillance.[51] Personal conduct thus played an integral role in the exercise of his professional authority.

This was most particularly evident in his relations with female parishioners. A stock of popular images of lecherous, hypocritical priests combined to make the sexual reputation of parish clergymen inherently vulnerable.[52] Such stereotypes could take on a cultural life of their own in village discourse, making possible a direct link between abuse of authority and sexual misconduct. This formed a powerful theme in a number of the stories circulated about Foulkes. It was rumoured, for instance, that on several occasions he had approached Catherine Collins of Green Lane in Stanton Lacy, 'whilst her husband was absent tempting her to commit Adultery with him', adding that she should not fear for her moral well-being since he 'being a minister' could save her soul 'for two pence'.[53] The assimilation of such tales with a persuasive stock of cultural

48. HRO, HD4/25 *Foulkes* v. *Chearme*, Allegation brought by Robert Foulkes, 19/12/1676; Adam Fox, 'Custom, memory and the authority of writing', in Griffiths *et al.*, eds, *The Experience of Authority*, pp. 89–116.

49. Ingram, 'From reformation to religious toleration', p. 113.

50. HRO, HD4/26 Articles of Exception brought by Robert Foulkes, 26/2/1678.

51. Foulkes, *Alarme for Sinners*, p. 16; Spurr, *Restoration Church*, p. 197.

52. Hindle, 'Shaming of Margaret Knowsley', pp. 397, 401; Spurr, *Restoration Church*, p. 184.

53. HRO, HD4/2/16 Deposition of William Hopton, 28/10/1676. Cf. HD4/26 Deposition of Elizabeth Atkinson, 18/9/1677; Foulkes, *Alarme for Sinners*, p. 21.

stereotypes no doubt assisted their plausibility and conditioned their audience to identify such behaviour as scandalous. [54]

Most attention, however, was focused upon Foulkes's familiarity with Anne Atkinson. When later pamphlet accounts of the case discussed the nature of the relationship between Foulkes and Atkinson, they commonly believed that Foulkes had been 'left Guardian' to an orphaned 'young gentlewoman', who lived in his house as 'a Servant or Boarder'. Representing the relationship in these terms seems to have been purposely designed to set the adultery in a recognisable household context, familiar from conduct literature and the pulpit, to emphasise its disruptive effects. More specifically it enabled pamphlets to present rapacious male sexual agency as a danger to household stability, collapsing the mutuality and trust that cemented the relations between masters and servants. Hence one pamphlet depicted Foulkes as 'making use of some Authority' derived from 'that trust' between guardian and ward, to 'debauch her to his bed'.[55] In fact, the social connections between Robert Foulkes and Anne Atkinson were more complicated than the master–servant or guardian–ward relationship would suggest.

Anne was the daughter of Thomas Atkinson, Foulkes's predecessor as vicar of Stanton Lacy who had died in 1657. Her date of birth is unclear, although she seems to have been born of Thomas's first wife who died in 1642, putting her in her early thirties when the scandal broke in 1676.[56] She lived not in Foulkes's house, but with her stepmother Elizabeth Atkinson, in a household that also accommodated a number of the Atkinsons' tenants. The widow Elizabeth and her spinster daughter Anne, although single women, were far from marginal figures in parish life. Both held leases of impropriation which gave them considerable power as landholders, and each had a number of male tenants.[57] Before the sexual relations between Robert Foulkes and Anne Atkinson came to light, there seems to have been close connections between the two families deriving from their membership of the same clerical social network and sustained by a reciprocity of economic interests.[58]

54. See also Hindle, 'Shaming of Margaret Knowsley', p. 401.

55. *A True and Perfect Relation*, p. 5; but cf. Foulkes, *Alarme for Sinners*, p. 20.

56. *Shropshire Parish Registers . . . Stanton Lacy*, p. 57; cf. HRO, *Office* v. *Atkinson* HD4/26 Allegation against Anne Atkinson, 1/10/1678, gives her age as 28, but it would appear that she was older.

57. HRO, HD4/26 Articles of Exception brought by Robert Foulkes, 26/2/1678; HD4/26 Deposition of Elizabeth Atkinson, 10/3/1677. On the power wielded by some single women see Capp, 'Separate domains?', p. 119; more generally, Amy Louise Erickson, *Women and Property in Early Modern England* (London and New York, 1993).

58. See, for instance, HRO, HD4/26 Deposition of Elizabeth Atkinson, 10/3/1677; ibid., Deposition of John Atkinson, 17/9/1677.

However, as for Foulkes, the ambiguities of Anne's social position could lead her into disputes with others and make her conduct suspicious. In the first place, Anne's continued spinsterhood beyond the normal age of marriage seems to have been a matter of public concern and cast doubt on her sexual reputation. Indeed, one of the charges brought against Foulkes was that his familiarity with Anne had damaged her chances of marriage.[59] Furthermore her independence as a property-holder placed her in an ambivalent position in the social and gender hierarchy which may have put her male tenants in an awkward position. One of the ways in which this was made manifest was through competition for space in the matriarchal Atkinson household. When Richard Chearme, who, along with his wife, lodged in the Atkinsons' house, tried to appropriate several ground floor rooms, normally used by Anne as dressing rooms, for his own use, this led to a bitter dispute in which the vicar finally had to mediate to protect the women's interests.[60]

On another occasion, Anne's leaseholding and Foulkes's public support for her rights brought her into conflict with another powerful local figure, William Hopton, son of the supposedly dishonest churchwarden. Hopton was employed as a bailiff by the Earl of Craven and was another man sensitive of his social status. Although officially described as a yeoman, he liked to style himself as a gentleman, perhaps as a result of the prestige he felt was conferred upon him by his office and the well-connected social circles in which he moved, even boasting the Bishop of Hereford as a friend.[61] Nevertheless, as a rent collector, Hopton was a potentially unpopular figure, and his financial honesty was publicly called into question on a number of occasions, with tales spreading that he had once 'runne his country' with Craven's money. When Anne believed that Hopton was trying to forge leases to the lands she and her stepmother held in Stanton with a view to building houses, she, with the help of Foulkes, exposed his fraudulent dealings to his employer, the Earl of Craven, who took disciplinary action.[62] When men like Richard Chearme and William Hopton sought revenge for their humiliation at the hands of Foulkes and Atkinson, they turned to the weapon of gossip, spreading rumours that would hit home at their enemies' weakest spot – their sexual reputation.

---

59. HRO, HD4/25 Libel against Robert Foulkes, 1/8/1676.
60. HRO, HD4/26 Articles of Exception brought by Robert Foulkes, 26/2/1678.
61. HRO, HD4/3/16 Deposition of William Hopton, 28/10/1676; HD4/26 Deposition of Richard Chearme, 19/3/1677.
62. HRO, HD4/26 Articles of Exception brought by Robert Foulkes, 26/2/1678; HD4/26 Deposition of Elizabeth Atkinson, 18/9/1677.

A social setting in which status was open to fluctuation, in which a festering tension characterised the relations between a number of leading village personalities, thus contributed to the vibrancy of the rumours that broke about Foulkes and Atkinson. A further factor arose from the very lack of direct evidence for their sexual involvement. It is often pointed out that rumour thrives best when facts are uncertain, where the imagination is left to run wild.[63] Not one villager of Stanton Lacy brought to testify in this case could describe Foulkes and Atkinson *in flagrante*. Rather, most of the witnesses brought to testify against Foulkes had their depositions structured around either suspicious circumstances or 'common fame' of Anne's bastard, supposedly born many miles away in the north Shropshire parish of West Felton.[64]

The circumstantial evidence largely focused on observing Foulkes and Atkinson in 'private and suspicious places', mostly being alone together in and around the house of Elizabeth Atkinson performing the gestures of intimacy: kissing, 'dallying' and fondling. Hence on New Year's Eve 1675, Grace Humphreys, a servant of Elizabeth Atkinson, spied them 'alone in the hall' of the house, 'without any Candle but a small fire in the said room' and 'the said Robert Foulkes was embraceing the said Anne with his Armes about her Middle and holding their faces close to each other'.[65] On another occasion, Foulkes and Atkinson were seen 'walking togeather alone hand in hand very familiarly in private places as in Meadows or Leasows [pastures] through which there was noe common or public way'.[66] However, this form of evidence was highly subjective and open to different interpretation by witnesses. Being 'alone' did not necessarily imply privacy even in such supposed refuges of intimacy as the bedchamber. Hence Anne's brother John could depose that he had seen them together 'publickly' in her chamber.[67] Equally, gestures such as the kiss might imply sociability rather than scandalous intimacy. While kissing an unmarried female parishioner might be interpreted as a 'scandall' to Foulkes's function as vicar, it might

63. Merry, 'Rethinking', p. 275; Rosnow and Fine, *Rumor and Gossip*, p. 16; Scott, *Domination*, p. 144.

64. The difficulty of obtaining direct proofs made such evidence admissible in cases of adultery. See Ayliffe, *Parergon*, pp. 50–2; Ingram, *Church Courts*, pp. 243–5.

65. HRO, HD4/2/16 Deposition of Grace Humphreys, 30/10/1676; see also ibid., Deposition of Margaret Chearme, 28/10/1676; ibid., Deposition of Mary Hopton 28/10/1676; ibid., Deposition of Richard Chearme, 30/10/1676.

66. HRO, HD4/26 Deposition of William Hopton, 21/3/1677.

67. HRO, HD4/26 Deposition of John Atkinson, 17/9/1677; see also ibid., Deposition of Francis Atkinson, 26/2/1677.

have been perfectly normal and well-mannered behaviour in the context of Foulkes's status as a 'gentleman', since, as one witness pointed out, 'he might salute her by way of courtesie'.[68] Many depositions thus hinged not so much on evidence of sexual immorality *per se* as on far less tangible notions of indiscretion – the ways in which different aspects of his character, his behaviour, even his body language, when viewed in the context of the expectations defined by his professional calling and social status, could be constructed as being to 'the great scandall of all honest, sober and discreet people'.[69] When so much of the evidence depended on subjective interpretation, when so many facts remained unknown, the situation became ripe for rumour.

How, then, were rumours actively used in the disputes between Foulkes and his parishioners? When defending himself in the Hereford church court against the charges of adultery, Foulkes portrayed himself as the victim of a conspiracy or 'combination' of 'Malevolent infamous and wicked persons' headed by William Hopton. The cabal also included Hopton's brother and father (both named Richard), and the churchwarden Richard Chearme. Together, the vicar believed, with 'anger, malice, revenge and deadly hatred' they 'spreade abroade to all persons' the 'fame' or 'rumoure' of sexual immorality with the avowed aim of ruining his reputation and depriving him of his position.[70] Although the truth of these claims is now hard to substantiate, there is much evidence in the depositions of witnesses to suggest ways in which these men might have manipulated opinion about Foulkes and how the vicar himself turned to sexual rumour concerning his enemies in an attempt to divide and discredit them. Examining the use of rumour, and the situations in which it could be activated, may therefore permit a fascinating insight into the ways in which sexual reputation might infuse factional strife between men and play a part in the assessment of authority.

William Hopton was in an excellent position to spread rumours about Foulkes and Atkinson among a wide and socially diverse audience. His work as a rent collector for the Earl of Craven brought him into contact with substantial figures outside Stanton Lacy which

68. HRO, HD4/26 Deposition of Elizabeth Atkinson, 18/9/1677.
69. HRO, HD4/2/16 Deposition of William Hopton, 28/10/1677. The categories and interpretation of circumstantial evidence are discussed further in my forthcoming doctoral thesis, 'Representations of adultery in England *c.*1660–*c.*1740'.
70. HRO, HD4/26 Personal Answers of Robert Foulkes, 22/5/1677; HD4/26 Articles of Exception brought by Robert Foulkes, 26/2/1678.

enabled stories to be spread over some distance. He also kept an alehouse in the village which connected him with humbler members of the parish community.[71] Hopton and his allies seem to have viewed rumour as something to be used in symbiosis with more formal legal actions. This was evident when Hopton revealed his plans to make 'publick' the adultery of Robert Foulkes and Anne Atkinson on a visit to the house of Henry Bradley, vicar of Great Ness, in June 1676, shortly before official action began. When Bradley warned him that such 'extravagant' speech might end in an action for defamation, Hopton supposedly replied that 'he spoak the words on purpose that [Foulkes] . . . might sue him', believing that by goading Foulkes to such an action he might incriminate himself.[72] Other witnesses recalled that the 'fame' of the adultery between Foulkes and Atkinson was 'not very comon' before the legal actions began and that the Hoptons had told stories about their bastard child to 'lessen the creditt and good repute' of Robert Foulkes and to 'propagate the cause' against him.[73] Although 'fame' alone was not sufficient to convict a person of a crime in the church courts, given the specific circumstances of this case, brought after Foulkes had already been admonished by his ecclesiastical superiors on suspicion of adultery, the standards of proof were lowered allowing 'common fame' to play a greater role.[74] William Hopton thus made it 'his business in all places and companies' to 'spread abroad the fame' both 'publickly and privately'.[75]

The vicar's enemies also exploited the legitimate mechanisms of social control to garner information they could use against him, and to keep the minister and his lover in the public eye. One method was to urge magistrates to investigate Anne Atkinson's bastard. In June 1677 Richard Hopton senior, 'haveing oftentimes heard' that Anne Atkinson had given birth to a child in the parish of West Felton, 'and being desirous to understand the truth thereof', obtained a warrant to force the local magistrate to look into the matter.[76] As bringer of the warrant, Richard Hopton travelled to West Felton to sit in on the examination of witnesses, after which he was often

71. On Hopton's alehouse see HRO, HD4/26 Deposition of Elizabeth Atkinson, 18/9/1677.
72. HRO, HD4/26 Deposition of Henry Bradley, 5/9/1677; ibid., Deposition of William Bradley, 5/9/1677.
73. HRO, HD4/26 Deposition of Joseph Wall, 3/9/1677; ibid., Deposition of Ralph Fenton, 1/9/1677.
74. Ayliffe, *Parergon*, pp. 275–8; Ingram, *Church Courts*, p. 244.
75. HRO, HD4/26 Deposition of Ralph Fenton, 1/9/1677.
76. HRO, HD4/26 *Office* v. *Atkinson* Deposition of Richard Hopton, 25/9/1678.

heard to relate 'in a clamorous manner' and 'with exceeding much passion' a detailed story about the birth and subsequent upbringing of Anne's child.[77] Richard Hopton seems to have been concerned with spreading the 'report' of Anne's bastard for several years prior to these investigations, an interest that was presented in some depositions as verging on the obsessive. Hence one witness was apt to believe that he was 'labouring under some distemper of body and insanity of mind' when he talked about it.[78] This suggests that there was a thin line between rational enquiry carried out by men under the auspices of social control and a morbid fascination with vice that could be perceived as symptomatic of madness.

William Hopton was also able draw on the verbal skills of men with a name for rumour-mongering to disseminate the scandalous stories. When Richard Hopton travelled to West Felton he was accompanied by a farmer, Charles Pearce of East Field in Stanton Lacy, whose reputation for slander had been confirmed in December 1676 when he had been presented to the church court for 'evil speaking'.[79] Foulkes alleged that Pearce had been paid by William Hopton to 'disperse' rumour of his bastard throughout the parish and beyond. Other witnesses testified that Pearce had taken to his task with relish, even going so far as to produce a lock of hair, supposedly snipped from the child's head, to give his story credibility.[80]

Although Foulkes presented himself as a passive victim of scandalous stories, he was in fact highly adept at using sexual gossip and insult as weapons against his opponents. When Foulkes discovered that Richard Chearme had been telling people that he and Anne Atkinson had been 'alone togeather in a Bower', he called Chearme and his wife Margaret to his house one July evening in 1676 to exact verbal revenge. Turning on Margaret in her husband's presence, he told her 'that she was a whore and soe was his wife alsoe and that they were . . . [William] Hopton's whores', before insulting Richard as a 'Cuckold-like rogue'.[81] What is especially striking about this outburst is the way Foulkes was prepared to imply his own cuckoldry in order to attack the sexual reputation of William Hopton as an adulterer and exploit a sensitivity to rumour in Richard

77. HRO, HD4/26 Deposition of Ralph Fenton, 1/9/1677.

78. HRO, HD4/26 Deposition of Elizabeth Atkinson, 19/3/1677.

79. HRO, HD4/26 *Office* v. *Atkinson* Deposition of Charles Pearce, 25/9/1678; HD4/1 Box 40 Acts of Office (Archdeaconry of Ludlow) f. 80.

80. HRO, HD4/26 Personal Answers of Robert Foulkes, 22/5/1677; HD4/26 Deposition of Somerset Wall, 1/9/1677.

81. HRO, HD4/2/16 Deposition of Richard Chearme 30/10/1676; ibid., Deposition of Mary Chearme, 28/10/1676.

Chearme. Foulkes would later testify in court that he believed that his wife had been in cahoots with Hopton over the forging of Anne Atkinson's leases, so in one sense this exchange forged a link between Hopton's financial dishonesty and his sexual immorality.[82] Although the exchange was relatively private, Foulkes's words seem to have struck a chord, for Margaret Chearme deposed that the vicar's words caused her husband to 'turne her away from him for some time'.[83]

When describing this incident to the court, Richard Chearme characterised Foulkes's words as a drunken outburst, as further evidence of his fractious personality. But when placed in a wider context, Foulkes's words seem to have been more purposefully designed to weaken the alliance between Chearme and William Hopton, by presenting Hopton as a dangerous sexual rival and cuckold-maker. Several witnesses believed that Hopton had forced Chearme into an engagement to hound Foulkes out of office under the sinister threat that he would 'doe him all injury soe long as he lived at Stanton' if he ever sought to come to a private reconciliation with the vicar.[84] Foulkes had on previous occasions used less specific sexual slanders in an attempt to prevent the alliance forming between Chearme and the Hoptons. Around Easter 1676, before the legal proceedings began, Foulkes had warned Chearme privately that William Hopton, his brother and his father were a 'Parcell of Rogues and Knaves', suggesting that their sexual reputations were suspect. While literary sources might place female sexual voraciousness at the heart of masculine anxiety, fears about the competitiveness of male sexuality and of the dangers, real or imagined, of the unchastity of their rivals could provide a compelling rhetoric in men's disputes.[85]

Foulkes was able to draw from a pool of rumours circulating around the parish concerning the sexual conduct of William Hopton. Gossip about Hopton's behaviour was spread by both women and men, although women appear to have been more reluctant to broadcast such stories before a wide audience. Elizabeth Atkinson, for instance, was approached by 'one Mary late a servant to Mr Richard Gravent of Whitbach', who told her that Hopton had attempted to

82. HRO, HD4/26 Articles of Exception brought by Robert Foulkes, 26/2/1678.
83. HRO, HD4/2/16 Deposition of Mary Chearme, 28/10/1676.
84. HRO, HD4/26 Deposition of Joseph Wall, 1/9/1677; ibid., Deposition of Richard Garbett, 1/9/1677.
85. See also Rachel Weil, 'Sometimes a scepter is only a scepter: pornography and politics in Restoration England', in Lynn Hunt, ed., *The Invention of Pornography: Obscenity and the Origins of Modernity 1500–1800* (New York, 1993), pp. 125–53.

rape a kinswoman of hers upon the highway.[86] Most talk centred on imputations that Hopton himself had fathered a bastard. Gossip about Hopton's illegitimate offspring spread around the same local middling sort and lesser gentry networks of male sociability in which Foulkes and Hopton were both active. Hence John Atkinson, a minister in Ludlow, heard it from Samuel Brampton, a gentleman whom he described as an 'intimate acquaintance' of Hopton, that he 'had a bastard child by one Symonds a coffymans maid at Grai's inn Bar gate in London'.[87] The mystery of Hopton's bastard, mentally associated with a geographically distant anonymous and supposedly amoral metropolitan milieu, held a strong imaginative appeal in a range of village discourse, to provide curious speculation in homosocial conversation, or to be brought out as a potent weapon against Hopton in public confrontation. Hence Foulkes himself appropriated a wilder version of the rumour in an angry exchange of insults with Hopton in the road outside the vicar's house in the summer of 1676 when he called him 'dogg and damnd dogg whelp rogue sonn of a whore sonn of a dogg and told him that he had a bastard and that he murthered a bastard at London and he was sure the said William was damnd'.[88] Despite the perception of infanticide as a female crime *par excellence*, rumours of male involvement could clearly provide a pungent means of attacking an adversary's sexual reputation.

Just as Foulkes seems to have been prepared to expose himself as a cuckold to attack the sexual reputation of his rivals, there is some evidence that William Hopton might on occasion have exploited rumours about his own bastard to further his verbal attacks on Foulkes and Atkinson. Elizabeth Atkinson, for instance, deposed that 'she hath heard it credibly reported that . . . Hopton had a bastard child and that he in a vaunting manner should say in the churchyard of Stanton upon a Sunday that he would marry his sonn to . . . Anne Atkinsons daughter'.[89] Evidence such as this suggests that Hopton might well have taken a vicarious pleasure from the scandal and seen it as an opportunity to enhance his status through wit and self-display.[90] This is suggested by another incident

86. HRO, HD4/26 Deposition of Elizabeth Atkinson, 18/9/1677.
87. HRO, HD4/26 Deposition of John Atkinson, 17/9/1677.
88. HRO, HD4/2/16 Deposition of Richard Chearme, 30/10/1676; ibid., Deposition of William Hopton, 28/10/1676; ibid., Deposition of Joanna Wood, 30/10/1676.
89. HRO, HD4/26 Deposition of Elizabeth Atkinson, 18/9/1677.
90. For other examples of Hopton making light of his immorality in homosocial conversation see HRO, HD4/26 Deposition of John Atkinson, 17/9/1677.

in the churchyard of Stanton Lacy. One Sunday morning sometime in 1676, Foulkes delivered a sermon on the text 'resist the devil and he will fly from thee'. Afterwards as the villagers filed out of church, Hopton pointed to Anne Atkinson and loudly exclaimed, 'there the shee devill goes let him resist her'.[91] The vivid scriptural language of immorality on this occasion offered an opportunity to demonstrate verbal dexterity in the presence of most of the village's inhabitants. The appropriation of the vicar's words and the uttering of them in the churchyard, symbolically the moral centre of the community, made this a very public inversion of Foulkes's moral and spiritual authority.

Writing in a very different setting, from a prison cell days before his execution, Robert Foulkes called upon a common biblical formulation to present revelation as a necessary and inevitable consequence of secret sin. 'Nothing is so secret but shall be revealed', he warned future readers of *An Alarme for Sinners*, for 'what is done in closets shall be published on the house-top'.[92] The murderous end to his affair with Anne Atkinson, his trial and impending dreadful punishment, provided evidence enough for the providential inevitability of the exposure of all 'vicious' lives and practices. But while this argument fitted the demands of his final penitential narrative, it certainly simplified the ways in which scandal was actively sought out and deployed in later seventeenth-century England. This chapter, by shifting the perspective on Foulkes's life from the retrospective view of the printed narratives to a context in which 'facts' were less certain and open to a range of subjective interpretation, has sought to demonstrate the sheer complexity of the uses of rumour and reputation in local society. In sharp contrast to prevailing literary stereotypes, evidence from this case foregrounds the role of men in discovering and publicly deploying information about sexual impropriety against one another. When set against the backdrop of local political tensions and litigation, rumours about sexual offences were used by Foulkes and his opponents as a pungent means of voicing rivalries, expressing social grievances and undermining status and authority, as well as offering opportunities for wit and social display. In a social context where status was a fragile commodity and subject to fluctuation, recourse to gossip and rumour could become an empowering experience for disgruntled men, and

91. HRO, HD4/26 Deposition of George Connor, 3/9/1677.
92. Foulkes, *An Alarme for Sinners*, p. 8.

a means of restoring their potency. Laura Gowing has recently argued that the rhetoric of sexual dishonour was a forceful means of dissolving a woman's claims to status.[93] The evidence from this case study suggests that, when understood within a broader set of power relations through which stories acquired their meaning and reputations were made and lost, rumours of sexual impropriety could serve a similar function for men to use against other men whose authority was called into question, as a means of erasing dignity and undermining claims to respect on which honour and status depended. It may now be necessary to rethink the extent to which sexual reputation was constructed and discussed along purely gendered lines. In the later seventeenth century, sexual reputation could still play a visible role in political disputes. How the rhetoric of such conflicts changed over the course of the eighteenth century, when sexuality was arguably becoming less central to men's reputations, is a subject that awaits further micro-historical research.[94]

The assumption that rumour and gossip were 'weapons of the weak' ignores the fact that such communication could be most devastatingly used by the powerful, in this case by substantial local men. Men in this case spread tales with a good deal of confidence, 'publicly' as well as in private, in a 'clamorous' or 'extravagant' manner, sometimes in tandem with more formal legal proceedings. In contrast, women are depicted in a much quieter role, as much more private communicators of scandalous information, occasionally approached by men for the stories they could supply, or as providers of moral support for Isabella Foulkes once her husband's suspected philandering became public knowledge.[95] This may have reflected an altogether greater security with which such men could activate rumour and scandal, for which women were potentially more susceptible to judicial sanctions and public shaming.[96] It would, however, be a mistake to view men's rumour-mongering in this case as first and foremost concerned with social control. The actions of men like William Hopton demonstrated that formal and informal

93. Laura Gowing, 'Women, status and the popular culture of dishonour', *TRHS* 6th ser., VI (1996), pp. 225–34.

94. On the declining social importance of male sexual reputation see Dabhoiwala, 'Construction of honour', pp. 212–13.

95. For examples see HRO, HD4/26 Deposition of Elizabeth Atkinson, 18/9/1677; HD4/2/16 Deposition of Martha Dovey, 28/10/1676.

96. In this respect this case stands in marked contrast to Margaret Knowsley's attempts to expose the sexual misconduct of a powerful local minister in 1620s Nantwich which ended in her own humiliation: Hindle, 'Shaming of Margaret Knowsley', *passim*. The use of legal sanctions against vociferous women was, however, highly selective: Ingram, '"Scolding women"', p. 71.

mechanisms of parochial order could in fact be used to pursue revenge and individual interests. Furthermore, the words used to describe the words of men in the court records, as 'flying reportes', 'false rumoures', 'extravagant discourse', even 'insanity', suggest that the 'rationality' of male discourse was open to question, by both women and men, rather than something to be assumed. The scandalous life of Robert Foulkes, then, though convoluted and ultimately depressing, may alert historians to important aspects of men's lives in later seventeenth-century England previously taken for granted. As Foulkes himself put it, those who may read of his experiences, 'either insult upon my fall, or are much troubled at it', but either way, 'no body can be indifferent upon this occasion'.[97]

97. Foulkes, *Alarme for Sinners*, p. 13.

CHAPTER TEN

'The Majesty of the Masculine-Form': Multiplicity and Male Bodies in Eighteenth-Century Erotica[1]

KAREN HARVEY

For a field in which questions of difference between bodies have come to dominate, the term 'the history of the body' might appear to be an inappropriate title. As exemplified by Thomas Laqueur's book *Making Sex* (1990), the foreground of this field is occupied with how people in the past imagined the relationship between the male body and the female body. Laqueur constructed a narrative of change in which this relationship experienced a momentous transformation some time during the eighteenth century, spawning the two opposite sexes of modernity. Yet in the opening passages, one of the bodies which emerged as half of this binary model by the end of the book, is apparently removed from exploration. 'It is probably not possible', Laqueur wrote, 'to write a history of man's body and its pleasures because the historical record was created in a cultural tradition where no such history was necessary.'[2] The term 'the history of the body' is no misnomer, therefore, for a field in which one body – a female body – dominates. This chapter, in contrast, works on the assumption that all bodies are subject to the lending of meaning to physical matter. Male bodies were sites of construction and debate.[3]

1. For their support and helpful comments I thank Sarah Barry, Alan Bray, Sandra Cavallo, Michèle Cohen, Penelope Corfield, Brian Cowan, Tim Hitchcock, Martin Lengwiler, Lyndal Roper, Eve Setch, Nick Stargaardt, Nick Webb and all those who attended the conference 'Masculinities, 1660–1800'. I am particularly indebted to Amanda Vickery for her boundless encouragement and enthusiasm.
2. Thomas Laqueur, *Making Sex: Body and Gender from the Greeks to Freud* (Cambridge MA and London, 1990), p. 22.
3. This chapter investigates a 'discursive' body created in texts, but bodies are not blank slates onto which endless meanings can be scrawled. We cannot ignore the physicality of bodies. As R.W. Connell states, bodies are 'both objects and agents of practice'. See *Masculinities* (Cambridge, 1995), p. 61.

The exclusion of male bodies from the history of *the* body implies that these bodies possess both a constancy and a one-dimensionality which excludes them from the field of historical exploration. Correspondingly, female bodies are often considered to be more unstable and less resistant to having meanings ascribed to them.[4] While the idea of constancy can be used fruitfully in work on male bodies, much recent work has made strenuous efforts to erode the myth of the one-dimensional male body.[5] Most frequently, this is attempted by adopting the theme of a disparity between ideals of masculinity and male bodies on the one hand, and the actuality of experiences of men and their bodies on the other. A specific variation of this approach can be found in those analyses which employ the language and analytical tools of psychoanalysis. In these, male bodies and authority are symbolically represented by the singular, majestic and imposing phallus, while the actuality of male bodies as changeable, soft and various is overshadowed.[6] Phrased in various ways, historians of the male body attempt to prise open the association between 'ideology' and 'actuality',[7] between the 'imagination and experience' of men themselves and 'traditions of representation',[8] or between 'embodiment' and 'phallic signification'.[9] The unmasking of the breach appears to show discord to be at the foundation of masculinity, and produces one of the most powerful themes of this historiography, in which men are repeatedly portrayed as anxiously trying to live up to unattainable ideals.[10]

4. Kathleen Brown alludes to this difference in '"Changed . . . into the fashion of a man": the politics of sexual difference in a seventeenth-century Anglo-American settlement', *JHS* 6 (1995), pp. 189–90. The 'emptiness' of the female form lends it to use in allegory. See Gill Perry, 'Women in disguise: likeness, the Grand Style and the conventions of "feminine" portraiture in the work of Sir Joshua Reynolds', in Gill Perry and Michael Rossington, eds, *Femininity and Masculinity in Eighteenth-Century Art and Culture* (Manchester, 1994); and Marina Warner, *Monuments and Maidens: The Allegory of the Female Form* (1985).

5. See Joanna Bourke, *Dismembering the Male: Men's Bodies, Britain and the Great War* (1996); Lesley A. Hall, *Hidden Anxieties: Male Sexuality, 1900–1950* (Cambridge, 1991); Laurence Goldstein, *The Male Body: Features, Destinies, Exposures* (Michigan, 1994).

6. For critiques of this equation within a psychoanalytic perspective, see Kaja Silverman, *Male Subjectivity at the Margins* (New York, 1992); and Susan Bordo, 'Reading the male body', in Goldstein, ed., *The Male Body*. Bordo, for example, seeks to challenge 'the singular, constant, transcendent rule of the phallus' ('Reading the male body', p. 265).

7. Hall, *Hidden Anxieties*, p. 2.   8. Bourke, *Dismembering the Male*, pp. 11, 29.

9. Bordo, 'Reading the male body', pp. 265, 296.

10. In *Anxious Masculinity in Early Modern England* (Cambridge, 1996), Mark Breitenberg claims that the 'necessary and inevitable condition' of 'anxious masculinity' results from the failure of constructs of manhood to paint over 'the fissures

This chapter implicitly questions these distinctions between 'discursive' ideals and anxious experience. It draws on around ten texts in both prose and poetry, published between 1722 and 1779, which are united in their deeply satirical use of extended metaphors to portray the genitals. Priced between sixpence and two shillings, these were not extremely expensive texts, though neither were they cheap ephemeral items. While they work on many different levels, their price and content suggest that readers were members of an educated, urban middling group or elite. If readers were to appreciate all the satirical jibes made, for example, an extensive knowledge of a range of other genres would be required. Moreover, it is likely that this sub-genre of erotica was deeply masculine in authorship, readership and content. Though a large proportion of these texts was published anonymously or pseudonymously, all the known authors of this material were male. Information on actual readers is more elusive, especially when one trick of the erotic book trade was to make false statements regarding the intended readership. Nevertheless, there are other suggestive clues. Though distinctions between different types of material should not be ignored, it is significant that references to consumers (rather than purveyors) of sexually revealing or obscene material in this period always refer to men, never to women.[11] In view of this, it may seem odd that images of reading which appear within the material invariably feature women as readers. Yet, as this chapter seeks to show, these fictional readers constitute one of a range of techniques which indicate an intended actual readership of men.[12] 'Masculine in readership' does not exclude the possibility of a woman reading these texts, rather it suggests that the content of this material was 'male-centred' and implies that the intended actual reader was male.[13]

and contradictions of patriarchal systems' (p. 2). Hall in *Hidden Anxieties*, and Andrew Campbell and Nathan Griffith, 'The male body and contemporary art', in Goldstein, ed., *The Male Body*, make a similar claim. See Ewa Lajer-Burcharth, 'The aesthetics of male crisis: the Terror in the republican imagery and Jacques-Louis David's work from prison', in Perry and Rossington, eds, *Femininity and Masculinity* for an example of a psychoanalytic approach to this idea of breach and anxiety.

11. Jean Marie Goulemot, *Forbidden Texts: Erotic Literature and its Readers in Eighteenth-Century France* (1991; Engl. trans. Cambridge, 1994), pp. 13–29, 95; Robert Darnton, *The Forbidden Best-Sellers of Pre-Revolutionary France* (London and New York, 1995), pp. 217–31.

12. For a more thorough exploration of the readership of erotica, see ch. 2 of my 'Representations of bodies and sexual difference in eighteenth-century written English erotica' (Ph.D. thesis, Royal Holloway, University of London, 1999).

13. The trope of sight explored below is exemplary of this: while female sight serves the needs of male bodies by transforming them, male sight only satisfies the needs of the male looker, and not the female body. The use of sight, then, is asymmetrical.

The lack of explicitness apparently rendered by these extended metaphors has been regarded as indicative of the relative timidity of the English with regards to things sexual, and has led historians to exclude them from the category of pornography.[14] Though the use of the term 'erotica' in this chapter is in accord with this exclusion, it does not imply a less explicit form of pornography.[15] Rather, these two bodies of material are envisaged as portraying sex, desire and bodies with distinctive strategies. At the heart of these distinctions is pornography's claims to explicitness and realism in its depiction of bodies and sex. Through techniques such as the obscene word and descriptions of the sex act, an illusion of greater proximity to the body is created, and sex takes on a realistic quality.[16] Erotica also creates an illusion, but it is an illusion which places bodies and sex at a distance. A variety of strategies might be employed in this process: bodies might be made conspicuously absent by being clothed in garments, placed outside the narrative, or (in this case) 'veiled' through the use of extended metaphors.

Yet while this chapter explores 'discursive' bodies created in written texts, it tries to move away from the idea that these bodies constituted an 'ideal' to which men anxiously tried to aspire. Rather, it is driven by a desire to explore how these texts and the images of bodies they contained functioned for men. Reflecting the emphasis of the authors, the parts of male bodies which appear most obviously here are the genitals. Yet these authors were not speaking of genitals, sex and reproduction alone: they used those body parts

14. For surveys of this material see Peter Wagner, *Eros Revived: Erotica of the Enlightenment in England and France* (1988), pp. 191–200; Roger Thompson, *Unfit for Modest Ears: A Study of Pornographic, Obscene and Bawdy Works Written or Published in England in the Second Half of the Seventeenth Century* (1979), pp. 190–4; and Patrick Kearney, *A History of Erotic Literature* (1982), pp. 53–7. For more studied analyses see Paul-Gabriel Boucé, 'Chthonic and pelagic metaphorization in eighteenth-century erotica', in R.P. Maccubin, ed., *'Tis Nature's Fault: Unauthorized Sexuality during the Enlightenment* (Cambridge, 1987); and Bridget Orr, 'Whore's rhetoric and the maps of love: constructing the feminine in Restoration erotica', in Clare Brant and Diane Purkiss, eds, *Women, Texts and Histories, 1575–1760* (London and New York, 1992). For instances where this material is briefly enlisted in wider arguments, see Laqueur, *Making Sex*, p. 172; and Tim Hitchcock, *English Sexualities, 1700–1800* (Basingstoke, 1997), pp. 12–14.

15. There is much confusion over terms in the historiography. Wagner uses the term 'erotica' to encompass four types of literature: erotic, pornography, bawdy and obscene (*Eros Revived*, p. 5). In *Forbidden Texts*, Jean Marie Goulemot uses 'erotica' interchangeably with the word 'pornographic'.

16. Lucienne Frappier-Mazur, 'Truth and the obscene word in eighteenth-century French pornography', in Lynn Hunt, ed., *The Invention of Pornography: Obscenity and the Origins of Modernity, 1500–1800* (New York, 1993); Joan DeJean, 'The politics of pornography: *L'Ecole des Filles*', in Hunt, ed., *The Invention of Pornography*.

metonymically to stand for entire male bodies. Moreover, it is on to these body parts that concerns about masculinity in wider cultural, social, economic and political contexts were projected.[17] In exploring some of these concerns, this chapter shows that a multiplicity of male bodies were valorised and reviled in a system with many axes: male bodies were ranked along the lines of size, age, nationality and fertility. Moreover, there were a multiplicity of states – of imposing erectness and soft vulnerability – in which male genitals might be imagined and cherished.[18]

Images of male bodies in eighteenth-century erotica are invariably accompanied by representations of women as sexual beings, which might offer tantalizing material for historians of women. Yet caution should be exercised before these images are celebrated as 'positive'. The simultaneous existence of chillingly grotesque females, for example, resists any simple assessment of 'positive' or 'negative'. Indeed, the use of images of female sexuality to undermine women in the early modern period forces us to question the notion that such images were intrinsically 'positive'.[19] Moreover, viewing these images in terms of women only fails to take account of how masculinity is forged in relation to femininity.[20] It does not recognise that such images have often been used as strategies in text, art, or film.[21] In the depiction of some male bodies as objects

17. This method of reading images of the body for meaning is not an anachronism. Sarah R. Cohen describes how bodies were read for meaning in this period in 'Body as "Character" in early eighteenth-century French art and performance'. *Art Bulletin* LXXVIII (1996), pp. 454–66.

18. This is distinct from representations of female bodies. The aura of competition which infuses comparisons of male bodies is not so obvious in portrayals of female bodies, and though female genitals are not always immobile, it is in representations of male genitals that movement becomes an absolutely crucial attribute.

19. James Grantham Turner, '"News from the exchange": commodity, erotic fantasy and the female entrepreneur', in John Brewer and Ann Bermingham, eds, *The Consumption of Culture, 1600–1800: Image, Object, Text* (London and New York, 1995). For a later period, Klaus Theweleit discusses how the perceived sexual independence of proletarian women in the writing of volunteer German soldiers after 1918, marked them out as agents of destruction who prompted reactions of the utmost violence. See *Male Fantasies I: Women, Floods, Bodies, History* (1977; Engl. trans. Cambridge, 1987), pp. 70–9.

20. The images of women created by the German volunteer armies are examined by Theweleit in this way. 'As the woman fades out of sight', he writes, 'the contours of the male sharpen . . . It could almost be said that the raw material for the man's "transformation" is the sexually untouched, dissolving body of the woman he is with', *Male Fantasies I*, p. 35.

21. For two classic examples for art and film respectively, see John Berger's *Ways of Seeing* (1972), in which he states that when a man looked at a painting of a female nude, 'What he saw reminded him that he was a man' (p. 57); and Laura Mulvey's 'Visual pleasure and narrative cinema', in Anthony Easthope, ed., *Contemporary Film*

of desire in eighteenth-century erotica, images of women were strategically deployed to disarm certain accusations that such depictions might have provoked. Images of female insatiability, of female
sight and touch, and of women as the privileged viewers of male
bodies allowed the male body to be shown in states of grandeur
and plenitude, but also of receptive movement and vulnerability.
What appear to be asymmetrical concerns with women's bodies in
the historical record, therefore, are seen as vocal comments on
male bodies, and ways in which the concerns of the male authors
and readers could be displayed vicariously.

Perhaps the most striking feature of the representation of
male bodies in eighteenth-century erotica is the irresistibility they
are granted, most frequently conveyed in the biblical story of the
Fall. Using the metaphor of eel, serpent, or tree, penises are presented as the intrinsically attractive objects of female adoration.
The electrical eel is lauded as the original serpent which 'tempted
the divine EVE, in the living garden of EDEN', though in *The Old
Serpent's Reply to the Electrical Eel* (1777) this is disputed, the serpent
stating unequivocally, 'I debauch'd fair Lady Eve'.[22] The arbor vitae,
as the name indicates, is the tree 'whose Fruits were so alluring
to our first Mother', while in another poem one woman exempts
Eve from responsibility in the Fall because the tree would have

---

Theory (London and New York, 1993), in which 'woman' is a 'silent image' onto
which 'man' can impose a meaning which underpins his identity (p. 112). A more
recent and historically pertinent analysis is Ann Bermingham's 'The aesthetics of
ignorance: the accomplished woman in the culture of connoisseurship', *Oxford Art
Journal* 16 (1993), pp. 3–20, in which she claims 'commodified bodies of women'
were 'positioned in relation to certain specific constructions of masculine subjectivity' (p. 5). Work on women as allegorical figures also provides a stark reminder that
images of women cannot be read in any simple way. As Marina Warner points out,
'Justice is not spoken of as a woman, nor does she speak as a woman . . . because
women were thought to be just, any more than they were considered capable of
dispensing justice', *Monuments and Maidens*, p. xix. Marcia Pointon has argued that
reading images of women in this 'cynical' way leaves no room for the control that
some women may have had over the construction and use of those images. See
'Killing pictures', in John Barrell, ed., *Painting and the Politics of Culture: New Essays on
British Art 1700–1850* (Oxford and New York, 1992), p. 60. Yet, should this control
be removed – as it would seem to be in eighteenth-century erotica – the cynical
reading of images of women as constructed in a particular way to serve a particular
function remains appropriate.

22. *The Electrical Eel: or, Gymnotus Electricus. Inscribed to the Honourable Members of
the R***l S*****y; by Adam Strong, Naturalist* (No publication details, 1774), pp. ii–
iii. *The Old Serpent's Reply to the Electrical Eel* (Printed for M. Smith, 1777), p. 14. Hereafter, all places of publication are London unless otherwise stated. The publishers'
names have been retained to distinguish between editions published in the same
year.

been too tempting to resist.[23] Not surprisingly, women rapturously lament the loss of the penis in *An Elegy on the Lamented Death of the Electrical Eel*:

> Women to thee shall dedicate their lives,
> And on their knees with gratitude revere,
> Thou wert the comfort of both maids and wives,
> And brush'd away the widow's ready tear.[24]

Such lamentation is understandable, in view of the influence of the tree of life. The arbor vitae, for example, is a thing of which 'the virtues are so many, a large Volume might be wrote of them'.[25] It has the capacity to solve domestic disputes, uniting husband and wife who are both 'in sullen pout', and has influences in world affairs: through its use, 'The most destructive Wars have been ended'.[26] Indeed, women are castigated should they not accept the calibre of male genitals:

> If your Ideas of them be
> Not full of Grace and Dignity;
> Attend, and it shall soon be shewn
> The Fault's not Nature's, but your own.[27]

This attraction stems from a number of attributes. Often the charm emanates simply from beauty. A painting of a penis in *A Chinese Tale* (1740) prompts the outburst:

> The World's great *Primum Mobile*;
> That Master-piece! that Source of Passion!
> That Thing that's never out of Fashion.[28]

The penis is variously described as 'That dear enchanting Rod', 'a Tree in all its Beauty', and 'strong, lusty, [and] beautiful'.[29] In the

---

23. *Arbor Vitae: or, the Natural History of the Tree of Life* (Printed for E. Hill, 1741), p. 8; *Wisdom Revealed: or, the Tree of Life Discover'd and Describ'd . . . By a Studious Enquirer into the Mysteries of Nature* (Printed for W. Shaw, 1732), p. 24.

24. *An Elegy on the Lamented Death of the Electrical Eel, or Gymnotus Electricus* by Lucretia Lovejoy [pseudonym], sister to Mr. Adam Strong, author of the Electrical Eel. (Printed for Fielding and Walker, 1777), p. 5.

25. *Arbor Vitae*, p. 9.   26. Ibid., pp. 21, 10.

27. *Adam's Tail: or, the First Metamorphosis* (Printed for John Bell, 1774), p. 2.

28. William Hatchett, *A Chinese Tale. Written originally by that prior of China the facetious Sou ma Quang* (For J. Cooper, 1740), pp. 22–3.

29. *Little Merlin's Cave. As it was latel'y discover'd by a Gentleman's gardener, in Maidenhead-Thicket to which is added, A Riddle: or a Paradoxical character of an Hairy Monster, often found under Holland* [Generally attributed to Ned Ward] 4th edn (Printed for T. Read, 1737), p. 4; *Wisdom Revealed*, p. 24; *Teague-Root Display'd: Being some Useful and Important Discoveries tending to illustrate the doctrine of Electricity* (Printed for W. Webb, 1746), p. 14.

hierarchical relationship established between male and female bodies, this beauty is one trait which distinguishes men. When differentiating between male and female bodies, the author of *Teague-Root Display'd* claims that 'the Female is not so beautiful a Root' and has 'a very shocking Appearance'.[30] Another author writes, 'the chiefest Perfections of the Female-Sex' are incomparable to 'the Majesty of the Masculine-Form'.[31] In the frontispiece to *A Voyage to Lethe* (1741) – which comprises a series of metaphorical descriptions of sex couched in a narrative of a voyage – this majesty is indicated visually. The pseudonymous author and supposed captain of the ship – Captain Samuel Cock – is depicted indicating conspicuously to his gun: a weapon used elsewhere in this book to indicate the penis and male ejaculation (Figure 1).[32] The confident pride with which this man appears to display his gun, though perhaps suggesting a degree of vulnerability and an apprehension about sex, lends the penis considerable strength, grandeur and dignity.[33]

Perhaps not surprisingly, size is also an important asset of desirable male genitals.[34] They are deemed most attractive when 'stiff, erect and high', 'most streight of lovely Size' and 'Of such a size – of such a length'.[35] Cloe's curiosity regarding the tree of life is most urgent on the issue of size: 'But will you never tell the Size?', she excitedly interrupts the narrator.[36] Another illustration from *A*

30. *Teague-Root Display'd*, pp. 14, 15.

31. Charles Cotton, 'Of the Situation of Bettyland', in *The Potent Ally: or, Succours from Merryland* (Printed by direction of the author, 'Paris' [London], 1741), pp. 28–9. Originally published as *Erotopolis* (1684). The superiority of male bodies is further indicated by the use Richard Bradley's distinction of tree and shrub to represent the male and female genitals respectively, in which the tree commanded greater perfections. This is used in *Arbor Vitae* and *The Natural History of the Frutex Vulvaria, or Flowring Shrub* (Date and publication details of the edition used have been damaged. *c.*1741). Originally published 1732. See Richard Bradley, *Philosophical Account of the Works of Nature* (Printed for W. Mears, 1721), pp. 35–7.

32. 'Capt. Samuel Cock' [Pseudonym], *A Voyage to Lethe* (Printed for J. Conybeare, 1741), p. 31.

33. Weapons appear elsewhere in this material to represent penises. See 'Philogynes Clitorides' [Pseudonym], 'Kynomotenia' and 'Armour', in *The Potent Ally: or, Succours from Merryland. With three essays in praise of the cloathing that country; and the story of Pandora's box. To which is added The Present state of Bettyland* ('Paris' [London], 1741).

34. George Rousseau has suggested that in the late eighteenth-century priapic tradition, the stress on fertility in representations of the penis had abated and Priapus 'was merely personified as a pigmy with a huge cock'. See 'The sorrows of Priapus', in his *Perilous Enlightenment: Pre- and Post-Modern Discourses. Sexual, Historical* (Manchester, 1991), p. 93. As explained below, however, the stress on size did not preclude a deep concern with fertility in erotica.

35. *Mimosa*, pp. 2, 3; *Arbor Vitae*, p. 12; *The Electrical Eel*, p. 25.

36. *Wisdom Revealed*, p. 9.

FIG. 1   'Captain Samuel Cock, F.R.S.', Frontispiece, *A Voyage to Lethe* (1741). British Library Cup. 1001. c.4
Reproduced by kind permission of the British Library

Voyage to Lethe suggests similar themes (Figure 2). Appearing in a book in which a range of inanimate objects are used to indicate male (and female) genitals, this image can be read as a depiction of the penis. The placing of a three-cornered hat at the base of the monument which a native covetously attempts to remove, might be another clue, as the penis was described as 'three-cornered' else-where.[37] The men on the voyage inspect two native helmeted statues which loom over them. The impressive height of one monument is reinforced by the presence of an explorer, whose outstretched cane reaches only as far as the statue's nose.

Indeed, size is an important factor in differentiating between male bodies. The author of *Arbor Vitae: or, the Natural History of the Tree of Life* writes, 'The Height here in *England*, rarely passes nine, or even eleven Inches, and that chiefly in Kent; whereas in *Ireland*, it comes to far greater Dimensions'.[38] Certainly, Ireland seems to produce the most esteemed male plants. The author of *Teague-Root Display'd* confides: 'I have seen it in most Countries of *Europe*; but I never met with any so good as in *Ireland*: There it arrives to the greatest *Perfection*'.[39] Other geographical distinctions can be found. A male teague-root 'thrives best in our more Northern Countries', whereas in the warmer climates of Spain and Italy 'it's suddenly ripe, and as soon rotten; and does not retain its Beauty, Vigour, nor Virtue, half as long as in Climates where the Heat is less intense'.[40] The mimosa plant, alternatively, is distinguished by English and French varieties, the latter apparently being revered by English women.[41] Nevertheless, the author reasserts the quality of English plants:

> The *motion* may not be so *strong*,
> The *pods* so full, the *stem* so long;
> So *succulent* the *root*.
> Yet Lady B—YMORE declares,
> Our *stamen* is as good as theirs;
> As exquisite the *fruit*.[42]

Significantly, it is the fruit of the English plant which serves to redeem it and ensure its attractiveness.

---

37. *Teague-Root Display'd*, p. 14.
38. *Arbor Vitae*, p. 3. Also see *Wisdom Revealed*, p. 9.
39. *Teague-Root Display'd*, pp. 13–4.
40. Ibid., p. 13. The same distinction is applied to female bodies in *The Natural History of the Frutex Vulvaria*, pp. 6–7.
41. *Mimosa*, p. 13.   42. Ibid., p. 13.

FIG. 2   The penis as majestic monument, *A Voyage to Lethe* (1741). British Library Cup. 1001. c.4
Reproduced by kind permission of the British Library

Indeed, perhaps most crucially, favourable depictions of male genitals stress their potential to carry out a reproductive function. This is exemplified in the keen interest these authors express not only in the penis, but in the scrotum and testicles. The description of the teague-root is typical of this:

> the Top of it is a beautiful Carnation-Colour, and softer than the soft-est Down: At the Bottom of the Root issue two round Globes, that are pendulous in a Bag, where they seem to be loose, tho' bound to the Stem of the Root, by small yielding Fibres: The Outside of this Bag is wrinkly, and cover'd with a Kind of Down, much resembling Hair.[43]

It is this fertility which ensures the superiority of the penis over imitations. In one comparison between the penis and dildo, the genuine article is superior because the dildo cannot produce the vital and productive fluid of semen.[44]

Satirising recent fascination in the sexual life of plants, authors of erotica referred to contemporary botanical books, partly because it allowed considerable emphasis to be placed upon fertility.[45] But only certain plants were suitable. One author advised his readers that an illustration of the tree of life could be found in a recent text by the botanist Richard Bradley (Figure 3).[46] Bradley wrote, 'It is wonderful to see this Plant rise out of the Earth in a Pillar-like Form, shooting directly upwards, . . . till it will attain to the height of about twenty Foot'.[47] In a later book he described it as having 'an extraordinary Face', and 'coming nearer the Perfection we look for' than other plants.[48] Bradley's admiring tone, together with the beautiful, large, dignified and superior nature of the plant, made it a suitable image in the depiction of male genitals.

The emphasis placed on the value of male semen further reveals a concern for fertility. The tree of life in *Wisdom Revealed* admin-isters the '*succus Genitalis*', through which younger plants are produced, while the sperm of the mimosa is described as 'the most

---

43. *Teague-Root Display'd*, p. 14. Also see *Wisdom Reveal'd*, p. 8 and *Arbor Vitae*, pp. 1–2.

44. *Monsieur Thing's Origin*, p. 19.

45. Philip Miller, for example, had reported on plant fertilisation in 1721, and published his *Catalogus Plantarum* in 1730, Wagner, *Eros Revived*, p. 193. For a more detailed consideration of the parasitic nature of this material, see Boucé, 'Chthonic and pelagic metaphorization'.

46. *Wisdom Revealed*, p. 7. The illustration referred to appears in Richard Bradley's *Philosophical Account*, and in a slightly altered form (used here) in his earlier *The History of Succulent Plants . . . Decade I* (Printed for the author, 1716).

47. Bradley, *The History of Succulent Plants*, p. 1.

48. Bradley, *Philosophical Account*, p. 23.

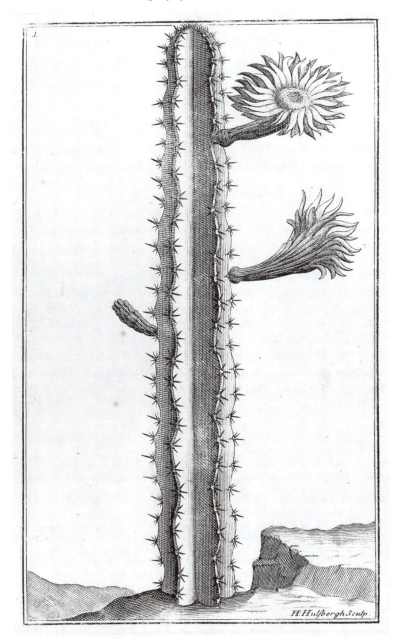

FIG. 3   The upright torch thistle, Richard Bradley, *The History of Succulent Plants* (1716)
Reproduced by kind permission of the British Library

animating sap'.[49] Women's handling of male trees is designed to 'invigorate their *Sap*, and make their *Juices* full of volatile particles, and apt to impregnate'.[50] Indeed, in *The Man-Plant* (1752), the description of women's eggs as 'Capsules of the male-seed', and of semen as the 'Spark or Particle of Fire', resembles an older Aristotelian vision of conception, in which the active male sperm works on the imperfect female's menstrual blood.[51] And just as beauty and size were qualities to be fought over, so in the trio of texts which use the metaphors of eel and serpent for male genitals, the old serpent asserts his more powerful reproductive capabilities *vis-à-vis* the eel.[52]

On occasion, men provide more than the active substance in conception, and are envisaged as the sole agents of reproduction, arresting women of their role.[53] In *Adam's Tail*, the story of the creation of woman is re-written with a twist, so that woman is created not from the earth or from Adam's rib, but is literally moulded from superfluous matter discarded from his genitals.[54] The (fictional) experiment reported in *The Man-Plant* aimed to produce a baby boy without a womb in which it would gestate, making women superfluous to this process. The impulse behind this was reinforced in the mythical stories of the births of Bacchus, Orion and Erichthonius (in which women are absent) recounted at the close of the book.[55] This stress on the superiority of men's contribution to conception and reproduction echoed the greater perfection of the male form encountered earlier.[56]

49. *Wisdom Revealed*, pp. 11, 12; *Mimosa*, p. vi
50. *The Natural History of the Frutex Vulvaria*, p. 4.
51. *The Man-Plant: or, Scheme for Increasing and Improving the British Breed*, by Vincent Miller [Pseudonym] (Printed for M. Cooper, 1752), pp. 16–17.
52. *The Old Serpent's Reply to the Electrical Eel*, p. 16.
53. There are also interesting examples of men describing themselves as giving birth, to babies and to knowledge. See *The Man-Plant*, p. 32; *Teague-Root Display'd*, p. 10; and *Merryland Displayed: or, plagiarism, ignorance, and impudence detected. Being observations upon a pamphlet intituled A New Description of Merryland* (2nd edition, Printed for the Author, Bath, 1741), pp. 9, 10. For discussions of similar images see Marie Mulvey Roberts, 'Pleasures engendered by gender: homosociality and the club', in Roy Porter and Marie Mulvey Roberts, eds, *Pleasure in the Eighteenth Century* (Basingstoke, 1996), and Mary Fissell, 'Gender and generation: representing reproduction in early modern England', *G&H* 3, 1995, pp. 440–1. Female fertility also has important cultural ramifications, see Breitenberg, *Anxious Masculinity*, and, for an anthropological perspective, Francoise Héritier-Augé, 'Older women, stout-hearted women, women of substance', in M. Feher, ed., *Fragments for a History of the Human Body: Part Three* (New York, 1989).
54. *Adam's Tail*, p. 9.   55. *The Man-Plant*, pp. 42–9.
56. Laqueur sees changes in ideas about conception as crucial in an alleged transformation in thinking about sex differences. See *Making Sex*, and 'Orgasm, generation, and the politics of reproductive biology', *Representations* 14 (1986),

Indeed, though the images of fertile female bodies which often appear in this material are ostensibly telling us about women, these images can be read as comments on men's own concerns. The image of the moist opening in the illustration from the 1737 edition of *Little Merlin's Cave* accompanied a riddle in which the topic was the female genitals, but it is emphatically about fertility and men's important role in this (Figure 4). Seated to the right, the narrator of the riddle is prominently armed with a spade, while directly behind in the distance a plough is being drawn across the field. Both the spade and the plough were used as metaphors for the penis in this material, and the act of farming moist land could represent the act of impregnating women. This stress on productive sex was reinforced in the slightly modified version which appeared in a later poem on the male genitals (Figure 5). The scene remains substantially the same, but at the foot of the waterfall and directed at the entrance to the cave, there has been added a penis and testicles thinly disguised as a tree. The implications of fertility are now underlined, and the plants are shown to 'do best in the same Bed'.[57]

At times, motivating impulses behind this stress on male fertility appear to be revealed. Behind the experiment to discover a new way of gestating babies in *The Man-Plant*, lies a desire to furnish the country with healthy baby boys who will possess:

> all that Strength of Sinew which strung the Arms of those Progenitors of ours, who antiently made such a Figure at the battles of *Crecy* and *Agincourt*, or of those who more lately drove whole Squadrons of their Enemies into the *Danube*, . . . Barbarous, rude, rough Work! and quite unfit for the dainty Hands of our present pretty Men; hands blanched with Almond-paste, brillianted with Diamonds, and be-delicated with *Dresden* Ruffles.[58]

The author unfavourably compares the fighting strength of Britain's present population with their ancestors. Similarly, in *The Natural History of the Frutex Vulvaria* (1741), a book ostensibly concerned with female genitals, the author claims that English trees 'are held in the utmost Contempt in all foreign Countries'.[59] He continues, 'Since the *Peace of Utrecht* we have never done any *Great Feats*, but seem to be damnably *off our Mettle*. All these Misfortunes the *Naturalists* and *Botanists* ascribe (how truly I know not) to the Degeneracy of

pp. 1–41. However, in the material examined here, though male sperm is the active agent, a variety of views of conception coexist and the material sits uncomfortably with Laqueur's narrative.

57. *Arbor Vitae*, pp. 2–3.   58. *The Man-Plant*, pp. 38–9.

59. *The Natural History of the Frutex Vulvaria*, p. 3.

FIG. 4   The female body as the fertile landscape, Frontispiece, *Little Merlin's Cave* (1737)
Reproduced by kind permission of the British Library

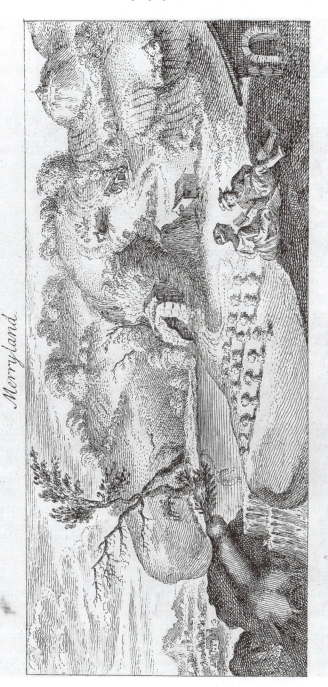

FIG. 5   Merryland', Frontispiece, *Arbor Vitae* (1741)
Reproduced by kind permission of the British Library

our *Trees of Life*.'[60] The interest in the fertility of female bodies and any positive portrayals of women's sexuality in this text are framed by a desire to control this reproductive capacity in order to ensure the health of men's bodies and a sturdy, thriving nation. Fears of a threat to the nation and the declining quality and quantity of the population infuse these images of male genitalia.[61]

The premium placed on size, beauty and fertility, the ways in which these factors are sometimes connected, and their use in differentiating between male bodies are evident in the unfavour-able descriptions of old male bodies. The genitals of old men are invariably portrayed as unattractive, withered objects of ridicule. The electrical desire that provides the potency of male plants in *Teague-Root Display'd* is weak in older men:

> Old Men are but slightly agitated by it; that is, the Effects of the Electrical Fire does not meet in their Bodies with a sufficient Quantity of *Pabulum* to make the Flame conspicuous to any but themselves. . . . The Old ones take a vast Pleasure in being electrify'd; tho' their natural Fires which should embrace the magick spark, is quite exhausted.[62]

Flaccidity in old age is treated harshly in these texts, and efforts made to enhance the potency of older men are portrayed as desperate.[63] Preventing the attainment of size, beauty and fertility, this lack of mutability and erection undermines the status of these bodies, further reinforcing the majesty and reproductive capacity of younger, potent male bodies.

Certain male bodies – those with large, beautiful and fertile genitals – are valorised in eighteenth-century erotica and presented as ador-able objects of desire. These same factors are enlisted in a competit-ive system of comparisons along the axes of sex, place and age. Yet to objectify male bodies in this way was problematic in conventional eighteenth-century aesthetics. Here the beautiful was gendered as female: it was 'the gratifying object of desire, easy and pleasing to look at, readily appropriated and unthreatening'.[64] The sublime,

60. Ibid., p. 4.
61. It is significant that in this material, British men are often measured against the French. See Linda Colley's *Britons: Forging the Nation, 1707–1839* (1994), which explores how British people 'defined themselves against the French' (p. 5), and Arline Meyer, 'Re-dressing classical statuary: the eighteenth-century "hand-in-waistcoat" portrait', *Art Bulletin* LXXVII, 1 (1995), pp. 45–63.
62. *Teague-Root Display'd*, p. 21. See also *Arbor Vitae*, p. 4.
63. See *Teague-Root Display'd*, p. 22; *Arbor Vitae*, p. 4; and *Wisdom Revealed*, pp. 18–19.
64. Alex Potts, *Flesh and the Ideal: Winckelmann and the Origins of Art History* (New Haven and London, 1994), p. 115. Potts is providing a gloss on Burke's *A Philosophi-cal Enquiry in to the Origin of our Ideas of the Sublime and Beautiful* (1757).

on the other hand, was masculine: 'an image of power, of austere elevation, of something that resisted being appropriated to conventional forms of gratification and consumption'.[65] To show male bodies as anything other than sublime threatened to disrupt this system.

In eighteenth-century erotica, however, the difficulties of presenting male bodies as beautiful objects of desire were partly overcome by the inclusion of desiring women. The motif of women's insatiable desire ensures that male bodies appear to be revealed for the pleasure of women. This valorisation of male bodies through images of women's desire is clear in the use of women's senses to reveal desirable male bodies. The pagoda which acts as a symbol for the penis in *An Elegy on the Lamented Death of the Electrical Eel* is 'rais'd to allure the ladies' ravished sight', while the imaginary female reader of *Mimosa* is informed of the effect looking at the plant will have on her:

> You feel the *thrill* in every *part*;
> It sends the *tremor* to your heart.[66]

Women also derive great pleasure from touching male genitals. Electrical metaphors prove particularly suited to this theme: 'let one of the nicest Ladies take a Male-Root into her Hand, and she becomes instantly Electrical, and you may observe the quick and sudden Flashes of Electrical Fire dart from her Eyes'.[67] With the possibility of such a forceful impact, women are shown yearning to touch male genitals:

> Where is there one – not longs to feel,
> The vigour of th' electric Eel,
> T' extract the fire by touch?[68]

Such images do not strictly conform to the gendered distinctions of the beautiful and sublime, because male bodies are being viewed as gratifying objects. Yet the disruptive implications of this are muted. What emerges more clearly than the objectification of men is the de-humanising desires of women, while in the context of a male author and masculine readership, any suggestions of women actually appropriating the male body are undermined and shown to be a device strategically deployed by men.

Women's looks or touches, however, do not simply satiate women's desires. Crucially, the female senses of sight and touch

65. Ibid., p. 114.
66. *An Elegy on the Lamented Death of the Electrical Eel*, p. 8; *Mimosa*, p. 2.
67. *Teague-Root Display'd*, p. 18.   68. *The Electrical Eel*, p. 19.

elicit a metamorphosis of male genitalia.[69] The look of the female reader has considerable impact on the mimosa:

> Enamour'd of your melting eye,
> It grows more stiff, erect, and high,[70]

and it is Eve's stare which coaxes the electrical eel from the water:

> 'Til from the pond the lengthen'd Eel,
> Bewitch'd, began her pow'r to feel,
> And from the mud he grew.[71]

A woman's touch has a similar impact. When a male teague-root comes 'under the Electrical Influence of the Female', for example, it 'becomes as stiff as a Poker'.[72] In the same way, the efforts of women with regards to the mimosa 'rear this *plant* to an amazing height', while a lady handling the tree of life will cause it to grow:

> . . . twice as big, and twice as long,
> And more than twenty times as Strong.[73]

Women's looks or touches constitute the catalysts for the trans-formation of the penis into an aroused state, a state in which it is admired. Male bodies are presented as needing the attention of women, therefore, as much as women are portrayed as the lusty admirers of these bodies. This served to externalise the impetus for male desire, fastening responsibility firmly to women. Excessive desire in this period undermined manhood: temptations were located outside the male body and the charms of such temptations had to be repudiated.[74] Showing male bodies in states of arousal risked appearing to relinquish this restraint and self-control. In eighteenth-century erotica, the reason for their potentially effeminising aroused state was externalised, and embodied in other sexually insatiable characters, who were gendered as female.

Gendering narrators and readers of accounts of male bodies as female served a similar purpose. A sexual response to female

69. Similar claims are made regarding the role of female perception in male validation in the twentieth century. See Silverman, *Male Subjectivity*, p. 8; and Bordo, 'Reading the male body', p. 275.

70. *Mimosa*, p. 2.   71. *The Electrical Eel*, p. 6.

72. *Teague-Root Display'd*, p. 15.   73. *Mimosa*, p. iii; *Wisdom Revealed*, p. 12.

74. Alan Bray, 'To be a man in early modern society. The curious case of Michael Wigglesworth', *HWJ* 41 (Spring 1996), pp. 155–65; John Barrell, 'The dangerous goddess: masculinity, prestige and the aesthetic in early eighteenth-century Britain', in his *Birth of Pandora and the Division of Knowledge* (Basingstoke and London, 1992), p. 66.

bodies by men was often deemed reasonable in this period.[75] Yet women viewing male bodies as objects of desire was suspect.[76] A woman attending life classes to sketch male bodies, for example, was considered unacceptable, and a female artist would avoid the depiction of brawny, sexual, adult men.[77] In descriptions of the male form by travel writers and art critics in the eighteenth century, men had praised softer male bodies through the voices of imaginary women in order to 'keep imputations of effeminacy at bay'.[78] Similarly, women are often established as the privileged viewers of male bodies in erotica. The first line of the ode to the electrical eel ('Ye lovely maids, ye amorous dames, . . . Ye widows') imagines a fictional female readership; while the closing line of *Adam's Tail* ('Thus, Ladies! I have told my Story') serves to frame the descriptions of male genitals in the same way.[79] Finally, in another poem, the author refuses to show the tree to men, but comments that any lady who required further details 'may have the Experiment made familiar to her Senses, by applying to the Author, (who has never fail'd of giving satisfaction)'.[80] This female presence sanctioned the representation of male bodies in a variety of states. The transformation rendered on men by a woman's look or touch allowed the penis to be shown as a receptive, feeling organ capable of movement. If ladies approach male genitals in *Wisdom Revealed*, 'beneath her Hand they shrink and crouch'.[81] Echoing this, the mimosa possesses a 'remarkable property of *receding* from the touch, and giving *signs* as it were of *animal* life and *sensation*'; though, of course, just as it will 'feelingly *recede*', it will 'just as quickly *rise*'.[82] Differing considerably from the enormous, permanently erect penises that seem characteristic of pornography, and existing alongside the concern for size in this erotic material, such descriptions emphasise the changeability and receptivity of the mimosa, showing it to be a tender thing of feeling.[83]

75. Linda Walsh, '"Arms to be kissed a thousand times": reservations about lust in Diderot's art criticism', in Perry and Rossington, eds, *Femininity and Masculinity*, pp. 165, 170.

76. Chloe Chard, 'Effeminacy, pleasure and the classical body', in Perry and Rossington, eds, *Femininity and Masculinity*, p. 157; Wendy Wassyng Roworth, 'Anatomy is destiny: regarding the body in the art of Angelica Kauffman', in Perry and Rossington, eds, *Femininity and Masculinity*, pp. 43, 44, 50.

77. Ibid., p. 43.

78. Chard, 'Effeminacy, pleasure', p. 152; Potts, *Flesh and the Ideal*, p. 123.

79. *An Elegy on the Lamented Death of the Electrical Eel*, p. 1; *Adam's Tail*, p. 27.

80. *Wisdom Revealed*, p. i.   81. Ibid., p. 12.   82. *Mimosa*, pp. 1, 13.

83. Rachel Weil, '"Sometimes a sceptre is only a sceptre": pornography and politics in Restoration England', in Hunt, ed., *The Invention of Pornography*. Weil writes

These texts allowed men to look at sexually desirable male bodies, by placing these bodies in a strictly heterosexual context: male bodies were craved for by women, revealed only to women, and responded only to women. As Alan Bray's contribution to this volume suggests, this heterosexual backdrop was not necessary to expressions of close physical contact between men in an earlier period. Nevertheless, this eighteenth-century erotica remains firmly within a male homosocial context in which men could admire their own and other male bodies. And while there are images which might have worked to police male bodies, this material appears to have functioned as a space in which certain male bodies were unquestioningly validated, in guises of both erect completeness and sensitive receptivity. In the overwhelming stress on fertility and the state of the population, a degree of concern and anxiety can be detected. Yet these texts served to assuage and reassure men, as much as they gave men something to live up to. Indeed, just as these texts validated male bodies, it could be argued that the very act of reading these texts served to reinforce their readers' masculinity.

By the 1780s, a small group of elite men had become fascinated with the ancient rites and rituals in which Priapus – the God of fertility – was worshipped. In some ways, these erotic texts resemble this respectable, though contentious, interest more than they do pornography.[84] Lacking the repetitive and supposedly realistic depiction of the sex act that is generally regarded as defining pornography, their presentation of desirable male bodies was couched in a style we might call learned bawdiness. The use of metaphor and satire were combined with an obvious erotic element, to produce a genre in which sex was spoken of in a sometimes crude, sometimes humorous way, but always maintaining the appearance of restraint. One might argue, therefore, that these erotic texts served to buttress the reader's self-control, to confirm men's learning and wit, promising to titillate and to tease, rather than provoke them into careless, disruptive, de-masculinizing sexual abandon.

---

that this pornographic material is partly characterised by 'the huge and magnificent penises, the women literally dying to be penetrated, and, importantly, the equation of sex with power over and violence against women' (p. 31).

84. Rousseau, 'The sorrows of Priapus'; Francis Haskell, 'The Baron d'Hancarville: an adventurer and art historian in eighteenth-century Europe', in his *Past and Present in Art and Taste: Selected Essays* (New Haven and London, 1988); and Eugene Michael O'Connor, *Symbolum Salacitatis: A Study of the God Priapus as a Literary Character* (Frankfurt, 1989). The stress on fertility in the ancient poems remains crucial in the later material.

PART FIVE

Conclusion

The Old Adam and the New Man: Emerging Themes in the History of English Masculinities, 1750–1850[1]

JOHN TOSH

Historical work on English masculinities stands at something of a cross-roads. A small body of high-quality and varied work has been carried out, but with a very uncertain sense of how the field is constituted, and how these specialist contributions might inform our received readings of the past. This uncertainty is not, however, due to intellectual timidity, but stems rather from the nature of gender itself. Feminist scholarship has demonstrated beyond question that gender permeates all cultural and social forms and all human experience. As the implications of that proposition have been explored, so women's history has fragmented, undermining the confidence with which only a few years ago scholars invoked 'patriarchy' or 'difference' as comprehensive conceptual frameworks.[2] Masculinity, like femininity, is historically expressed in complex and confusing variety, with comparable dangers to conceptual coherence. But there is a further problem which applies to masculinity specifically. Because men have historically been dominant in the public sphere, masculinity carries public meanings of great political moment, in addition to its bearing on personal conduct and self-imagining. Whereas femininity has often been defined to exclude women from economic activities and civic responsibilities, representations of masculinity have necessarily straddled the public/private divide, covering the entire spectrum from men's domestic

1. I am grateful to Ludmilla Jordanova, Robert Shoemaker and the editors of this volume for their helpful suggestions on an earlier draft of this chapter.
2. For a review of the different directions in women's history, see K. Offen and R. Pierson, eds, *Writing Women's History: International Perspectives* (Basingstoke, 1991).

conduct at one extreme, to the manly virtues which should characterise the body politic at the other. In tackling the subject of
masculinity in such different ways, historians have shown no less
than a proper respect for its complexity – and its multiple points of
contact with the conventional content of their subject.

Recent work on the period 1750–1850 bears out this general
picture. 'Masculinity' stands for a bewildering diversity of approaches:
the gendering of public discourse about the state of the nation, the
marking of class difference, the experience of sexuality, the exercise of household authority, the rise of the work ethic, and so on.[3]
This diversity is, I repeat, necessary and welcome. But the point has
perhaps been reached when a broader synthesis can be attempted,
not least as a means of directing future work. The period 1750–
1850 is one which invites a thematic overview with particular insistence. At the level of popular stereotype, no greater contrast could
be imagined than that between the uninhibited 'Georgian' libertine
and his sober frock-coated 'Victorian' grandson; if only at the level
of social mores there are clearly significant changes to be explained.
More centrally, this period is the focus for historical debates about
the transition to modernity in England. Was there a shift in masculinity commensurate with the contemporary transformations in
economy and politics? Can we speak of a 'new man' to match a new
politics and a new kind of production? More broadly, we might
consider what light this period sheds on the relative autonomy of
gender in historical explanation. Were changes in the gender order
merely contingent on higher-level changes determined elsewhere?
Might it make more sense to conceive of gender as a structure of
practices and attitudes which was particularly *resistant* to change?

Hitherto the attempt to identify major changes in masculinity
during this period has followed one of two paths, with few signs of
convergence. The first treats changes in masculinity as in some way
related to changes in the class structure of England, in particular
the transition from a landed to a commercial society. It charts
the rise to ascendancy of a bourgeois masculinity which eclipsed –
without ever entirely displacing – its aristocratic predecessor. The
second path interprets masculinity in the context of a growing
polarisation of sexual difference, embracing body, mind, and the
gendering of social space. Science and the arts were at one in

---

3. Compare, for example, the deployment of masculinity in L. Davidoff and
C. Hall, *Family Fortunes: Men and Women of the English Middle Class, 1780–1850* (1987)
with K. Wilson, *The Sense of the People: Politics, Culture and Imperialism in England,
1715–1785* (Cambridge, 1995).

making the binary opposition between male and female a dominant idiom of culture, and this imposed new rigidities on the understanding of masculinity, as also of femininity. In this chapter I evaluate the claims of each of these perspectives to offer a viable history of masculinity. In each case I draw back from the more ambitious claims of transformative change advanced by some historians, while acknowledging that both perspectives address significant issues. I then turn to a third perspective, that of gender identity, which has been implicit rather than fully articulated in recent work. Here the key question is whether the period 1750–1850 marked a significant stage in the shift from masculinity as social reputation to masculinity as an interiorised sense of personal identity. Once again, the record turns out to be contradictory, indicating a greater scope for masculine individuality but not necessarily any greater freedom of choice in determining how that individuality should be defined. I conclude by suggesting that our historical understanding might be better served by recognising the relative impermeability and endurance of many structures of gender, instead of expecting (or hoping) to bring to light dramatic trajectories of social transformation.

Analysing masculinity through the lens of class is much the most established approach. The grand theme here is the transition from a genteel masculinity grounded in land ownership to a bourgeois masculinity attuned to the market. The new commercial society was made possible by, and in turn reinforced, a new manhood. The man of substance and repute came to be someone who had a steady occupation in business or the professions, instead of receiving rents or trading in stocks. In its most schematic form – in the writings of the sociologist R.W. Connell for instance – the change is from personal to bureaucratic authority, from sociability to domesticity, and from sexual license to respectability.[4] In essentials this is the framework of the most significant analysis of masculinity to date, Leonore Davidoff and Catherine Hall's *Family Fortunes.* Their book is certainly not schematic or unduly linear – indeed much of its strength lies in its close attention to occupational and religious variation; but this very diversity on the ground serves only to throw into relief the two key elements of the new masculinity: the elevation of work as a 'calling', and the moralising of home as the focus

4. R.W. Connell, 'The big picture: masculinities in recent world history', *Theory & Society* 22 (1993), pp. 597–623. See also his *Masculinities* (Oxford, 1995), pp. 191–203.

of men's non-working lives.[5] These were the constituents of an integrated gender code: domestic steadiness was conducive to success in business, while the rigours of bread-winning were rewarded by the comforts of home. The bourgeois character of this new configuration is neatly illustrated by the history of the term 'effeminacy'. In the eighteenth century one of the give-away symptoms of this condition was 'luxury' – the unbridled desire to acquire and spend; by 1850 this meaning of effeminacy had disappeared, suggesting a much easier relationship between normative masculinity and the values of commercial society.[6] According to this account, by the mid-nineteenth century, middle-class masculinity was firmly in the ascendant. The expansive sociability, luxury and sexual laxity associated with the aristocracy had become a vestige of the past, as more and more men from the landed classes conformed to the new pattern.

Lower down the social scale a comparable process is suggested by the much smaller corpus of work which has attended to the masculinity of the labouring classes. Anna Clark has shown how in London around the turn of century artisan culture was focused on the workshop and the tavern, at the expense of home and neighbourhood. Journeymen whose attainment of full masterhood was blocked by the conditions of trade continued to affect a bachelor style of life, including heavy convivial drinking, well after marriage. By the 1840s, however, artisan culture was well on the way to transforming itself 'from drunken misogyny to respectable patriarchy'. The 'moral force' wing of the Chartist movement staked the working man's claim to the vote on his sober and self-controlled domesticity. This reflected not only conditions in London, but the pattern of working-class masculinity in the mill towns of Lancashire where the responsibilities of bread-winner were reflected in a high value on marriage and a demand for the 'family wage'. By 1850 the lineaments of a 'mature' (i.e. modern) working class were discernible. The growing gulf between working men who subscribed to domesticity and those who continued to adhere to what Clark calls 'pugilist and pub culture' anticipated the great Victorian divide between 'respectable' and 'rough'.[7]

5. Davidoff and Hall, *Family Fortunes*. The phrase 'new men' appears from time to time, e.g. p. 113.

6. J. Barrell, *The Birth of Pandora and the Division of Knowledge* (1992), pp. 64–5; M. Cohen, *Fashioning Masculinity: National Identity and Language in the Eighteenth Century* (1996).

7. A. Clark, *The Struggle for the Breeches* (Berkeley CA, 1995), pp. 25–34, 271. See also M. Anderson, *Family Structure in Nineteenth-Century Lancashire* (Cambridge, 1971).

Would that things were quite so simple. The application of a class analysis to the history of masculinity during this period looks much less secure today than it did ten years ago. The fit between class and gender is more awkward. For a start, the 1780s seem somewhat less significant as a turning-point in the rise of bourgeois masculinity. Dutiful attention to business and a prioritisation of home pursuits had been the standard – and in many cases the practice – of men of the middling sort since the early eighteenth century. Margaret Hunt shows how domesticity was favoured by these men not so much from home-loving sentiment, as from a hard-headed awareness of the danger which the pleasures of the town posed to credit and reputation; 'rational domesticity' embodied many of the values which the Evangelicals would claim as their own a hundred years later.[8] As for the eighteenth-century gentry, Anthony Fletcher has reminded us that they were hardly the bearers of a uniform masculinity: at one extreme stood the boorish homosociality of the hunting squire; at the other the civility of the refined gentleman bent on improving his mind and his land.[9] This latter group has been the subject of an illuminating case study by Amanda Vickery. She demonstrates how in north-east Lancashire around the end of the century gender distinctions between commercial and landed families were less striking than their common attachment to domestic comfort, field sports and public service.[10] Revisionist work on the nineteenth century has also complicated the picture. Dror Wahrman, for example, has shown how in the 1820s the middle class had no monopoly of family values; the agitation on behalf of Queen Caroline traded on a popular equation of manliness with chivalry towards the 'weaker' sex, rather than a specifically middle-class sense of affronted propriety. Finally, the contrast between gentle and bourgeois modes of masculinity needs to be tempered by a recognition of the continuities between them, most notably the ethic of public service; as Stefan Collini points out, the Victorian elite's cult of 'character' stood in the eighteenth-century tradition of civic virtue.[11]

8. M. Hunt, *The Middling Sort: Commerce, Gender, and the Family in England, 1680–1780* (Berkeley CA, 1996).

9. A. Fletcher, *Gender, Sex and Subordination in England, 1500–1800* (1995), pp. 325–9.

10. A. Vickery, 'Women of the local elite in Lancashire, 1750–1825' (Ph.D. thesis, University of London, 1991).

11. D. Wahrman, '"Middle-class" domesticity goes public: gender, class and politics from Queen Caroline to Queen Victoria', *JBS* 32 (1993), pp. 396–432; S. Collini, *Public Moralists: Political Thought and Intellectual Life in Britain, 1850–1920* (Oxford, 1991), ch. 3.

To say the picture has been over-simplified, however, does not mean that it is wrong. After *Family Fortunes* it is hard to deny that the maturing of the English middle class was a gendered process, in the sense of having been deeply conditioned by the structure of relations between men and women. Equally, the shift in the class alignment of the British elite between 1750 and 1850 caused the definition of masculinity to be understood in new ways. One which has been sadly neglected is the decline of bearing arms as a core attribute of masculinity. Along with the exercise of household authority, the bearing of arms had been the central attribute of manhood since feudal times. Military manliness was still at a premium during the Napoleonic Wars, but it rapidly lost ground after 1815.[12] With the abandonment of the duel, the growing professionalisation of the armed forces, and the reform of policing, the exercise of violence became specialised: as Connell puts it, 'Mr Gladstone did not fight duels, nor lead armies'.[13] The increasing popularity of fox-hunting among businessmen and professionals during the Victorian period qualifies the picture somewhat, particularly if we take seriously the argument – put forward by military men of the time – that riding to hounds was a preparation for a 'real' cavalry charge. But compared with fighting, hunting was a very inferior test of manhood: 'all the excitement of war with only half its danger', as the hunting journalist R.S. Surtees conceded.[14] The dominant forms of masculinity were becoming increasingly detached from military training and from the expectation of taking up arms. This is borne out by the vogue for medieval chivalry which, far from socialising men to military ways, displaced valour and danger into a safe haven of agreeable fantasy.[15] The decline of arms as a facet of masculinity bears the unmistakeable imprint of bourgeois values in the ascendant. It also depended on the unusually long period of peace between Waterloo and the Crimea. Notions of the heroic had to be adjusted accordingly. In Thomas Carlyle's immensely influential lectures *On Heroes* (1840) hardly any space was given to martial valour – the honours went to the man of letters, the prophet and the statesman. The first military figure to seize the public imagination since Wellington was Sir Henry Havelock of Indian Mutiny fame, and the impact of the new masculinity is clear; the public was moved as

12. L. Colley, *Britons: Forging the Nation, 1707–1837* (1992), pp. 178, 193.
13. Connell, 'The big picture', p. 609. On the end of duelling, see D.T. Andrew, 'The code of honour and its critics: the opposition to duelling in England, 1700–1850', *SH* 5 (1980), pp. 409–34.
14. Colley, *Britons*, p. 172; R.S. Surtees, quoted in Davidoff and Hall, *Family Fortunes*, p. 406.
15. M. Girouard, *The Return to Camelot: Chivalry and the English Gentleman* (1981).

much by the edifying spectacle of an elderly man returning to duty in order to support wife and children, as by the race to relieve Lucknow.[16] Behind this re-definition of the heroic lies a shift in men's attitudes to weapons and combat which merits much closer attention.

On its own terms, then, the historiography I have been describing so far has much to commend it. But I have a more fundamental unease about it. In the last resort what it does is to present the gendered dimensions of a transition whose logic is determined elsewhere – in the economy, in elite politics, in religion. This is certainly much to be preferred to a reading of the past which is wholly innocent of gender. But is gender in the last analysis superstructural and epiphenomenal? Possibly it is, but if so the proposition must be subject to much more rigorous testing. In particular we need to consider very carefully those facets of masculinity which did *not* significantly change during the transition to bourgeois ascendancy. There were important aspects of gender which proved impermeable to the play of class politics at this time.

Take, first, the issue of household authority. The married state called for the exercise of what Boswell called 'manly firmness'.[17] Like the bearing of arms, this had been a touchstone of masculinity throughout Western history, but unlike the bearing of arms it remained fairly resilient during this period. Adult gender identity for men involved forming a household, maintaining it, protecting it, and controlling it. As a socially validated status, masculinity depended on these attributes as strongly as ever. New patterns of work and leisure changed the context, but not the fundamental requirement. The theory of middle-class domesticity might be based on marital harmony achieved through complementary roles, but the reality had to take account of men's continuing insistence on mastery in the home. The courts were shocked by cases in which an angry husband usurped his wife's control over children and servants or threatened her with violence. But these cases were only the tip of the iceberg. As A. James Hammerton suggests, the conventions of domesticity imposed strains on masculine self-esteem which, if anything, increased rather than diminished the incidence of household tyranny.[18] Enough work has now been done on domestic violence at various periods between the late seventeenth and the

16. G. Dawson, *Soldier Heroes: British Adventure, Empire and the Imagining of Masculinities* (1994), pp. 134–44.

17. J. Bailey, ed., *The Shorter Boswell* (1925), p. 26.

18. A.J. Hammerton, *Cruelty and Companionship: Conflict in Nineteenth-Century Married Life* (1992), chs 3 and 4.

mid-nineteenth centuries to point to some very enduring continuities.[19] Through the shifting relationship between class and gender
during this period, masculinity remained deeply wedded to the
exercise of private patriarchy.

My second instance of enduring masculinity is the sexual *rite
de passage* of young men on the threshold of manhood. In terms of
peer-group standing this was no less a badge of masculine status
than the household headship which was meant to follow a few years
later. In the mid-eighteenth century it would seem that sowing wild
oats was often commended not only by a well-born young man's
companions, but by his parents also.[20] The life of the libertine was
grounded in the first instance in a period of youthful sexual experimentation which was widely condoned. The standards of nineteenth-
century bourgeois masculinity were much less accommodating, but
their impact on the conduct of the young needs to be questioned.
By the 1850s libertinage had long ceased to be a culturally validated lifestyle, yet many of its governing assumptions still prevailed
among young men. Except for those from devout families, they
were under pressure to lose their virginity, and repeated 'conquests'
were a form of display intended to impress other males. This is
the main explanation for the vast scale of Victorian prostitution,
whose clients encompassed every variant of bachelorhood from the
common soldier living in barracks to the well-heeled bourgeois
awaiting the means to marry in style.[21] (The cheating husband
was less to the fore than his posthumous notoriety suggests.) Repeated appeals to young men to turn to religion, to study, to sport,
to business advancement, to 'manly science'[22] – in short to anything
which distracted them from vice – testify to the undiminished
appeal of the 'gay life'. In 1848 Ralph Waldo Emerson was shocked
to hear Dickens and Carlyle accept as a matter of course the lack
of chastity in England's young men; Dickens went so far as to express fears for the health of a young man who remained chaste.[23]

19. E. Foyster, 'Male honour, social control and wife-beating in late Stuart
England', *TRHS* 6th ser., VI (1996), pp. 215–24; M. Hunt, 'Wife-beating, domesticity
and women's independence in eighteenth-centry London', *G&H* 4 (1992), pp. 10–
33; Clark, *Struggle for the Breeches*; Hammerton, *Cruelty and Companionship*.

20. Fletcher, *Gender, Sex and Subordination*, pp. 342–6.

21. I explore the relationship between prostitution and bachelorhood at greater
length in ch. 6 of my forthcoming book, *A Man's Place: Masculinity and the Middle-
Class Home in Victorian England* (London and New Haven, 1999).

22. A. Thackray, 'Natural knowledge in cultural context: the Manchester model',
American Historical Review 79 (1974), p. 690.

23. *Journals and Miscellaneous Notebooks of Ralph Waldo Emerson*, vol. 10 (Cambridge
MA, 1973), pp. 50–1.

This time-honoured feature of apprentice manhood was certainly proof against the morally challenging discourse of middle-class masculinity.[24]

Both these features of what might be called resilient masculinity were, of course, fundamentally to do with the assertion of men's power over women. Sexual mastery and household authority are surely at the very heart of face-to-face patriarchy. Their persistence prompts the reflection that recent historians may have over-played the idea of masculinity as a variable discursive construction. The alternative is not an essentialist conception of sexual difference, but a recognition that some of the salient structures of gender are grounded in social arrangements and psychic needs which are particularly resilient: they are of course subject to change and modification, but on a time-scale which may not relate very closely to other historical trajectories. This is where Connell has made perhaps his most original contribution. The phrase 'hegemonic masculinity' is sometimes used to refer to the prescribed masculine attributes of whichever class happens to be dominant at a given time. Connell deploys the term in a more pointed way to highlight the reach and durability of the gender order. 'Hegemonic masculinity' in his account denotes those masculine attributes which serve to sustain men's power over women in society as a whole; and a vital measure of their success is that they elicit support and conformity regardless of economic or political status.[25] Household authority and sexual predation were in this sense facets of hegemonic masculinity, and they persisted through substantial changes in the class formation between 1750 and 1850. The work of Antony Simpson and Anna Clark shows how both these features loomed large in the masculinity of the labouring classes throughout the period. As regards the dominant masculinities of late Georgian and early Victorian England, we need to balance the implications for change of the new class order against those traditional attributes of masculinity which remained in essentials unchanged.[26]

24. Cf. L. Roper, 'Blood and cod-pieces', in her *Oedipus and the Devil* (1994), ch. 5.

25. R.W. Connell, *Gender and Power* (Oxford, 1987), pp. 183–8. See also J. Tosh, 'What should historians do with masculinity? Reflections on nineteenth-century Britain', *HWJ* 38 (1994), pp. 191–2. Connell's concept of 'hegemonic masculinity' is also very illuminating with regard to the relationship between dominant and subordinate masculinities.

26. A. Simpson, 'Masculinity and control: the prosecution of sex offenses in eighteenth-century London' (Ph.D. thesis, New York University, 1984); Clark, *Struggle for the Breeches*.

Alongside the convergence of class and gender has developed a second broad strand of work on masculinity which places sexual difference at the heart of its analysis. There are three elements here. First, the emergence of a stable sexed opposition between the male and the female body, in place of a traditional Galenic continuum in which men's bodies were superior to, but not radically different from, those of women. Thomas Laqueur has been criticised for locating the transition from what he calls a 'one-sex' to a 'two-sex' model in the late eighteenth century, instead of taking account of the gradual undermining of the Galenic model over the previous 200 years.[27] Yet Laqueur's chronology is apt, for the full implications of the revolution in anatomical knowledge were not registered until after 1750. Only then did the complementary notions of female sexual passivity and an all-powerful male libido become the received wisdom of educated society.[28] The intellectual victory of the two-sex model may have arisen from a need to redefine woman as fundamentally different, but the consequences were certainly not confined to women. The stage was set for men to locate the sexual energy required for both pleasure and procreation primarily in themselves, not only by demeaning the sexuality of women, but by prioritising penetrative sex, and (less certainly) by increasing still further the odium attached to homosexual acts.[29] It was an appropriation which would become increasingly burdensome to men as sexuality itself became pathologised during the Victorian period.

The second dimension of the polarising tendency, closely related to the first, concerned sexual character. With the two-sex model came an increasingly dichotomised notion of mind and temperament. For men this meant an intensified emphasis on rationality as against emotionality, energy rather than repose, constancy instead of variability, action instead of passivity, and taciturnity rather than talkativeness. In the light of this changed character alignment, several male activities had to be reassessed. The sedentary profession

---

27. T. Laqueur, *Making Sex: Body and Gender from the Greeks to Freud* (Cambridge MA, 1990); Fletcher, *Gender, Sex and Subordination*, pp. 34–43.

28. Interestingly, Trumbach points out that after 1750 men were no longer arrested for consorting with prostitutes; the implication is that men were considered less responsible for their sexual urges. R. Trumbach, 'Sex, gender and sexual identity in modern culture: male sodomy and female prostitution in Enlightenment London', *JHS* 2 (1991), p. 195.

29. T. Hitchcock, *English Sexualities, 1700–1800* (Basingstoke, 1997); Simpson, 'Masculinity and control'.

of letters was one; the libertine style of life was another.[30] Of much wider relevance, and very little discussed so far, was the role of father. Here the traditional masculine concern with instruction and discipline had to be balanced against the tendency of the new sexual economy to concentrate all nurturing qualities in the mother.[31] Underlying these dichotomies was a conviction of essential difference which structured the sexed mind as well as the sexed body.[32] As Mary Wollstonecraft complained, the writers of her day maintained that 'the sexes ought not to be compared' on the grounds that men were superior to women 'not in degree, but in essence'.[33] And if men were marked off by natural difference from women, it followed that their manliness was more secure – which helps to explain why the discourse of effeminacy was so much less prominent in the nineteenth century than the eighteenth.[34]

This framework has the great advantage of foregrounding the relational aspect of gender: within an insistent metaphor of polarisation, masculinity can only be understood in relation to its 'other', and during this period the feminine became a much more pervasive 'other' than the child, the slave or the savage, each of which provided alternative reverse images of man. But while the conceptual implications of the 'two-sex' model continue to fascinate historians, it is worth pausing to ask whether sexual polarisation was anything more than a discursive trope. Did it reflect the reality of relations between men and women? This question is particularly insistent when we turn to the third dimension of polarisation, the development of separate spheres. The possibility that everyday social behaviour reflected new and fundamental beliefs about sexual difference has a tempting symmetry about it. But on closer inspection this is no more convincing than the assumed convergence of gender and class, with which I began. Recent critiques by Amanda Vickery and Robert Shoemaker have focused mainly on the inconsistency

30. N. Clarke, 'Strenuous idleness: Thomas Carlyle and the man of letters as hero', in M. Roper and J. Tosh, eds, *Manful Assertions: Masculinities in Britain Since 1800* (1991); A. Clark, *Women's Silence, Men's Violence: Sexual Assault in England, 1770–1845* (1987).

31. For a beginning, see J. Tosh, 'Authority and nurture in middle-class fatherhood: the case of early and mid Victorian England', *G&H* 8 (1996), pp. 48–64.

32. Fletcher, *Gender, Sex and Subordination*, pp. 390–400; Cohen, *Fashioning Masculinity*, pp. 79–83.

33. Mary Wollstonecraft, *A Vindication of the Rights of Woman*, ed. C.H. Poston (New York, 1988), p. 63.

34. For eighteenth-century effeminacy, see C.D. Williams, *Pope, Homer and Manliness* (1993), and Wilson, *Sense of the People*, pp. 185–205.

between separate spheres ideology and the roles actually performed in public by middle-class women. Indeed it may be that the incessant flow of prescriptive texts on this subject was designed (vainly) to draw women back into the home.[35]

But the really interesting questions about separate spheres concern men. This is because the relationship between domesticity and masculinity has always been so ambiguous. A fine balancing of advantages and drawbacks recurs again and again in prescriptive accounts of men in the home from the early eighteenth century through to the late nineteenth, pointing to a real conflict of interests. In Margaret Hunt's recent account, domesticity among the eighteenth-century middling sort held out the prospect of comfort (dependent of course on attentive service), economy (as against the sometimes crippling cost of male conviviality), and respectability (especially as regards sexual reputation); 'rational domesticity' of this type was conducive to what Hunt calls the 'almost inhuman level of self-discipline' needed for success in the high-risk conditions of early capitalism.[36] It is also worth pointing out that the practice of domesticity by fathers served to moderate the fear that sons brought up in a feminine setting would prove deficient in manliness later in life.[37] All these arguments in favour of domesticity were recognised well before turn-of-the-century Evangelicalism raised the profile of home as a moral refuge from the contamination of city life. The contrary arguments were fewer perhaps, but they were weighty. The danger of domesticity to true manliness applied not just to sons, but to the head of the household himself; the man who spent too much time in the company of wife and daughters might become effeminised, at the expense of both his manly vigour and his familial authority.[38] Furthermore, as we have seen, in real life male domesticity was often a recipe for marital conflict, since the husband who was constantly at home was more likely to impose himself in matters of domestic management and thus to antagonise his wife.

Above all, the home-loving man was losing out on all-male conviviality – both its social pleasures and the business contacts which

---

35. A. Vickery, 'Golden age to separate spheres?: a review of the categories and chronology of English women's history', *HJ* 36 (1993), pp. 383–414; R.W. Shoemaker, *Gender in English Society, 1650–1850: The Emergence of Separate Spheres?* (1998).

36. Hunt, *Middling Sort*, pp. 202, 217.

37. See Williams, *Pope, Homer and Manliness*, p. 33.

38. M. Hunt, 'English urban families in trade, 1660–1800' (Ph.D. thesis, New York University, 1986), p. 250; Williams, *Pope, Homer and Manliness*, pp. 36–8, 94.

it often oiled. Leonore Davidoff has recently commented that 'domesticity', unlike so many key-words, has no conceptual 'other'.[39] In broad terms this is correct, but from men's perspective there *is* a binary opposite – the somewhat infelicitous neologism 'homo-sociality'. ('Fraternalism' is an older and more attractive term, but it is best reserved for more institutionalised forms of male associa-tion based on an ideology of brotherhood.[40]) Passing time with male companions was the traditional leisure occupation of men at all levels of society, whether in the informal conviviality of an alehouse or in more elaborate craft associations and fraternities. This reflected the central role of peer approval in confirming mascu-line status, as well as the need for support networks for men who were seeking to survive and prosper in business or employment. The conflict between homosocial activities and the claims of home and family provided one of the staple themes of didactic writers from the mid-eighteenth century until the High Victorian period.[41] The era of domesticity did not of course sweep away these homo-social underpinnings, but it did necessitate some careful balancing. Henry Fox, we are told, dealt with the potential conflict by trans-planting his club to his house, where he regularly entertained his cronies despite the intermittent jealousy of his wife.[42] One can see a scaled-down version of this procedure in the dining practices of wealthy bourgeois in the late eighteenth century. In urban Scot-land, according to Stana Nenadic, the expensive mahogany dining-table made its appearance at this time, as middle-class men displayed their wealth and hospitality to their business associates, but in the early nineteenth century this was superseded by mixed-sex dining.[43]

The truth was that for men domesticity and homosociality were inherently in a state of tension, because they answered to different needs. It is a misreading of 'separate spheres' to see this situation as aberrant. Between 1750 and 1850 home and public space were subject to progressively sharper differentiation. The term 'separate spheres' is a convenient recognition of this trend, fully supported by the contemporary sense that the home was unique and indispens-able. But this should not be allowed to prejudge the gender issue.

39. L. Davidoff, *Worlds Between: Historical Perspectives on Gender and Class* (Cam-bridge, 1995), p. 228.

40. M.A. Clawson, 'Early modern fraternalism and the patriarchal family', *Feminist Studies* 6 (1980), pp. 368–91.

41. Tosh, *A Man's Place*, chs 2 and 6.

42. S. Tillyard, *Aristocrats* (1995), pp. 32–3.

43. S. Nenadic, 'Middle-rank consumers and domestic culture in Edinburgh and Glasgow, 1720–1840', *P&P* 145 (1994), pp. 122–54.

How much time, and of what quality, men spent in the home is a separate question, not to be answered by collapsing separate spheres with gender polarisation. At one extreme stood the middle-class suburbanite who needed reminding that public duty might from time to time require him to forsake his creature comforts.[44] If any-one lived out the dictates of 'separate spheres', it was the London journeymen at the other end of the spectrum; denied their due as masters, these artisans married just the same, but continued to act as if they were still bachelors, according to a fraternal ethos of drunken misogyny which kept them out of the home most of the time.[45] In between came the affluent public-spirited men of the established middle-class – the ones who loom so large in the historiography of the Victorian bourgeoisie.[46] These men acknow-ledged the claims of both home and associational life. This double call certainly exposed them to competing demands on their time, but we are imposing an artificial contradiction if we suppose that it also transgressed an accepted principle of 'separate spheres'. The point is rather that men operated at will in *both* spheres; that was their privilege.

The third strand of my agenda is much less securely rooted in the current historiography. Issues to do with identity have attracted comparatively little attention from scholars, despite their central place in writing about contemporary masculinity.[47] Much of the best work on masculinity in our period has treated it primarily as a public discourse – a metaphor for the nation's virility in the case of the eighteenth century, and a set of prescriptions for the virtuous and profitable life in the nineteenth century. There has been much less interest in the terms on which individual men internalised the discourse. All that can be said with confidence is that a fundamental shift occurred between the seventeenth and twentieth centuries. In the sixteenth and seventeenth centuries masculinity was regarded as a matter of reputation; it had first to be earned from one's peers and then guarded jealously against defamation, in court or in com-bat. Domestic disorder, which later generations would regard as a personal predicament, was then seen as a serious blow to a man's

---

44. For an attack on this lifestyle, see John Angell James, *The Family Monitor, or a Help to Domestic Happiness* (Birmingham, 1828), p. 22.

45. Clark, *Struggle for the Breeches*, pp. 25–34.

46. R.J. Morris, *Class, Sect and Party: The Making of the British Middle Class, 1820–1850* (Manchester, 1990); H.L. Malchow, *Gentlemen Capitalists: The Social and Political World of the Victorian Businessman* (1991).

47. A good example is R. Chapman and J. Rutherford, eds, *Male Order* (1988).

standing in the community.[48] In the twentieth century, by contrast, masculinity has come to be experienced as an aspect of subjectivity, sensitive to social codes no doubt, but rooted in the individual's interiority; an 'insecure' masculinity is one which is assailed by inner doubt (particularly about sexuality) rather than by threats and aspersions from other men. These issues have been placed on the agenda by Anthony Fletcher, but very little work has been done.[49] We know little about the pace and timing of this change in the nature of gender identity. Does the apparent lack of pricliness in matters of honour on the part of the Victorians mean that their masculinity was more securely anchored within than that of their Georgian forebears? Was the period 1750–1850, so crucial for the development of class identities, also critical in the gradual transition from masculinity as reputation to masculinity as interiority?

The evidence of language should obviously not be ignored, but it offers no easy answers. It so happens that the word 'masculinity' itself entered the English language in the middle of the eighteenth century. But the term implied none of the interiority which is so strongly indicated today.[50] According to the *OED*, 'masculinity' was an importation from France, and its primary meaning was gender privilege, as in matters of inheritance. My impression is that the word was little used until the late nineteenth century.[51] Prior to the twentieth century, the only abstract nouns which did duty for masculinity were the traditional ones of 'manhood' and 'manliness'. From the perspective of gender identities, these are perplexing terms. Both of them – and particularly 'manliness' – embraced moral or cultural as well as physical facets of being a man: courage as well as virility (or 'vigour'), for example. The adjectival form 'manly' was used interchangeably with 'masculine', and with the same duality.[52]

This ambiguity reflects an important truth about early modern England. Reputation and honour may have been the measure of all things, but they did not rest on behaviour and appearance alone. They depended on the solid inner qualities which were always implicit in 'manliness', such as courage, resolution and tenacity. Ambiguities in the language reinforced this: not only manliness itself, but unequivocally physical labels like 'sturdy', and 'robust'

---

48. The most comprehensive recent discussion is Fletcher, *Gender, Sex and Subordination*, chs 8–11.

49. Ibid., pp. 322–3.   50. Here I differ from Fletcher. Ibid., p. 322.

51. For a corresponding observation with regard to the USA, see G. Bederman, *Manliness and Civilization* (Chicago IL, 1995), pp. 17–19.

52. *OED*, entries for 'masculinity', 'manliness', 'manhood', 'manly' and 'masculine'.

acquired moral dimensions. It was the consistent aim of boys' education to internalise these moral qualities – to make them second nature so that they could be expressed in action instinctively and convincingly. Virtue was held to be inseparable from manliness.[53] The same applied to the code of civility which became dominant among gentlemen during the eighteenth century. For all the stress on social accomplishments, civility was widely recognised to depend on an inner moral sense.[54] Taciturnity, as Michèle Cohen shows, was increasingly valued as a pointer to the gentleman's 'self-discipline and his strength'.[55] In the last analysis honour and reputation were worthless without virtue and wisdom.

However, respect for inner qualities is not the same as interiority. Modern notions of masculinity (and femininity also) emphasise the inner consciousness of the individual. Masculinity may be culturally determined, in the sense of featuring only a limited repertoire of traits, but it is also understood to be an expression of the self, and up to a point a matter of individual choice, tormenting or liberating as the case may be. Authenticity is the exacting standard by which contemporary gender identities are judged. In the eighteenth century, on the other hand, the most authoritative forms of manliness and civility demanded the *repression* of the self.[56] The indulgence of the self which characterised so much youthful behaviour was seen as a passing phase, brought to a close when reason and intellect prevailed over impulse. Again and again control of the passions, restraint of the appetites and moderation in sex were emphasised. A man who would have authority over others must first master himself. The charge of effeminacy was laid against the man who relaxed all restraint and surrendered to his every desire.[57] Individual men certainly faced a choice, but it was cast in the stark binary form of manliness against effeminacy, self-indulgence against self-discipline – or vice against virtue, as in the Choice of Hercules, a popular theme in the visual arts of the period.[58] The only context

53. Fletcher, *Gender, Sex and Subordination*, ch. 15; G.C. Brauer, *The Education of a Gentleman* (New York, 1959).

54. Fletcher, *Gender, Sex and Subordination*, pp. 332–5. See also Cohen, *Fashioning Masculinity*, pp. 55–6.

55. Ibid., pp. 104–5.

56. The vogue for 'sensibility' among educated men around mid-century certainly validated a less severe code of living, but how far its influence extended from literary convention into social behaviour is far from clear.

57. Fletcher, *Gender, Sex and Subordination*, p. 411; D. Donald, *The Age of Caricature: Satirical Prints in the Age of George III* (1996), p. 81.

58. R. Paulson, *Emblem and Expression: Meaning in English Art of the Eighteenth Century* (1975), pp. 38–40, 73; Barrell, *Birth of Pandora*, pp. 65–6. Cf. P.J. Greven, *The Protestant Temperament* (New York, 1977), pp. 243–50.

in which something like a choice of identity was on offer was the molly-house homosexual sub-culture of the metropolis, with its own spaces, its own argot and its own dress-codes. While the molly-house presents some fascinating anticipations of modern sexual identity,[59] it seems to have been wholly exceptional, and it cannot be taken to signify that sexuality was widely understood to be the core of a man's identity: that proposition was probably entertained only in the literary circles influenced by Rousseau and other advanced thinkers.[60] Rank, marital status and honour were more significant than sexuality, and each of them was firmly rooted in external circumstance and social standing.

By the end of the period the traditional manifestations of the code of honour were in decline. In the upper levels of society duel-ling had virtually disappeared by the 1840s; and its plebeian equival-ent of fist-fighting was also less common than it had been.[61] The curtailment of interpersonal violence was part of a broader reform of manners for which the Evangelicals claimed most of the credit. Since the Evangelicals also had an articulate sense of the values they wished to see prevail in the place of honour, their programme is particularly relevant here. Manliness in its popular form was high on their hit-list of corrupt practices. From the Evangelical perspect-ive, the fatal flaw in traditional manliness was that it was built on the chimera of reputation; the world which judged a man's actions was not imbued with virtue and refinement, as the exponents of civility complacently assumed, but was mired in vice and hypocrisy. In place of reputation, the Evangelicals elevated *character* – by which they meant the inner resources of heart and mind transformed by God's saving grace. Instead of being guided by the opinion of others, the serious Christian was urged to listen only to the inward monitor of conscience, and to appear to the world as he really was. If this gave him authority, it was genuine authority from within, instead of the counterfeit currency of reputation. 'Manliness is superiority and power certainly', conceded Isaac Taylor in 1820, 'but it is power and superiority of character, not of vociferation.'[62] All this could only be achieved by means of unremitting self-scrutiny through

59. A. Bray, *Homosexuality in Renaissance England*, revised edn (1995); R. Norton, *Mother Clap's Molly House* (1992).
60. For a less conservative interpretation, see L. Jordanova, *Sexual Visions* (Hemel Hempstead, 1989), p. 12.
61. A. Clark, 'The rhetoric of Chartist domesticity', *JBS* 31 (1992), pp. 62–88, and *Struggle for the Breeches*.
62. Isaac Taylor, *Advice to the Teens: or Practical Helps Towards the Formation of One's Own Character*, 3rd edn (1820), p. 93.

private prayer and contemplation. The inner man was represented as in constant struggle with the world and its expectations.[63]

One of the most significant expressions of the Evangelical sense of self was the moralising of work. Traditionally work had very demeaning associations: it implied burdensome toil, or a servile dependence on patronage (as in 'place' or 'situation'). The new social morality emphasised 'independence'; that is, the autonomy which came from running one's own business, practising a profession, or (more tenuously) marketing a hard-won skill. Here Evangelical morality converged with the requirements of political economy which attributed economic vitality to the self-motivated, rational, independent actor. Work was now re-defined as 'occupation' and – even more pointedly – as 'calling'. Entrepreneurs (no less than clergy) believed that they laboured under the direction of Divine Providence. The Bradford wool-comber Isaac Holden thought of himself first and foremost as a 'Man of Business', a phrase which implied a sanctified vocation and not merely knowledge of the mundane expedients required to run a mill. As the stormy history of his marriage shows, Holden's masculine self was in the last analysis constructed by his work, rather than his family or his Methodist faith.[64] The dignifying of occupation within an Evangelical worldview was surely the starting-point for the modern secular notion that a man's masculinity is vested in his working identity.[65]

Yet there were severe limits to the Evangelicals' respect for the masculine self. It is certainly true that they cultivated a greater awareness of the self than anyone else, but the desired outcome was not self-expression, but a repression of the self far more severe than anything laid down by the gentlemanly code of restraint. For the Evangelical, the self was the seat of all impure thoughts and vain ambitions; he was in a state of war with his inner impulses. Nowhere was this conflict more keenly felt than with regard to sexuality. The mores of the libertine were of course shunned, but so too was the sexual latitude permitted under the code of civility. Evangelicals were expected to marry, lifelong celibacy being regarded as popish deviance; but no experimentation and no deviation from the heterosexual norm were countenanced. Sexuality was a perilous impulse to be curbed – a burden, not a form of self-expression.

63. For the place of character and reputation in Evangelical thinking, see M. Morgan, *Manners, Morals and Class in England, 1774–1858* (1994), pp. 63–71, 100–3, 107–8.
64. J. Tosh, 'From Keighley to St-Denis: separation and intimacy in Victorian bourgeois marriage', *HWJ* 40 (1995), pp. 193–206.
65. Davidoff and Hall, *Family Fortunes*, pp. 229–34.

Nor did Evangelicalism set much of a premium on individual choice. Of course, becoming a serious Christian involved a decision, and much was made of the responsibility of the individual to turn to God. Yet, like the Choice of Hercules between vice and virtue, the approach to conversion did not open up a range of possibilities, only the sharp alternatives of salvation or perdition, true or counterfeit manliness. Once within the fold, the options for Evangelical men were very restricted. The worship of 'character' did not denote a generous appreciation of human diversity, but a narrow definition of carefully prescribed attributes. Nor did the new respect for the dignity of work introduce a significant element of individual choice of occupation. Evangelicalism did not undermine the father's right to endow the next generation with a station in life. It was still commonplace for sons to enter the family business, or to be placed by their fathers under kinsmen or business associates. The real turning-point here was the growing bureaucratisation of the professions from the mid-nineteenth century onwards, which increased the range of practical choice open to young men, while restricting the scope for paternal influence. Prior to that point personal identity, in the sense of individual choice, was marginal to the working lives of middle-class men.

The paradox of Evangelicalism is that it imposed an almost impossibly demanding personal discipline and yet was credited with wide influence. It is certainly true that the Evangelical outlook spread far beyond those who recognised the full authority of 'serious religion'. But a condition of this influence was a dilution of the challenging – even confrontational – quality of the original message. This is especially true of the key concept of character, which quickly became sullied with just those associations of 'reputation' which the Evangelicals had fought so hard against. What had begun as a rallying-call for moral integrity became shorthand for the qualities which were at a premium in commercial society. 'Character' was in effect taking over some of the ground previously occupied by birth and rank as markers of social status. As Stefan Collini points out, 'to be known as a man of character was to possess the moral collateral which would reassure potential business associates or employers'; and he continues, 'character was an ascribed quality, possessed and enjoyed in public view'.[66] In practice 'character' was interpreted to conform with the much more self-serving and socially attuned requirement of 'independence'. Victorian manliness retained that blend of innate and ascribed qualities which had characterised all

66. Collini, *Public Moralists*, p. 106.

the most influential definitions of masculinity for centuries. It is hard to see compelling evidence for a new sense of interiority as yet. That would only come much later, with the decline of religious discipline and the further growth in urban individualism.

Masculine identity in this sense was very much a middle-class possession, available to the 'improving' upper echelons of the lower orders, but scarcely relevant to the broad mass of working people. Yet momentous changes were taking place at this level. Working-class men were relatively far removed from the discursive shifts that enveloped men of the middle class (many indeed were beyond the reach of organised religion); but they had been exposed to much greater disruption in their patterns of living and working. The ways in which a sense of manhood was invested in skill, in bread-winning and in fraternal solidarity arose from specific material conditions and were central to the whole process of class formation.[67] Drink, sex and resort to violence carried distinctive meanings. The suggestion has also been made that men who were forced off the land into the cities sought compensation for their lost status by demanding greater authority within the home.[68] What is far from clear is how much of this was new, and how much represented a re-working of established patterns. Much more comprehensive work on eighteenth-century plebeian masculinities will have to be carried out before this question can be tackled.

For understandable reasons gender historians have sought to uncover major transformations and turning-points which will hold the same intellectual excitement as the better known stories of economic and political change. Reviewing the work done so far on the period 1750–1850 suggests some of the limitations to this approach. There is certainly plenty in this period to support a dynamic interpretation. At a discursive level, gender was a flexible and effective idiom for arguments about human nature and national character, which changed quite sharply during this period.[69] In terms of social practice, major changes occurred in the gendering of work, which I have scarcely touched on here.[70] But, while being alert to

67. K. McClelland, 'Masculinity and the "representative artisan" in Britain, 1850–80', in Roper and Tosh, *Manful Assertions*, pp. 74–91.
68. Simpson, 'Masculinity and control', esp. pp. 604–20. Cf. A. Tolson, *The Limits of Masculinity* (1977), p. 31.
69. See, for example, Jordanova, *Sexual Visions*, chs 1–2; Wilson, *Sense of the People*; M. Poovey, *Uneven Developments: The Ideological Work of Gender in Mid-Victorian England* (Chicago IL, 1988).
70. For an up-to-date review of the issues, see Shoemaker, *Gender in English Society*.

the evidence of major change, we need to register the weight of those structures of gender which changed little and which obstructed or qualified changes in other areas. Masculinities were subject to less change than the shifting pattern of class hegemony would imply. Sexual polarisation was much more characteristic of medical and prescriptive writing than of actual social relations. And the development of masculine interiority in place of the code of honour was contradictory, to say the least. At this stage in the debate, a certain caution in embracing ambitious models of change would be more consistent with respect for the place of gender in history.

This is a less defensive posture than it may seem at first sight. For allowing gender a deeper anchorage in the social fabric opens the way to understanding the ways in which gender transcends class. Here I am not primarily thinking of the 'two-sex' model which, in prioritising sexual difference over other distinctions, implied that the essentialised masculinity shared by master and man might count for more than the division of rank between them.[71] Taken to such an extreme, two-sex thinking becomes an abstraction with little purchase on social experience. My argument is about persistence rather than change. For a period when so much social and discursive change was taking place, too little attention has been given to those structures of masculinity which were hegemonic in the sense that they moulded consciousness and behaviour at all levels of society. Predatory sexuality among the young and domestic patriarchy among the fully mature are two such structures. We need to know more about the culture and social practice of young unmarried men – the homosocial networks, the appropriated public spaces, the drinking and whoring, the balance between comradeship and competition, in short the apprentice culture which Joan Lane has recently reconstructed in outline for early modern England.[72] And we need much more content to our picture of domestic patriarchy, not only the incidence of marital violence but the dynamics of household authority which fuelled grievance, insecurity, provocation and assault.

The argument here is not that the troubling transition to adult masculinity, or the enforcement of domestic patriarchy, operated in precisely the same way everywhere, but that class distinctions only make sense when seen in the context of certain shared (and

71. A. Clark discusses this implication of Laqueur's thesis. Clark, *Struggle for the Breeches*, p. 2.
72. J. Lane, *Apprenticeship in England, 1660–1914* (1996). Cf. Roper, 'Blood and cod-pieces'.

enduring) patterns of gendered behaviour.[73] Historians of gender have tended to feel uneasy with models of continuity, not only because they find change more alluring, but because persistence and stasis imply a trans-historical essentialism. But when anthropologists observe recurrent patterns, they do not leap to the conclusion that all societies are 'the same', or that the common traits they have uncovered are biologically programmed; as David Gilmore has shown, men almost universally perform the functions of protecting and providing for dependents, but manhood ideologies vary according to the social and material environment.[74] As historians we should be equally ready to recognise the embeddedness and durability of certain aspects of gender. Taking the measure of masculinities in England between 1750 and 1850 means engaging with the old Adam quite as much as the new man.

73. The argument here is not dissimilar to that of Judith Bennett with regard to the low skill and low status of women's work from the thirteenth to the nineteenth centuries. J.M. Bennett, ' "History that stands still": women's work in the European past', *Feminist Studies* 14 (1988), pp. 269–83.

74. D.P. Gilmore, *Manhood in the Making* (New Haven CT, 1990), pp. 222–5. See also M.Z. Rosaldo, 'Women, culture and society: a theoretical overview', in M.Z. Rosaldo and L. Lamphere, eds, *Women, Culture and Society* (Stanford CA, 1974).

Further Reading

General and theoretical

ARIES, P. and DUBY, G., eds, *History of Private Life*, vol. 3, R. Chartier *et al.*, eds, *Passions of the Renaissance* (Cambridge, 1989).

BARKER, H. and CHALUS, E., *Gender in Eighteenth-Century England: Roles, Representations and Responsibilities* (1997).

BARKER-BENFIELD, G.J., *The Culture of Sensibility: Sex and Society in Eighteenth-Century Britain* (Chicago IL, 1992).

BARRELL, J., 'The dangerous goddess: masculinity, prestige and the aesthetic in early eighteenth-century Britain', in his *Birth of Pandora and the Division of Knowledge* (Basingstoke and London, 1992).

BRAY, A., 'To be a man in early modern society. The curious case of Michael Wigglesworth' *HWJ* 41 (1996) 155–65.

BREITENBERG, M., *Anxious Masculinity in Early Modern England* (Cambridge, 1996).

BREWER, J., *The Pleasures of the Imagination: English Culture in the Eighteenth Century* (1997).

BROWN, K., ' "Changed . . . into the fashion of a man": the politics of sexual difference in a seventeenth-century Anglo-American settlement' *JHS* 6 (1995) 171–93.

BULLOUGH, V.L. and BULLOUGH, B., *Cross-Dressing, Sex, and Gender* (Philadelphia PA, 1993).

BUTLER, J., *Gender Trouble: Feminism and the Subversion of Identity* (1990).

CLARK, A., *The Struggle for the Breeches: Gender and the Making of the British Working Class* (Berkeley CA, 1995).

COHEN, M., *Fashioning Masculinity: National Identity and Language in the Eighteenth Century* (1996).

CONNELL, R.W., *Masculinities* (Cambridge, 1995).

CONNELL, R.W., 'The big picture: masculinities in recent world history' *Theory & Society* 22 (1993) 597–623.

EPSTEIN, J. and STRAUB, K., eds, *Body Guards: The Cultural Politics of Gender Ambiguity* (1991).

FLETCHER, A., *Gender, Sex and Subordination in England, 1500–1800* (New Haven and London, 1995).

GILMORE, DAVID D., *Manhood in the Making: Cultural Concepts of Masculinity* (1990).

HILL, B., *Women, Work and Sexual Politics in Eighteenth-Century England* (1989).

HITCHCOCK, T., 'Redefining sex in eighteenth-century England' *HWJ* 41 (1996) 72–90.

HITCHCOCK, T., *English Sexualities, 1700–1800* (Basingstoke and London, 1997).

HUFTON, O., *The Prospect Before Her: A History of Women in Western Europe*, vol. 1 (1995).

LAIPSON, P., 'From boudoir to bookstore: writing the history of sexuality' *Comparative Studies in Society and History* 34, 4 (Oct. 1992) 636–44.

LANGFORD, P., *A Polite and Commercial People: England 1727–1783* (Oxford, 1989).

LAQUEUR, T., *Making Sex: Body and Gender from the Greeks to Freud* (Cambridge MA, 1990).

MACFARLANE, A., *Marriage and Love in England, 1300–1840* (Oxford, 1986).

MANGAN, J.A. and WALVIN, J., eds, *Manliness and Morality: Middle-Class Masculinity in Britain and America, 1800–1940* (Manchester, 1987).

McKEON, M., 'Historicizing patriarchy: the emergence of gender difference in England, 1660–1760' *E-CS* 28 (1995) 295–322.

MOSSE, G.L., *The Image of Man: The Creation of Modern Masculinity* (Oxford, 1996).

NUSSBAUM, F.A., *The Brink of all we Hate* (Lexington KY, 1984).

NUSSBAUM, F.A., *The Autobiographical Subject: Gender and Ideology in Eighteenth-Century England* (1989).

OFFEN, K. and PIERSON, R., eds, *Writing Women's History: International Perspectives* (Basingstoke and London, 1991).

ORGEL, S., *Impersonations: The Performance of Gender in Shakespeare's England* (Cambridge, 1996).

PERRY, G. and ROSSINGTON, M., eds, *Femininity and Masculinity in Eighteenth-Century Art and Culture* (Manchester, 1994).

ROGOFF, I. and VAN LEER, D., 'Afterthoughts: a dossier on masculinities' *Theory and Society* 22, 5 (Oct. 1993) 739–62.

ROPER, L., *Oedipus and the Devil: Witchcraft, Sexuality and Religion in Early Modern Europe* (1994).

ROPER, M. and TOSH, J., eds, *Manful Assertions: Masculinities in Britain Since 1800* (1991).

SHOEMAKER, R., *Gender in English Society, 1650–1850* (Harlow, 1998).

SHOEMAKER, R. and VINCENT, M., eds, *Gender and History in Western Europe* (1998).

SIMONS, P., 'Homosociability and erotica in Italian Renaissance portraiture' in J. Woodall, ed., *Portraiture: Facing the Subject* (Manchester, 1997).

SNELL, K.D.M., *Annals of the Labouring Poor: Social Change and Agrarian England, 1660–1900* (Cambridge, 1985).

SOLKIN, D.H., *Painting For Money: The Visual Arts and the Public Sphere in Eighteenth-Century England* (New Haven and London, 1993).

STONE, L., *The Family, Sex and Marriage in England, 1500–1800*, 1st edn (1977).

THOMAS, K., 'The double standard' *JHI* XX (1959) 195–216.

TOSH, J., 'What should historians do with masculinity? Reflections on nineteenth-century Britain' *HWJ* 38 (1994) 179–202.

TRUMBACH, R., 'London's sapphists: from three sexes to four genders in the making of modern culture' in J. Epstein and K. Straub, eds, *Body Guards: The Cultural Politics of Gender Ambiguity* (1991).

TRUMBACH, R., 'Sex, gender, and sexual identity in modern culture: male sodomy and female prostitution in Enlightenment London' *JHS* II, 2 (1991) 186–203.

TRUMBACH, R., 'The birth of the queen: sodomy and the emergence of gender equality in modern culture, 1660–1750' in M. Duberman, M. Vicinus and G. Chauncy Jr, eds, *Hidden From History: Reclaiming the Gay and Lesbian Past* (1991).

VICKERY, A., *The Gentleman's Daughter: Women's Lives in Georgian England* (New Haven and London, 1998).

Honour and reputation

AMUSSEN, S., ' "The part of a Christian man": the cultural politics of manhood in early modern England' in S. Amussen and M. Kishlansky, eds, *Political Culture and Cultural Politics in Early Modern England: Essays Presented to David Underdown* (Manchester, 1995).

AMUSSEN, S., *An Ordered Society: Gender and Class in Early Modern England* (Oxford, 1988).

BRANT, C., 'Speaking of women: scandal and the law in mid-eighteenth century' in C. Brant and D. Purkiss, eds, *Women, Texts and Histories, 1575–1760* (London and New York, 1992).

CLARK, A., 'Whores and gossips: sexual reputation in London, 1770–1825' in A. Angerman *et al.*, eds, *Current Issues in Women's History* (1989).

DABHOIWALA, F., 'The construction of honour, reputation and status in late seventeenth- and early eighteenth-century England' *TRHS* 6th series, VI (1996) 201–13.

FOYSTER, E., 'A laughing matter? Marital discord and gender control in seventeenth-century England' *RH* 4, 1 (1993) 5–21.

FOYSTER, E., 'Male honour, social control and wife beating in late Stuart England' *TRHS* 6th series, VI (1996) 215–24.

FREIST, D., *Governed by Opinion: Politics, Religion and the Dynamics of Communication in Stuart London, 1637–1645* (London and New York, 1997).

GOWING, L., 'Women, status and the popular culture of dishonour' *TRHS* 6th series, VI (1996) 225–34.

GOWING, L., *Domestic Dangers: Women, Words and Sex in Early Modern London* (Oxford, 1996).

GOWING, L., 'Gender and language of insult in early modern London' *HWJ* 35 (1993) 1–21.

GOWING, L., 'Language, power and the law: women's slander litigation in early modern London' in J. Kermode and G. Walker, eds, *Women, Crime and the Courts in Early Modern England* (1994).

GOWING, L., 'Secret births and infanticide in seventeenth-century England' *P&P* 156 (1997) 87–115.

GRIFFITHS, P., *Youth and Authority: Formative Experiences in England, 1560–1640* (Oxford, 1996).

HINDLE, S., 'The shaming of Margaret Knowsley: gossip, gender and the experience of authority in early modern England' *CC* 9, 3 (1994) 391–419.

INGRAM, M., *Church Courts, Sex and Marriage in England, 1570–1640* (Cambridge, 1987).

JAMES, M., 'English politics and the concept of honour, 1485–1642', first published as *P&P* supplement no. 3 (1978) and reprinted in his *Society, Politics and Culture in Early Modern England* (Cambridge, 1986).

MELDRUM, T., 'A woman's court in London: defamation at the Bishop of London's consistory court, 1700–1745' *LJ* XIX, 1 (1994) 1–20.

MITCHISON, R. and LEAH, L., *Sexuality and Society Control: Scotland 1660–1780* (Oxford, 1989).

MORRIS, P., 'Sodomy and male honor: the case of Somerset, 1740–1850' *JH* XVI, 1/2 (1989) 383–406.

SHARPE, J.A., *Defamation and Sexual Slander in Early Modern England: The Church Courts at York*, Borthwick Papers 58 (York, 1980).

WALKER, G., 'Expanding the boundaries of female honour in early modern England' *TRHS* 6th series, VI (1996) 235–56.

WILTENBURG, J., *Disorderly Women and Female Power in the Street Literature of Early Modern England and Germany* (Charlottesville VA, 1992).

Homosexuality

BINGHAM, C., 'Seventeenth-century attitudes towards deviant sex, with a comment by Bruce Mazlish' *Journal of Interdisciplinary History* I, 3 (1971) 447–72.

BOON, L.J., 'Those damned sodomites: public images of sodomy in the eighteenth-century Netherlands' *JH* XVI, 1/2 (1989) 237–48.

BOUCÉ, P.-G., 'Aspects of sexual tolerance and intolerance in XVIIIth-century England' *BJE-CS* III (1980) 173–91.

BRAY, A., 'Homosexuality and the signs of male friendship in Elizabethan England' *HWJ* 29 (1990) 1–19.

BRAY, A., *Homosexuality in Renaissance England*, revised edn (1995).

BREDBECK, G.W., *Sodomy and Interpretation: Marlowe to Milton* (Ithaca NY, 1991).

BURG, B.R., 'Ho hum, another work of the devil: buggery and sodomy in early Stuart England' *JH* VI, 1/2 (1980/81) 69–78.

COHEN, E., *Talk on the Wilde Side: Towards a Genealogy of Discourse on Male Sexualities* (1993).

CORBER, R.J., 'Representing the "unspeakable": William Godwin and the politics of homophobia' *JHS* I (1990–91) 85–101.

CROMPTON, L., '*Don Leon*, Byron, and homosexual law reform' *JH* VIII, 3/4 (1983) 53–72.

CROMPTON, L., ed., 'Jeremy Bentham's essay on "Paederasty" (Part 2)' *JH* IV, 1 (1978) 91–107.

CROMPTON, L., ed., 'Offences against one's self: Paederasty (Part 1)' *JH* III, 4 (1978) 389–405.

CROMPTON, L., 'Homosexuals and the death penalty in colonial America' *JH* I, 3 (1976) 277–94.

CROMPTON, L., 'Jeremy Bentham's essay on "Paederasty": an introduction' *JH* III, 4 (1978) 383–8.

DUBERMAN, M., VICINUS, M. and CHAUNCY, G., JR, eds, *Hidden From History: Reclaiming the Gay and Lesbian Past* (1991).

GILBERT, A.N., 'Buggery in the British Navy, 1700–1861' *JSH* X, 1 (1976) 72–98.

GILBERT, A.N., 'Conceptions of homosexuality and sodomy in Western history' *JH* VI, 1/2 (1980/81) 57–68.

GILBERT, A.N., 'Sexual deviance and disaster during the Napoleonic Wars' *Albion* IX, 1 (1977) 98–113.

GOLDBERG, J., ed., *Queering the Renaissance* (Durham NC, 1994).

GOLDBERG, J., ed., *Reclaiming Sodom* (New York, 1994).

GOLDBERG, J., *Sodometries: Renaissance Texts, Modern Sexualities* (Stanford CA, 1992).

GOLDBERG, J., 'Sodomy and society: the case of Christopher Marlowe', *Southwest Review* 69 (1984) 371–8; reprinted in D. Kasten and P. Stallybrass, eds, *Staging the Renaissance* (New York, 1991).

HEKMA, G., 'Sodomites, platonic lovers, contrary lovers: the backgrounds of the modern homosexual' *JH* XVI, 1/2 (1989) 433–55.

HERRUP, C.B., 'Law and morality in seventeenth-century England' *P&P* 106 (1985) 102–23.

HIGGENS, P., *A Queer Reader* (1993).

HOWSON, G., *The Thief-Taker General: The Rise and Fall of Jonathan Wild* (1970).

HUUSSEN, A.H., Jr, 'Sodomy in the Dutch Republic during the eighteenth century' in R.P. Maccubbin, *'Tis Nature's Fault: Unauthorized Sexuality during the Enlightenment* (Cambridge, 1987).

HUUSSEN, A.H., 'Prosecution of sodomy in eighteenth-century Frisia, Netherlands' *JH* XVI, 1/2 (1989) 249–62.

KOPELSON, K., 'Seeing sodomy: *Fanny Hill*'s blinding vision' *JH* XXIII, 1/2 (1992) 173–83.

LAKE, P., 'Deeds against nature: cheap print, Protestantism and murder in early seventeenth-century England' in K. Sharpe and P. Lake, *Culture and Politics in Early Stuart England* (1994).

McINTOSH, M., 'The homosexual role' *Social Problems* 16 (1968) 182–92.

MONTER, E.W., 'Sodomy and heresy in early modern Switzerland' *JH* VI, 1/2 (1980/81) 41–57.

MORRIS, P., 'Sodomy and male honor: the case of Somerset, 1740–1850' *JH* XVI, 1/2 (1989) 383–406.

MURRAY, S.O., 'Homosexual acts and selves in early modern Europe' *JH* XVI, 1/2 (1989) 457–77.

NOORDAM, D.J., 'Sodomy in the Dutch Republic, 1600–1725' *JH* XVI, 1/2 (1989) 207–28.

NORTON, R., *Mother Clap's Molly House: The Gay Subculture in England, 1700–1830* (1992).

OAKS, R.F., '"Things Fearful to Name": sodomy and buggery in seventeenth-century New England' *JSH* XII, 2 (1978) 268–281.

OAKS, R.F., 'Defining sodomy in seventeenth-century Massachusetts' *JH* VI, 1/2 (1980/81) 79–83.

OAKS, R.F., 'Perceptions of homosexuality by Justices of the Peace in colonial Virginia' *JH* V, 1/2 (1979/80) 35–42.

OOSTERHOFF, J., 'Sodomy at sea and at the Cape of Good Hope during the eighteenth century' *JH* XVI, 1/2 (1989) 229–35.

PARKER, W., 'Homosexuality in history: an annotated bibliography' *JH* VI, 1/2 (1980/81) 191–210.

REY, M., 'Parisian homosexuals create a lifestyle, 1700–1750: the police archives' in R.P. Maccubbin, ed., *'Tis Nature's Fault: Unauthorized Sexuality during the Enlightenment* (Cambridge, 1987).

REY, M., 'Police and sodomy in eighteenth-century Paris: from sin to disorder' *JH* XVI, 1/2 (1989) 129–46.

ROCKE, M., *Forbidden Friendships: Homosexuality and Male Culture in Renaissance Florence* (Oxford, 1996).

ROUSSEAU, G.S., '"In the House of Madam Vader Tasse, on the Long Bridge": a homosocial university club in early modern Europe' *JH* XVI, 1/2 (1989) 311–47.

ROUSSEAU, G.S., 'The pursuit of homosexuality in the eighteenth century: "Utterly Confused Category" and/or rich repository?' in R.P. Maccubbin, ed., *'Tis Nature's Fault: Unauthorized Sexuality during the Enlightenment* (Cambridge, 1987).

RUBINI, D., 'Sexuality and Augustan England: sodomy, politics, elite circles and society' *JH* XVI, 1/2 (1989) 349–82.

SEDGWICK, E.K., *Between Men: English Literature and Male Homosocial Desire* (New York, 1985).

SEDGWICK, E.K., *Epistemology of the Closet* (Berkeley CA, 1990).

SENELICK, L., 'Mollies or men of mode? Sodomy and the eighteenth-century London stage' *JHS* I, 1 (1990) 33–67.

SMITH, B., *Homosexual Desire in Shakespeare's England: A Cultural Poetics* (Chicago IL, 1991).

SMITH, B., 'Making a difference: male/male desire in tragedy, comedy, and tragi-comedy' in S. Zimmerman, ed., *Erotic Politics: Desire on the Renaissance Stage* (New York, 1992).

SMITH, N., 'Sexual mores in the eighteenth century: Robert Wallace's "Of Venery"' *JHI* IXL, 3 (1978) 419–34.

SPENCER, C., *Homosexuality: A History* (1995).

SPRAGUE, G.A., 'Male homosexuality in Western culture: the dilemma of identity and subculture in historical research' *JH* X, 3/4 (1984) 29–43.

STEWART, A., *Close Readers: Humanism and Sodomy in Early Modern England* (Princeton NJ, 1997).

TRUMBACH, R., 'London's sodomites: homosexual behaviour and Western culture in the eighteenth century' *JSH* XI, 1 (1977) 1–33.

TRUMBACH, R., 'Sex, gender, and sexual identity in modern culture: male sodomy and female prostitution in Enlightenment London' *JHS* II, 2 (1991) 186–203.

TRUMBACH, R., 'Sodomitical assaults, gender roles, and sexual development in eighteenth-century London' *JH* XVI, 1/2 (1989) 407–29.

TRUMBACH, R., 'Sodomitical subcultures, sodomitical roles, and the gender revolution of the eighteenth century: the recent historiography' in R.P. Maccubbin, ed., *'Tis Nature's Fault: Unauthorized Sexuality during the Enlightenment* (Cambridge, 1987).

TRUMBACH, R., 'The birth of the queen: sodomy and the emergence of gender equality in modern culture, 1660–1750' in M. Duberman, M. Vicinus and G. Chauncy Jr, eds, *Hidden From History: Reclaiming the Gay and Lesbian Past* (1991).

VAN DER MEER, T., 'The persecution of sodomites in eighteenth-century Amsterdam: changing perceptions of sodomy' *JH* XVI, 1/2 (1989) 263–307.

Sexuality, demography and the body

ADAIR, R., *Courtship, Illegitimacy and Marriage in Early Modern England* (Manchester, 1996).

BEALL, O.T., Jr, *'Aristotle's Masterpiece* in America: a landmark in the folklore of medicine' *William and Mary Quarterly* XX (1963) 207–22.

BENNETT, P. and ROSARIO, V.A., II, eds, *Solitary Pleasures: The Historical, Literary and Artistic Discourses of Autoeroticism* (New York, 1995).

BOUCÉ, P-G., 'Imagination, pregnant women, and monsters, in eighteenth-century England and France' in G.S. Rousseau and Roy Porter, eds, *Sexual Underworlds of the Enlightenment* (Manchester, 1987).

BOUCÉ, P-G., 'Some sexual beliefs and myths in eighteenth-century Britain' in P-G. Boucé, ed., *Sexuality in Eighteenth-Century Britain* (Manchester, 1982).

CASH, A.H., 'The birth of Tristram Shandy: Sterne and Dr Burton' in P-G. Boucé, ed., *Sexuality in Eighteenth-Century Britain* (Manchester, 1982).

CRAWFORD, P., 'Attitudes to menstruation in seventeenth-century England' *P&P* 91 (1981) 47–73.

CRAWFORD, P., 'Attitudes to pregnancy from a woman's spiritual diary, 1687–8' *LPS* 21 (1978) 43–5.

CRAWFORD, P., 'Printed advertisements for women medical practitioners in London, 1670–1710' *Society for the Social History of Medicine*, Bulletin 35 (1984) 66–70.

CRAWFORD, P., 'Sexual knowledge in England, 1500–1750' in R. Porter and M. Teich, eds, *Sexual Knowledge, Sexual Science: The History of Attitudes to Sexuality* (Cambridge, 1994).

DONNISON, J., *Midwives and Medical Men. A History of Inter-Professional Rivalries and Women's Rights* (New York, 1977).

DUDEN, B., 'A repertory of body history' in M. Feher, ed., *Fragments for a History of the Human Body*, Part Three (New York, 1989).

ECCLES, A., *Obstetrics and Gynaecology in Tudor and Stuart England* (Kent OH, 1982).

ENGELHARDT, T., 'The disease of masturbation: values and concepts of disease' *BHM* 48 (1974) 234–48.

EPSTEIN, J., *Altered Conditions: Disease, Medicine and Storytelling* (1995).

EPSTEIN, J., 'Either/or, neither/nor: sexual ambiguity and the ideology of gender' *Genders* 7 (1990) 101–142.

FRIEDLI, L., ' "Passing Women": a study of gender boundaries in the eighteenth century' in G.S. Rousseau and R. Porter, eds, *Sexual Underworlds of the Enlightenment* (Manchester, 1987).

ERICKSON, R.A., ' "The Books of Generation": some observations on the style of the English midwife books, 1671–1764' in P-G. Boucé, ed., *Sexuality in Eighteenth-Century Britain* (Manchester, 1982).

FILDES, V., *Wet Nursing: A History from Antiquity to the Present* (Oxford, 1988).

FISSELL, M., 'Gender and generation: representing reproduction in early modern England' *G&H* VII, 3 (1995) 433–56.

FISSELL, M., 'Readers, texts and contexts: vernacular medical works in early modern England' in R. Porter, ed., *The Popularization of Medicine, 1650–1850* (1992).

FORBES, T., 'The regulation of English midwives in the sixteenth and seventeenth centuries' *Medical History* 8 (1964) 235–44.

GALLAGHER, C. and LAQUEUR, T., eds, *The Making of the Modern Body: Sexuality and Society in the Nineteenth Century* (Berkeley, 1987).

GILLIS, J., 'Married but not churched: plebeian sexual relations and marital nonconformity in eighteenth-century Britain' in R.P. Maccubbin, *'Tis Nature's Fault: Unauthorized Sexuality During the Enlightenment* (Cambridge, 1987).

HARE, E.H., 'Masturbatory insanity: the history of an idea' *Journal of Mental Science* 108 (1962) 2–25.

HILL, B., 'The marriage age of women and the demographers' *HWJ* 28 (1989) 129–47.

JACQUART, D. and THOMASSET, C., *Sexuality and Medicine in the Middle Ages* (Cambridge, 1988).

JONES, A.R. and STALLYBRASS, P., 'Fetishizing gender: constructing the hermaphrodite in Renaissance Europe' in J. Epstein and K. Straub, eds, *Body Guards: The Cultural Politics of Gender Ambiguity* (1991).

JORDANOVA, L., 'The popularization of medicine: Tissot on onanism' *Textual Practice* I, 1 (1987) 68–79.

JORDANOVA, L., *Sexual Visions. Images of Gender in Science and Medicine between the Eighteenth and Twentieth Centuries* (1989).

KATES, G., 'D'Eon returns to France: gender and power in 1777' in J. Epstein and K. Straub, eds, *Body Guards: The Cultural Politics of Gender Ambiguity* (1991).

KELLER, E.F., *Reflections on Gender and Science* (New Haven CT, 1985).

LAQUEUR, T., 'Amor Veneris, vel Dulcedo Appeletur' in M. Feher, ed., *Fragments for a History of the Human Body*, Part Three (New York, 1989).

LAQUEUR, T., 'Bodies of the past' *BHM* 67 (1993) 155–61.

LAQUEUR, T., *Making Sex: Body and Gender from the Greeks to Freud* (Cambridge MA, 1990).

LAQUEUR, T., 'Orgasm, generation and the politics of reproductive biology' in C. Gallagher and T. Laqueur, eds, *The Making of the Modern Body: Sexuality and Society in the Nineteenth Century* (Berkeley CA, 1987).

LAQUEUR, T., 'The social evil, the solitary vice and pouring tea' in M. Feher, ed., *Fragments for a History of the Human Body*, Part Three (New York, 1989).

LASLETT, P., OOSTERVEEN, K. and SMITH, R., eds, *Bastardy and its Comparative History* (1980).

LENEMAN, L., 'The study of illegitimacy from Kirk Session records: two eighteenth-century Perthshire parishes' *LPS* 31 (1983) 29–33.

LESLIE, G., 'Cheat and imposter: debate following the case of the rabbit breeder' *The Eighteenth Century: Theory and Interpretation* XXVII, 3 (1986) 269–86.

LEVINE, D., ' "For Their Own Reasons": individual marriage decisions and family life' *JFH* (1982) 255–64.

LEVINE, D., *Family Formation in an Age of Nascent Capitalism* (New
York, 1977).

MACDONALD, R.H., 'The frightful consequences of onanism: notes
on the history of a delusion' *JHI* XXVIII, 3 (1967) 423–31.

MACLEAN, I., *The Renaissance Notion of Woman* (Cambridge, 1980).

MARTENSEN, R., 'The transformation of Eve: women's bodies, medicine and culture in early modern England' in R. Porter and
M. Teich, *Sexual Knowledge, Sexual Science: The History of Attitudes
to Sexuality* (Cambridge, 1994).

MARTENSEN, R., ' "Habit of Reason": anatomy and Anglicanism in
Restoration England' *BHM* 66 (1992) 511–35.

MCLAREN, A., *A History of Contraception From Antiquity to the Present
Day* (Oxford, 1990).

MCLAREN, A., *Reproductive Rituals. The Perception of Fertility in England from the Sixteenth Century to the Nineteenth Century* (1984).

MCLAREN, A., 'The pleasures of procreation: traditional and bio-
medical theories of conception' in W.F. Bynum and R. Porter,
eds, *William Hunter and the Eighteenth-Century Medical World* (Cambridge, 1985).

MERCHANT, C., *The Death of Nature: Women, Ecology and the Scientific
Revolution* (New York, 1980).

METEYARD, B., 'Illegitimacy and marriage in eighteenth-century
England' *Journal of Interdisciplinary History* X, 3 (1980) 479–89;
also the following debate with L. Stone and B. Meteyard, 'Illegitimacy in eighteenth-century England: again' *Journal of Interdisciplinary
History* XI, 3 (1981) 507–14.

MORT, F., *Dangerous Sexualities: Medical-Moral Politics in England* (1987).

NEUMAN, R.P., 'Masturbation, madness, and the modern concepts
of childhood and adolescence' *JSH* VIII (1975) 1–27.

OUTHWAITE, R.B., *Clandestine Marriage in England, 1500–1850* (1995).

PARFITT, G. and HOULBROOKE, R., eds, *The Courtship Narrative of
Leonard Wheatcroft* (Reading, 1986).

PERRY, R., 'Colonizing the breast: sexuality and maternity in
eighteenth-century England' *JHS* II, 2 (1991) 204–34.

PORTER, R., ' "The Whole Secret of Health": mind, body and medicine in *Tristram Shandy*' in J. Christie and S. Shuttleworth, eds,
Nature Transfigured (Manchester, 1989).

PORTER, R., 'A touch of danger: the man-midwife as sexual pred-
ator' in G.S. Rousseau and R. Porter, eds, *Sexual Underworlds of
the Enlightenment* (Manchester, 1987).

PORTER, R. and HALL, L., *The Facts of Life: The Creation of Sexual Knowledge in Britain, 1650–1950* (Princeton NJ, 1995).

PORTER, R., 'Love, sex and medicine: Nicolas Venette and his *Tableau de l'amour conjugal*' in P. Wagner, ed., *Erotica and the Enlightenment* (Frankfurt, 1990).

PORTER, R., 'Spreading carnal knowledge or selling dirt cheap? Nicolas Venette's *Tableau de l'amour conjugal* in eighteenth-century England' *Journal of European Studies* 14 (1984) 233–56.

PORTER, R., 'The literature of sexual advice before 1800' in R. Porter and M. Teich, eds, *Sexual Knowledge, Sexual Science: The History of Attitudes to Sexuality* (Cambridge, 1994).

PORTER, R., 'The sexual politics of James Graham' *BJE-CS* V, 2 (1982) 199–206.

PORTER, R., '"The Secrets of Generation Display'd": *Aristotle's Masterpiece* in eighteenth-century England' in R.P. Maccubin, ed., *'Tis Natures Fault: Unauthorized Sexualities During the Englightenment* (New York, 1985).

POTTER, R.G. and MILLMAN, S.R., 'Fecundability and the frequency of marital intercourse: a critique of nine models' *Population Studies* 39 (1985) 461–70.

QUAIFE, G.R., *Wanton Wenches and Wayward Wives: Peasants and Illicit Sex in Early Seventeenth-Century England* (1979).

RENDALL, J., *Women in an Industrializing Society: England, 1750–1880* (Oxford, 1990).

ROGERS, N., 'Carnal knowledge: illegitimacy in eighteenth-century Westminster' *JSH* XXIII, 2 (1989) 355–75.

ROPER, L., *Oedipus and the Devil: Witchcraft, Sexuality and Religion in Early Modern Europe* (1994).

SCHIEBINGER, L., 'Mammals, primatology and sexology' in R. Porter and M. Teich, eds, *Sexual Knowledge, Sexual Science: The History of Attitudes to Sexuality* (Cambridge, 1994).

SCHIEBINGER, L., *Nature's Body: Sexual Politics and the Making of Modern Science* (1994).

SCHIEBINGER, L., 'Skeletons in the closet: the first illustrations of the female skeleton in eighteenth-century anatomy' in C. Gallagher and T. Laqueur, eds, *The Making of the Modern Body: Sexuality and Society in the Nineteenth Century* (Berkeley CA, 1987).

SCHIEBINGER, L., *The Mind has no Sex? Women in the Origins of Modern Science* (Cambridge MA, 1989).

LAQUEUR, T., 'Sex and desire in the industrial revolution' in P. O'Brien and R. Quinault, eds, *The Industrial Revolution and British Society* (Cambridge, 1993).

SCHOFIELD, R., 'English marriage patterns revisited' *JFH* (1985) 2–20.

SHARPE, P., 'Locating the "missing marryers" in Colyton, 1660–1750' *LPS* 48 (1992) 49–59.

SHARPE, P., 'Marital separation in the eighteenth and early nineteenth centuries' *LPS* 45 (1990) 66–70.

SHORTER, E., *The Making of the Modern Family* (New York, 1975).

SMITH, H., 'Gynecology and ideology in seventeenth-century England' in B. Caroll, *Liberating Women's History* (Westport CT, 1978).

SMOUT, T.C., 'Scottish marriage, regular and irregular, 1500–1940' in R.B. Outhwaite, ed., *Marriage and Society: Studies in the Social History of Marriage* (1981).

STRAUB, K., *Sexual Suspects: Eighteenth-Century Players and Sexual Ideology* (Princeton NJ, 1992).

VEITH, I., *Hysteria: The History of a Disease* (Chicago MI, 1965).

WALL, R., 'Leaving home and the process of household formation in pre-industrial England' *CC* II, 1 (1987) 77–101.

WEIR, D.R., 'Rather never than late: celibacy and age at marriage in English cohort fertility, 1541–1871' *JFH* (1984) 340–54.

WILSON, A., 'Illegitimacy and its implications in mid-eighteenth-century London: the evidence of the Foundling Hospital' *CC* IV, 1 (1989) 103–64.

WILSON, A., *The Making of Man-Midwifery: Childbirth in England, 1660–1770* (Cambridge MA, 1995).

WRIGLEY, E.A. and SCHOFIELD, R.S., *The Population History of England, 1541–1871* (1981).

WRIGLEY, E.A., 'Marriage, fertility and population growth in eighteenth-century England' in R.B. Outhwaite, ed., *Marriage and Society: Studies in the Social History of Marriage* (1981).

WRIGLEY, E.A., 'The growth of population in eighteenth-century England: a conundrum resolved' *P&P* 98 (1983) 121–50.

WYATT, G., 'Bastardy and prenuptial pregnancy in a Cheshire town during the eighteenth century' *LPS* 49 (1992) 38–50.

Effeminacy

CARTER, P., 'Men about town: representations of foppery and masculinity in early eighteenth-century urban society' in H. Barker and E. Chalus, eds, *Gender in Eighteenth-Century England: Roles, Representations and Responsibilities* (1997).

CARTER, P., 'An "effeminate" or "efficient" nation? Masculinity and eighteenth-century social documentary' *Textual Practice* 11, 3 (1997) 429–43.

COHEN, M., *Fashioning Masculinity: National Identity and Language in the Eighteenth Century* (1996).

SHAPIRO, S., '"Yon Plumed Dandebrat": male "effeminacy" in English satire and criticism' *Review of English Studies* new series, XXXIX, 155 (1988) 400–412.

SHAPIRO, S., 'Gender and fashion in early modern Britain' *Journal of Popular Culture* 20 (1986–87) 113–28.

PARKER, P., 'On the tongue: cross gendering, effeminacy, and the art of words' *Style* 23, 3 (Fall 1989) 445–65.

SENELICK, L., 'Mollies or men of mode? Sodomy and the eighteenth-century London stage' *JHS* I, 1 (1990) 33–67.

WILSON, K., *The Sense of the People: Politics, Culture and Imperialism in England, 1715–1785* (Cambridge, 1995).

Education, socialisation and sociability

BEN-AMOS, I.K., *Adolescence and Youth in Early Modern England* (New Haven CT, 1994).

CLARK, P., *Sociability and Urbanity: Clubs and Societies in the Eighteenth-Century* (Victorian Studies Centre, University of Leicester, 1986).

CLARK, P., *The English Alehouse: A Social History 1200–1830* (1983).

CLAWSON, M.A., 'Early modern fraternalism and the patriarchal family' *Feminist Studies* 6 (1980) 368–91.

CLAWSON, M.A., *Constructing Brotherhood. Class, Gender and Fraternalism* (Princeton NJ, 1989).

D'CRUZE, S., 'The middling sort in eighteenth-century Colchester: independence, social relations and the community broker' in J. Barry and C. Brooks, eds, *The Middling Sort of People: Culture, Society and Politics in England, 1550–1800* (Basingstoke and London, 1994).

COHEN, M., 'The grand tour: constructing the English gentleman in eighteenth-century France' *History of Education* 21, 3 (1992) 241–57.

DWYER, J., *Virtuous Discourse: Sensibility and Community in Late Eighteenth-Century Scotland* (Edinburgh, 1987).

DWYER, J. and SHER, R.B., eds, *Sociability and Society in Eighteenth-Century Scotland* (Edinburgh, 1993).

JONES, L.C., *The Clubs of the Georgian Rakes* (New York, 1942).

KLEIN, L., 'Gender, conversation and the public sphere in early eighteenth-century England' in J. Still and M. Worton, eds, *Textuality and Sexuality: Reading Theories and Practices* (Manchester, 1993).

LANE, J., *Apprenticeship in England, 1660–1914* (1996).

STAVES, S., 'The secrets of genteel identity in *The Man of Mode.* Comedy of manners vs. the courtesy book' *Studies in Eighteenth-Century Culture* 19 (1989) 117–28.

VICKERY, A., *The Gentleman's Daughter: Women's Lives in Georgian England* (New Haven and London, 1998).

WEISNER, M.E., 'Guilds, male bonding and women's work in early modern Germany' *G&H* 1 (1989) 125–37.

WEISNER, M.E., 'Wandervogels and women: journeymen's concepts of masculinity in early modern Germany' *JSH* 24, 4 (1991) 767–82.

WESTHAUSER, K., 'Friendship and family in early modern England: the sociability of Adam Eyre and Samuel Pepys' *JSH* 27, 3 (1994) 517–36.

Separate spheres and domesticity

BREWER, J., 'This, that and the other: public, social and private in the seventeenth and eighteenth centuries' in D. Castiglione and L. Sharpe, eds, *Shifting the Boundaries: Transformations of the Language of Public and Private in the Eighteenth Century* (Exeter, 1995).

CLARK, A., *The Struggle for the Breeches: Gender and the Making of the British Working Class* (Berkeley CA, 1995).

DAVIDOFF, L., 'Regarding some "old husbands' tales": public and private in feminist history' in *Worlds Between: Historical Perspectives on Gender and Class* (Cambridge, 1995).

DAVIDOFF, L. and HALL, C., *Family Fortunes: Men and Women of the English Middle Class, 1780–1850* (1987).

EARLE, P., *The Making of the English Middle Class: Business, Society and Family Life in London, 1660–1730* (1989).

FLETCHER, A., *Gender, Sex and Subordination in England, 1500–1800* (New Haven CT, 1995).

GILLIS, J., *For Better, For Worse: British Marriages 1600 to the Present* (Oxford, 1985).

GOODMAN, D., 'Public sphere and private life: toward a synthesis of current historiographical approaches to the old regime' *History and Theory* 31, 1 (1992) 1–20.

HABERMAS, J., *Struckturwandel der Offentlichkeit* (1962). English translation, *The Structural Transformation of the Public Sphere: An Inquiry into a Category of Bourgeois Society* (Cambridge MA, 1989).

HUNT, M., *The Middling Sort: Commerce, Gender, and the Family in England, 1680–1780* (Berkeley CA, 1996).

KERBER, L.K., 'Separate spheres, female worlds, woman's place: the rhetoric of women's history' *JAH* 75, I (1988) 9–39.

KLEIN, L., 'Gender and the public/private distinction in the eighteenth century: some questions about evidence and analytic procedure' *E-CS* 29 (1995) 92–109.

KLEIN, L., 'Gender, conversation and the public sphere in early eighteenth-century England' in J. Still and M. Worton, eds, *Textuality and Sexuality: Reading Theories and Practices* (Manchester and New York, 1993).

LEWIS, J., 'Separate spheres: threat or promise?' *JBS* 30, 1 (1991) 105–15.

NADELHAFT, J., 'The Englishwoman's sexual civil war: feminist attitudes towards men, women and marriage 1650–1740' *JHI* 43, 4 (1982) 555–79.

SHAPIRO, A.-L., ed., *Feminist Revision History* (New Brunswick NJ, 1994).

SHOEMAKER, R., *Gender in English Society, 1650–1850* (Harlow, 1998).

SNELL, K.D.M., *Annals of the Labouring Poor: Social Change and Agrarian England, 1660–1900* (Cambridge, 1985).

STONE, L., *Broken Lives: Separation and Divorce in England, 1660–1857* (Oxford, 1993).

STONE, L., *Road to Divorce: England, 1530–1987* (Oxford, 1990).

STONE, L., *Uncertain Unions: Marriage in England, 1660–1753* (Oxford, 1992).

TOSH, J., 'From Keighley to St-Denis: separation and intimacy in Victorian bourgeois marriage' *HWJ* 40 (1995) 193–206.

TOSH, J., 'Authority and nurture in middle-class fatherhood: the case of early and mid Victorian England' *G&H* 8 (1996) 48–64.

VICKERY, A., 'Golden age to separate spheres? A review of the categories and chronology of women's history' *HJ* 36, 2 (1993) 383–414.

WAHRMAN, D., ' "Middle-Class" domesticity goes public: gender, class and politics from Queen Caroline to Queen Victoria' *JBS* 32 (1993) 396–432.

WILSON, K., *The Sense of the People: Politics, Culture and Imperialism in England, 1715–1785* (Cambridge, 1995).

Language and representation

BARRELL, J., ed., *Painting and the Politics of Culture: New Essays on British Art 1700–1850* (Oxford and New York, 1992).

BARRELL, J., ' "The Dangerous Goddess": masculinity, prestige, and the aesthetic in early eighteenth-century Britain' in *The Birth of Pandora and the Division of Knowledge* (1992).

BARRELL, J., *English Literature in History 1730–80: An Equal Wide Survey* (1983).

BOUCÉ, P.-G., 'Chthonic and pelagic metaphorization in eighteenth-century erotica' in R.P. Maccubin, ed., *'Tis Nature's Fault: Unauthorized Sexuality during the Enlightenment* (Cambridge, 1987).

CAMERON, D., 'Performing gender identity: young men's talk and the construction of heterosexual masculinity' in S. Johnson and U.H. Meinhof, eds, *Language and Masculinity* (Oxford, 1997).

COHEN, MICHÈLE, *Fashioning Masculinity: National Identity and Language in the Eighteenth Century* (1996).

COHEN, MURRAY, *Sensible Words: Linguistic Practice in England 1640–1785* (1977).

DARNTON, R., *The Forbidden Best-Sellers of Pre-Revolutionary France* (London and New York, 1995).

FARLEY-HILLS, D., ed., *Rochester: The Critical Heritage* (New York, 1972).

FISSELL, M., 'Gender and generation: representing reproduction in early modern England' *G&H* 1 (1995), 433–56.

FOXON, D., *Libertine Literature in England, 1660–1745* (New York, 1965).

GOULEMOT, J.M., *Forbidden Texts: Erotic Literature and its Readers in Eighteenth-Century France* (1991; Engl. trans. Cambridge, 1994).

GREENBLATT, S., *Renaissance Self-Fashioning: From More to Shakespeare* (Chicago and London, 1980).

HUNT, L., ed., *The Invention of Pornography: Obscenity and the Origins of Modernity, 1500–1800* (New York, 1993).

HUTSON, L., *The Usurer's Daughter: Male Friendship and Fictions of Women in Sixteenth-Century England* (1994).

JOHNSON, S., 'Theorizing language and masculinity: a feminist perspective' in S. Johnson and U.H. Meinhof, eds, *Language and Masculinity* (Oxford, 1997).

KAMENSKY, J., 'Talk like a man: speech, power, and masculinity in early New England' *G&H* 8, 1 (1996) 22–47.

KEARNEY, P., *A History of Erotic Literature* (1982).

KIMMEL, M.S., 'The contemporary "crisis" of masculinity in historical perspective' in H. Brod, ed., *The Making of Masculinities* (1987).

KLEIN, L., *Shaftesbury and the Culture of Politeness: Moral Discourse and Cultural Politics in Early Eighteenth-Century England* (Cambridge, 1994).

KUCHTA, D., 'The semiotics of masculinity in Renaissance England', in J.G. Turner, ed., *Sexuality and Gender in Early Modern Europe: Institutions, Texts, Images* (Cambridge, 1993).

KUCHTA, D., 'The making of the self-made man: class, clothing and English masculinity, 1688–1832' in V. de Grazia with E. Furlough, eds, *The Sex of Things: Gender and Consumption in Historical Perspective* (Berkeley and London, 1996).

ORR, B., 'Whore's rhetoric and the maps of love: constructing the feminine in Restoration erotica' in Clare Brant and Diane Purkiss, eds, *Women, Texts and Histories, 1575–1760* (London and New York, 1992).

PARKER, P., 'On the tongue: cross gendering, effeminacy, and the art of words' *Style* 23, 3 (Fall 1989) 445–65.

PINCUS, S., ' "Coffee Politicians Does Create": coffeehouses and Restoration political culture' *Journal of Modern History* 67 (1995) 807–34.

POINTON, M., 'The case of the dirty beau' in K. Adler and M. Pointon, eds, *The Body Imaged: The Human Form of Visual Culture Since the Renaissance* (Cambridge, 1993).

THOMPSON, R., *Unfit for Modest Ears: A Study of Pornographic, Obscene and Bawdy Works Written or Published in England in the Second Half of the Seventeenth Century* (1979).

TURNER, J.G., ' "News from the Exchange": commodity, erotic fantasy and the female entrepreneur' in John Brewer and Ann Bermingham, eds, *The Consumption of Culture, 1600–1800: Image, Object, Text* (London and New York, 1995).

WAGNER, P., *Eros Revived: Erotica of the Enlightenment in England and France* (1988).

WEIL, R., 'Sometimes a scepter is only a scepter: pornography and politics in Restoration England' in L. Hunt, ed., *The Invention of Pornography: Obscenity and the Origins of Modernity 1500–1800* (New York, 1993).

WILLIAMS, C.D., *Pope, Homer and Manliness* (1993).

Violence and misogyny

AMUSSEN, S.D., 'Punishment, discipline, and power: the social meanings of violence in early modern England' *JBS* 34 (1995) 1–34.

ANDREW, D.T., 'The code of honour and its critics: the opposition to duelling in England, 1700–1850' *SH* 5 (1980) 409–34.

BEATTIE, J., *Crime and the Courts in England 1660–1800* (Princeton NJ, 1986).

BEATTIE, J., 'Violence and society in early-modern England' in Anthony Doob and Edward Greenspan, eds, *Perspectives in Criminal Law* (Aurora, Ontario, 1985).

BENNETT, J.M., 'Misogyny, popular culture and women's work' *HWJ* 31 (1991) 166–88.

CHAYTOR, M., 'Husband(ry): narratives of rape in the seventeenth century' *G&H* 7, 3 (1995) 378–407.

CLARK, A., 'Humanity or justice? Wifebeating and the law in the eighteenth and nineteenth centuries' in C. Smart, ed., *Regulating Womanhood: Historical Writings on Marriage, Motherhood and Sexuality* (1992).

CLARK, A., *Women's Silence, Men's Violence: Sexual Assault in England, 1770–1845* (1987).

COCKBURN, J.S., 'Patterns of violence in English society: homicide in Kent 1560–1985' *P&P* 130 (1991) 70–106.

DOLAN, F., *Dangerous Familiars: Representations of Domestic Crime in England, 1550–1700* (Ithaca NY and London, 1994).

FEELEY, M. and LITTLE, D., 'The vanishing female: the decline of women in the criminal process, 1687–1912' *Law and Society Review* 25 (1991) 719–57.

FOYSTER, E., 'Male honour, social control and wife-beating in late Stuart England' *TRHS* 6th series, VI (1996) 215–24.

HARRIS, T., 'The bawdy house riots of 1668' *HJ* XXIX, 3 (1986) 537–56.

HUNT, M., 'Wife beating, domesticity and women's independence in eighteenth-century London' *G&H* I, 1 (1992) 10–33.

KIERNAN, V.G., *The Duel in European History: Honour and the Reign of the Aristocracy* (Oxford, 1988).

KING, P., 'Punishing assault: the transformation of attitudes in the English courts' *Journal of Interdisciplinary History* 27 (1996) 43–74.

McGOWEN, R., 'Punishing violence, sentencing crime' in N. Armstrong and L. Tennenhouse, eds, *The Violence of Representation: Literature and the History of Violence* (1989).

ROBERTS, M.M., 'Masonics, metaphor and misogyny: a discourse of marginality' in P. Burke and R. Porter, eds, *Languages and Jargons: Contributions to a Social History of Language* (Cambridge, 1995).

ROBERTS, M.M., 'Who wears the apron? Masonic misogyny and female Freemasonry' *Transactions of the Eighth International Congress of the Enlightenment* (Oxford: The Voltaire Foundation) II, 812–16.

SHARPE, J.A., 'The history of violence in England: some observations' *P&P* 108 (1985) 206–24.

SHOEMAKER, R.B., *Prosecution and Punishment: Petty Crime and the Law in London and Rural Middlesex, c.1660–1725* (Cambridge, 1991).

STONE, L., 'Interpersonal violence in English society' *P&P* 101 (1983) 22–33.

UNDERDOWN, D.E., 'The taming of the scold: the enforcement of patriarchal authority in early modern England' in A. Fletcher and J. Stevenson, eds, *Order and Disorder in Early Modern England* (Cambridge, 1985).

Index